TEACHING ENGLISH CREATIVELY

What does it mean to teach English creatively to primary school children?

Teaching English Creatively encourages and enables teachers to adopt a more creative approach to the teaching of English in the primary school. Fully updated to reflect the changing UK curricula, the second edition of this popular text explores research-informed practices and offers new ideas to develop imaginatively engaged readers, writers, speakers and listeners.

Underpinned by theory and research, and illustrated throughout with examples of children's work, it examines the core elements of creative practice and how to explore powerful literary, non-fiction, and visual and digital texts creatively. Key themes include:

- developing creativity in and through talk and drama;
- creatively engaging readers and writers;
- teaching grammar and comprehension imaginatively and in context;
- profiling meaning and purpose, autonomy, collaboration and play;
- planning, reviewing and celebrating literacy learning;
- ensuring the creative involvement of the teacher.

Inspiring and accessible, *Teaching English Creatively* puts contemporary and cutting-edge practice at the forefront and includes a wealth of innovative ideas to enrich English teaching.

Written by an experienced author with extensive experience of initial teacher education and English teaching in the primary school, it's an invaluable resource for any teacher who wishes to embed creative approaches to teaching in their classroom.

Teresa Cremin is Professor of Education (Literacy) at The Open University, UK, a Fellow of the English Association and a Director of the Cambridge Primary Review Trust.

THE LEARNING TO TEACH IN THE PRIMARY SCHOOL SERIES

Series editor: Teresa Cremin, The Open University, UK

Teaching is an art form. It demands not only knowledge and understanding of the core areas of learning, but also the ability to teach these creatively and foster learner creativity in the process. *The Learning to Teach in the Primary School Series* draws upon recent research that indicates the rich potential of creative teaching and learning, and explores what it means to teach creatively in the primary phase. It also responds to the evolving nature of subject teaching in a wider, more imaginatively framed twenty-first century primary curriculum.

Designed to complement the textbook *Learning to Teach in the Primary School*, the well-informed, lively texts in this series offer support for student and practising teachers who want to develop more creative approaches to teaching and learning. Uniquely, the books highlight the importance of the teachers' own creative engagement and share a wealth of research informed ideas to enrich pedagogy and practice.

Titles in the series:

Teaching English Creatively, 2nd Edition
Teresa Cremin

Teaching Mathematics Creatively, 2nd Edition
Linda Pound and Trisha Lee

Teaching Religious Education Creatively
Edited by Sally Elton-Chalcraft

Teaching Physical Education Creatively
Angela Pickard and Patricia Maude

Teaching Music Creatively
Pam Burnard and Regina Murphy

Teaching History Creatively
Edited by Hilary Cooper

Teaching Geography Creatively
Edited by Stephen Scoffham

Teaching Science Creatively
Dan Davies

TEACHING ENGLISH CREATIVELY

Second edition

Teresa Cremin with
David Reedy,
Eve Bearne and
Henrietta Dombey

Routledge
Taylor & Francis Group

LONDON AND NEW YORK

First published 2015
by Routledge
2 Park Square, Milton Park, Abingdon, Oxon OX14 4RN

and by Routledge
711 Third Avenue, New York, NY 10017

Routledge is an imprint of the Taylor & Francis Group, an informa business

First edition published by Routledge 2009

British Library Cataloguing in Publication Data
A catalogue record for this book is available from the British Library

Library of Congress Cataloging in Publication Data
Cremin, Teresa, 1959–
   Teaching English creatively/Teresa Cremin. – Second edition.
   pages cm. – (Learning to teach in the primary school series)
   ISBN 978-1-138-78701-8 (hardback) – ISBN 978-1-138-78702-5
   (paperback) – ISBN 978-1-315-76690-4 (e-book) 1. English language –
   Study and teaching (Elementary) – Great Britain. 2. Language arts
   (Elementary) – Great Britain. 3. Creative teaching – Great Britain. I. Title.
   LB1576.C778 2015
   372.60941 – dc23
   2014042664

ISBN: 978-1-138-78701-8 (hbk)
ISBN: 978-1-138-78702-5 (pbk)
ISBN: 978-1-315-76690-4 (ebk)

Typeset in Times New Roman and Helvetica Neue
by Florence Production Ltd, Stoodleigh, Devon

CONTENTS

CONTENTS ▪ ▪ ▪ ▪

LIST OF FIGURES

LIST OF FIGURES ▨ ▨ ▨ ■

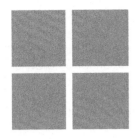

AUTHOR BIOGRAPHIES

Teresa Cremin (previously Grainger) is Professor of Education (Literacy) at the Open University and joint coordinator of the British Educational Research Association (BERA) Special Interest Group on Creativity. Teresa is also an Academician of the Academy of Social Sciences, a Fellow of the English Association, a Trustee of the United Kingdom Literacy Association (UKLA) and the Society for Educational Studies, and a board member of Booktrust and the Poetry Archive. Additionally, she is a Director of Research in the Cambridge Primary Review Trust. Teresa has always been concerned to make learning an imaginatively vital experience and seeks to foster the creative engagement of both teachers and younger learners in her research and consultancy work. Her research has involved investigating teachers' identities as readers and writers and the pedagogical consequences of increasing their reflective and aesthetic engagement as literate individuals. She has also examined teachers' knowledge of children's literature, the relationship between drama and writing, the development of voice and verve in children's writing, storytelling, poetry and the role of 'possibility thinking' in creative learning. Most recently, her projects have included: Creative Little Scientists, an EU project researching the synergies between creativity and enquiry-based approaches to science and mathematics teaching; the Helicopter Technique, exploring contemporary enactments of Vivian Gussin Paley's work on dictation and dramatisation; Prospero's island, researching immersive theatre; and the Carnegie Shadowing Scheme, examining the creative literary discussions of extracurricular reading groups.

Teresa's most recent books include *Building Engaged Communities of Readers: Reading for pleasure* (2014), written with colleagues, *The International Handbook of Research into Children's Literacy, Learning and Culture* (Wiley Blackwell, 2013), which she edited with Kathy Hall, Barbara Comber and Luis Moll, and *Writing Voices: Creating communities of writers* (Routledge, 2012) with Debra Myhill. Her forthcoming text, *Researching Literacy Lives*, was written with colleagues Marilyn Mottram, Fiona Collins, Sacha Powell and Rose Drury (Routledge, 2015).

Eve Bearne's research interests while at the University of Cambridge, Faculty of Education, have been children's production of multimodal texts and gender, language and literacy. She has also written and edited numerous books about language and literacy and children's literature and most recently co-authored *Visual Approaches to Teaching Writing: Multimodal literacy 5–11* with Helen Wolstencroft (Sage, 2008). She is currently the associate editor for publications for the UKLA and is a Fellow of the English Association.

Henrietta Dombey is Professor Emeritus of Literacy in Primary Education at the University of Brighton. Since the start of her teaching career, when she was confronted with a class of 7-year-olds with very little purchase on written language, she has been passionately interested in the teaching of reading and committed to a creative approach to it. This interest has encompassed attention to phonics, children's know-ledge of the syntax and semantics of written language, and the interactions between teachers, children and texts that appear to be productive of literacy learning. Henrietta has written extensively on many aspects of teaching reading.

David Reedy is currently president of the UKLA and a director of the Cambridge Primary Review Trust. Until recently, he was also principal adviser for primary schools in the London Borough of Barking and Dagenham. David's main research interests focus on effective talk for learning and the place of dialogic teaching in the primary classroom. His publications include *Guiding Reading – A handbook for teaching guided reading in KS2* (Institute of Education, 2006, with Angela Hobsbaum and Nikki Gamble), *Developing Writing For Different Purposes – Teaching about genre in the early years* (Paul Chapman, 2000, with Jeni Riley) and *Teaching Grammar Effectively in Primary Classrooms* (UKLA, 2013, with Eve Bearne).

SERIES EDITOR'S FOREWORD

Teresa Cremin

Over recent decades teachers working in accountability cultures across the globe have been required to focus on raising standards, setting targets, and 'delivering' prescribed curricula and pedagogy. The language of schooling, Mottram and Hall (2009: 109) assert, has predominantly focused upon 'oversimplified, easily measurable notions of attainment', which they argue has had a homogenising effect, prompting children and their development to be discussed 'according to levels and descriptors', rather than as children, as unique learners. Practitioners, positioned as passive recipients of the prescribed agenda appear to have had their hands tied, their voices quietened and their professional autonomy both threatened and constrained. At times, the relentless quest for higher standards has obscured the personal and affective dimensions of teaching and learning, fostering a mindset characterised more by compliance and conformity than curiosity and creativity.

However, creativity too has been in the ascendant in recent decades; in many countries efforts have been made to re-ignite creativity in education, since it is seen to be essential to economic and cultural development. This impetus for creativity can be traced back to the National Advisory Committee on Creative and Cultural Education (NACCCE, 1999), which recommended a core role for creativity in teaching and learning. Primary schools in England were encouraged to explore ways to offer more innovative and creative curricula (DfES, 2003) and new national curricula in Scotland also foregrounded children's critical and creative thinking. Additionally, initiatives such as Creative Partnerships, an English government-funded initiative to nurture children's creativity, inspired some teachers to reconstruct their pedagogy (Galton, 2012). Many other schools and teachers, encouraged by these initiatives, and determined to offer creative and engaging school experiences, have exercised the 'power to innovate' (Lance, 2006). Many have proactively sought ways to shape the curriculum responsively, appropriating national policies in their own contexts and showing professional commitment and imagination, despite, or perhaps because of, the persistent performative agenda (e.g. Cremin *et al.*, 2015; Neelands, 2009; Woods and Jeffrey, 2009).

Schools continue to be exhorted to be more innovative in curriculum construction and national curricula afford opportunities for all teachers to seize the space, exert their professionalism and shape their own curricula in collaboration with the young people with whom they are working. Yet for primary educators, tensions persist, not only because the dual policies of performativity and creativity appear contradictory, but also perhaps because teachers' own confidence as creative educators, indeed as creative individuals, has been radically reduced by the constant barrage of change and challenge. As Csikszentmihalyi (2011) notes, teachers lack a theoretically underpinned framework for creativity that can be developed in practice; they need support to develop as artistically engaged, research-informed curriculum co-developers. Eisner (2003) asserts that teaching is an art form, an act of improvisation (Sawyer, 2011), and that teachers benefit from viewing themselves as versatile artists in the classroom, drawing on their personal passions and creativity as they teach creatively. As Joubert too observes:

> Creative teaching is an art. One cannot teach teachers didactically how to be creative; there is no fail safe recipe or routines. Some strategies may help to promote creative thinking, but teachers need to develop a full repertoire of skills which they can adapt to different situations.
>
> (Joubert 2001: 21)

However, creative teaching is only part of the picture, since teaching for creativity also needs to be acknowledged and their mutual dependency recognised. The former focuses more on teachers using imaginative approaches in the classroom (and beyond) in order to make learning more interesting and effective, the latter, more on the development of children's creativity (NACCCE, 1999). Both rely upon an understanding of the notion of creativity and demand that professionals confront the myths and mantras that surround the word. These include the commonly held misconceptions that creativity is the preserve of the arts or arts education, and that it is confined to particularly gifted individuals.

Creativity, an elusive concept, has been multiply defined by educationalists, psychologists and neurologists, as well as by policy makers in different countries and researchers in different cultural contexts (Glăveanu, forthcoming). Debates resound about its individual and/or collaborative nature, the degree to which it is generic and/or domain specific, and the differences between the 'Big C' creativity of genius and the 'little c' creativity of the everyday. Notwithstanding these issues, most scholars in the field believe it involves the capacity to generate, reason and critically evaluate novel ideas and/or imaginary scenarios. As such, it encompasses thinking through and solving problems, making connections, inventing and reinventing, and flexing one's imaginative muscles in all aspects of learning and life.

In the primary classroom, creative teaching and learning have been associated with innovation, originality, ownership and control (Woods and Jeffrey 1996; Jeffrey 2006) and creative teachers have been seen, in their planning and teaching, and in the ethos which they create, to afford high value to curiosity and risk taking, to ownership, autonomy and making connections (Craft et al., 2014; Cremin et al., 2009; Cremin, 2015). Such teachers often work in partnership with others: with children, other teachers and experts from beyond the school gates (Cochrane and Cockett 2007; Davies et al., 2012; Thomson et al., 2012). These partnerships offer new possibilities, with teachers acquiring some of the repertoire of pedagogic practices

– the 'signature pedagogies' that artists use (Thomson and Hall, forthcoming). Additionally, in research exploring possibility thinking, which Craft (2000) argues drives creativity in education, an intriguing interplay between teachers and children has been observed. In this body of work, children and teachers have been involved in immersing themselves in playful contexts, posing questions, being imaginative, showing self-determination, taking risks and innovating – together (Burnard *et al.*, 2006; Cremin *et al.*, 2006; Chappell *et al.*, 2008; Craft *et al.*, 2012; Cremin *et al.*, 2013). As McWilliam (2009) argues, teachers can choose not to position themselves as the all-knowing 'sage on the stage', or the facilitator- like 'guide on the side'. They can choose, as creative practitioners do, to take up a role of the 'meddler in the middle', co-creating curricula in innovative and responsive ways that harness their own and foster the children's creativity. A new pedagogy of possibility beckons.

This series *Learning to Teach in the Primary School*, which accompanies and complements the edited textbook *Learning to Teach in the Primary School* (Cremin and Arthur, 2014), seeks to support teachers in developing as creative practitioners, assisting them in exploring the synergies between and potential for teaching creatively and teaching for creativity. The series does not merely offer practical strategies for use in the classroom, though these abound, but more importantly seeks to widen teachers' and student teachers' knowledge and understanding of the principles underpinning creative approaches, principles based on research. It seeks to mediate the wealth of research evidence and make accessible and engaging the diverse theoretical perspectives and scholarly arguments available, demonstrating their practical relevance and value to the profession. Those who aspire to develop further as creative and curious educators will find much of value to support their own professional learning journeys and markedly enrich their pedagogy and practice right across the curriculum.

ABOUT THE SERIES EDITOR

Teresa Cremin (Grainger) is a Professor of Education (Literacy) at the Open University and a past President of UKRA (2001–2) and UKLA (2007–9). She is currently Research Director of the Cambridge Primary Review Trust, co-convenor of the BERA Creativity SIG and a Trustee of Booktrust and UKLA. In addition, Teresa is a Fellow of both the English Association and the Academy of Social Sciences.

Her work involves research, publication and consultancy in literacy and creativity. Many of Teresa's current projects seek to explore the nature and characteristics of creative pedagogies, including for example, examining immersive theatre and related teaching techniques, children's make believe play in the context of storytelling and story acting, their everyday lives and literacy practices, and the nature of literary discussions in extracurricular reading groups. Additionally, Teresa is researching creative science practice with learners aged 3–8 years and possibility thinking as a driver for creative learning. Teresa is also passionate about, (and still researching), teachers' own creative development and their identity positioning in the classroom as readers, writers, and creative human beings.

Teresa has written and edited over 25 books and numerous papers and professional texts, most recently editing with colleagues *Researching Literacy Lives*: *Building Home-School Communities* (2015, Routledge*)*, *Teaching English Creatively*

(2nd edn, 2015, Routledge); *Building Communities of Engaged Readers: Reading for Pleasure* (2014, Routledge); and *The International Handbook of Research into Children's Literacy, Learning and Culture* (2013, Blackwell). *Storytelling in Early Childhood: Enriching Language, Literacy and Classroom Culture* is forthcoming (2016, Routledge). In addition, her book publications since 2000 include: *Writing Voices: Creating Communities of Writers* (2012, Routledge); *Learning to Teach in the Primary School* (2014, Routledge); *Teaching Writing Effectively*: *Reviewing Practice* (2011, UKLA); *Drama, Reading and Writing: Talking Our Way Forwards (2009, UKLA); Jumpstart Drama* (2009, David Fulton); *Creative Teaching for Tomorrow: Fostering a Creative State of Mind* (2009, Future Creative); *Documenting Creative Learning 5–11* (2007, Trentham); *Creativity and Writing: Developing Voice and Verve* (2005, Routledge); *Teaching English in Higher Education* (2007, NATE and UKLA); *Creative Activities for Character, Setting and Plot, 5–7, 7–9, 9–11* (Scholastic 2004); and *Language and Literacy: A Routledge Reader* (2001, Routledge).

REFERENCES

Burnard, P., Craft, A. and Cremin, T. (2006) 'Possibility thinking', *International Journal of Early Years Education*, 14(3): 243–62.

Chappell, K., Craft, A., Burnard, P. and Cremin, T (2008). 'Question-posing and question-responding: The heart of possibility thinking in the early years', *Early Years*, 283: 267–86.

Cochrane, P. and Cockett, M. (2007) *Building a Creative School: A dynamic approach to school improvement*, Stoke on Trent: Trentham Books.

Craft, A. (2000) *Creativity Across the Primary Curriculum*, London: Routledge.

Craft, A. Cremin, T. Hay, P. Clack, J. (2014) 'Creative primary Schools: Developing and maintaining pedagogy for creativity', *Ethnography and Education* 9(1):16–34.

Craft, A., Cremin, T., Burnard, P., Dragovic, T. and Chappell, K. (2012) 'Possibility thinking: Culminative studies of an evidence-based concept driving creativity?', *Education 3-13: International Journal of Primary, Elementary and Early* 41(5): 538–56.

Cremin, T. (2015) 'Creative teachers and creative teaching', in A. Wilson (ed.) *Creativity in Primary Education*, London: Sage, pp. 33–44.

Cremin, T. and Arthur, J. (2014) (eds) *Learning to Teach in the Primary School* (3rd edn), London: Routledge.

Cremin, T., Burnard, P. and Craft, A. (2006) 'Pedagogy and possibility thinking in the early years', *International Journal of Thinking Skills and Creativity*, 1(2): 108–19.

Cremin, T., Barnes, J. and Scoffham, S. (2009) *Creative Teaching for Tomorrow: Fostering a creative state of mind*, Deal: Future Creative.

Cremin, T., Chappell, K. and Craft, A. (2013) 'Reciprocity between narrative, questioning and imagination in the early and primary years: Examining the role of narrative in possibility thinking', *Thinking Skills and Creativity* 9: 136–51.

Cremin, T., Glauert, E., Craft, A., Compton, A. and Stylianidou, F. (forthcoming, 2015) 'Creative little scientists: Exploring pedagogical synergies between inquiry-based and creative approaches in Early Years science', *Education 3-13, International Journal of Primary, Elementary and Early Years Education*, Special issue on creative pedagogies.

Cremin, T. Mottram, M. Powell, S, Collins, R. and Drury, R. (2015) *Researching Literacy Lives: Building home school communities*, London: Routledge.

Csikszentmihalyi, M. (2011) 'A systems perspective on creativity and its implications for measurement', in R. Schenkel and O. Quintin (eds) *Measuring Creativity,* Brussels: The European Commission, pp. 407–14.

Davies, D., Jindal-Snape, D., Collier, C., Digby, R., Hay, P. and Howe, A. (2012) 'Creative environments for learning in schools', *Thinking Skills and Creativity.* http://dx.doi.org/10.1016/j.tsc.2012.07.004.

Department for Culture, Media and Sport (2006) *Government Response to Paul Roberts' Report on Nurturing Creativity in Young People*, London: DCMS.

Department for Education and Skills (DfES) (2003) *Excellence and Enjoyment: A strategy for primary schools*, Nottingham: DfES.

Eisner, E. (2003) 'Artistry in education', *Scandinavian Journal of Educational Research*, 47(3): 373–84.

Galton, M. (2010) 'Going with the flow or back to normal? The impact of creative practitioners in schools and classrooms', *Research Papers in Education* 25(4): 355–75.

Glăveanu, V. Sierra, Z. and Tanggaard, L. (forthcoming, 2015) 'Widening our understanding of creative pedagogy: A North–South dialogue', *Education 3–13: International Journal of Primary, Elementary and Early Years Education*, Special issue on creative pedagogies.

Jeffrey, B. (ed.) (2006) *Creative Learning Practices: European experiences*, London: Tufnell Press.

Jeffrey, B. and Woods, P. (2009) *Creative Learning in the Primary School*, London: Routledge.

Joubert, M.M. (2001) 'The art of creative teaching: NACCCE and beyond', in A. Craft, B. Jeffrey and M. Liebling (eds) *Creativity in Education*, London: Continuum, p. 21.

Lance, A. (2006): Power to innovate? A study of how primary practitioners are negotiating the modernisation agenda, *Ethnography and Education*, 1(3): 333–44.

Mottram, M. and Hall, C. (2009) 'Diversions and diversity: Does the personalisation agenda offer real opportunities for taking children's home literacies seriously?', *English in Education*, 43(2): 98–112.

National Advisory Committee on Creative and Cultural Education (NACCCE) (1999) *All Our Futures: Creativity, culture and education*, London: Department for Education and Employment.

Neelands, J. (2009) 'Acting together: ensemble as a democratic process in art and life', *Research in Drama Education* 14(2):173–89.

Sawyer, K. (2011) (ed.) *Structure and Improvisation in Creative Teaching*, New York: Cambridge University Press.

Thomson, P. and Hall, C. (forthcoming, 2015) 'Everyone can imagine their own Gellert: The democratic artist and "inclusion" in primary and nursery classrooms', *Education 3-13: International Journal of Primary, Elementary and Early Years Education*, Special issue on creative pedagogies.

Thomson, P., Hall, C., Jones, K. and Sefton-Green, J. (2012) *The Signature Pedagogies Project: Final report*, London: Creativity, Culture and Education.

Woods, P. and Jeffrey, B. (1996) *Teachable Moments: The art of creative teaching in primary schools*, Buckingham: Open University Press.

ACKNOWLEDGEMENTS

This book has benefited from many conversations and collaborations with colleagues in classrooms, in universities, in arts organisations and in policy contexts. I would like in particular to thank my three contributing authors, Eve Bearne, Henrietta Dombey and David Reedy, alongside whom I have travelled over many years. My thanks also to Maureen Lewis, who wrote the original non-fiction chapter and has generously allowed us to borrow from it.

I am also keenly aware of the contribution of the many teachers with whom I and my co-authors have worked on research and development projects over the years; together, our collective desire to play, innovate and open new doors on children's learning taught us a great deal about our own creativity and the children's. It is somewhat invidious to mention a few, but Tracey Dunn, Shamim Awan and Sarah Abraham from Birmingham, Nicola Mitchell and Carla Belling from Kent, as well as Laura Davies from Lambeth deserve a mention, as do my colleagues Andrew Lambirth from Greenwich University, Kathy Goouch from Canterbury Christ Church University and Anna Craft, previously at the Open University and Exeter University. Over the years, we experimented with ideas and possibilities, and I learned much from this collaborative and iterative process. Our curiosity also enabled us to explore the pedagogical consequences of more creative approaches to teaching and learning.

Thanks are also due to the UKLA, the Esmée Fairbairn Foundation, the Qualifications and Curriculum Authority, Creative Partnerships, CILIP, MBA, HLT, Canterbury Christ Church University, the Open University and the Arts Council England, for awarding funding grants that have enabled me to work alongside teachers in classrooms, observe them in action, document their pedagogic practice and seek to understand the relationship between their own engagement and stance and that of the younger learners.

I would also like to thank Helen Pritt and Sarah Tuckwell from Routledge, whose longstanding support and enthusiasm have helped this revised text become a reality, and my own family, whose playful approach to life and language fostered my own creative disposition.

TEACHING ENGLISH CREATIVELY

Teresa Cremin

INTRODUCTION

Teaching and learning English are, at their richest, energising, purposeful and imaginatively vital experiences for all involved, developing youngsters' competence, confidence and creativity, as well as building positive attitudes to learning. At its poorest, English teaching and learning can be dry, didactic experiences, focused on the instruction of assessable skills and paying little attention to children's affective or creative development as language learners and language users.

Following apparently safe routes to raise literacy standards, interspersed with occasional more creatively oriented activities, does not represent balanced literacy instruction. Such practice pays lip service to creative approaches and fails to acknowledge the potential of building on young children's curiosity, desire for agency and capacity to generate and innovate. Such practice ignores research that indicates the multiple benefits of teaching and learning creatively (e.g. Vass, 2004; Cremin, 2015; Galton, 2010; Craft, McConnon *et al.*, 2012; Thomson *et al.*, 2012). It also ignores policy recommendations that, in many, though not all, countries, encourage teachers to exercise their professional judgement and teach more creatively.

Teaching literacy creatively does not mean short-changing the teaching of the essential knowledge, skills and understanding of the subject; rather, it involves teaching literacy skills and developing knowledge about language in creative contexts that explicitly invite learners to engage imaginatively, nurture their commitment and stretch them cognitively and affectively. Creative teachers work to extend children's abilities as readers, writers, speakers and listeners and help them to express themselves effectively, to create as well as critically evaluate their own work.

Creativity emerges as children become absorbed in actively exploring ideas, initiating their own learning and making choices and decisions about how to express themselves using different media and language modes. In responding to what they read, view, hear and experience, children make use of their literacy skills and transform their knowledge and understanding in the process. It is the aim of this book to encourage and enable teachers to adopt a more creative approach to the teaching of English in the primary phase.

THE LITERACY AGENDA

For nearly two decades, primary teachers in England have experienced unprecedented prescription and accountability. The original National Curriculum (NC) (DfEE, 1989) framed and delineated the nature of the subject that was later reconceptualised as 'literacy' within the Literacy Strategies (DfEE, 1989; DfES, 2006). Both specified long lists of objectives to be taught and tested and required teachers to employ particular pedagogical practices, such as shared and guided reading. The new NC (DfE, 2013), although purportedly offering increased professional freedom, lays out in detail the core knowledge about language to which teachers must attend and, despite asserting teachers are to make their own pedagogical choices (DfE, 2010), specifies the use of systematic synthetic phonics. In contrast, in Northern Ireland (DENI, 2011), the language and literacy curriculum is much briefer and simply outlines minimum content, thus affording maximum flexibility for teachers. The literacy and English framework (Education Scotland, 2012) within the Scottish Curriculum for Excellence explicitly seeks to develop children's critical and creative thinking, as well as their competence in listening and talking, reading, writing and their personal, interpersonal and team-working skills. Yet there have been challenges for teachers in developing this curriculum because, as Priestly and Humes (2010) note, although it was framed as an open, discovery-oriented curriculum, more directed objectives followed. In Wales, the curriculum is currently under review in order to complement the approach taken in the new National Literacy Framework. The pressure created by any new or shifting curricula, changing national assessment systems and the demands of day-to-day teaching in accountability cultures are likely to constrain teachers' and children's experience of creativity and reduce professional autonomy and artistry.

THE CREATIVITY AGENDA

The first edition of this book was published in 2010, during what some have called a creative decade (Craft *et al.*, 2013). At this time, a plethora of policies and practices, influenced by economic and political goals, became prominent in government policies across the UK, most of which sought to ensure creativity was recognised, fostered and promoted (e.g. Ofsted, 2003; Roberts, 2006). The establishment of the Creative Partnerships (CP) initiative also sought to offer opportunities for the young to develop their creativity, in this case by building partnerships with creative organisations, businesses and individuals. It also sought to demonstrate the role creativity and creative people can play in transforming teaching and learning (e.g. Ofsted, 2006).

The definition of creativity employed by these documents was that coined in the report *All Our Futures: Creativity, culture and education*, namely that creativity is 'imaginative activity fashioned so as to produce outcomes that are both original and of value' (NACCCE, 1999: 30). This report suggested that the curriculum needed rebalancing, and, as a consequence, many primary schools worked to achieve this, though many schools remain at the early stages of adopting more creative approaches to teaching and learning, hampered by heavy prescription, league tables and tests and targets.

Nonetheless, academic explorations of creative teaching and teaching for creativity have continued to expand, both in the UK (e.g. Cremin, Barnes *et al.*, 2009; Jeffrey and Woods, 2009; Davies *et al.*, 2012; Thomson *et al.*, 2012; Craft *et al.*, 2013; Cremin *et al.*, 2013) and abroad (e.g. Lin, 2011; Sawyer, 2011; Kuntz *et al.*, 2013), and teachers still seek innovative ways to shape the curriculum in response to children's needs. In one study, which explored how schools have sought to maintain pedagogy for creativity, three characteristics emerged. These were: co-construction between and with children, frequently involving real-life contexts for learning, high value placed on children's control/agency/ ownership, and teachers' high expectations of children knowing 'how to' engage creatively, in other words valuing children's motivation and capabilities (Craft *et al.*, 2013). These key strands affirm earlier research (Jeffrey and Woods, 2009) and were seen in each school's development of creativity, mainly through the arts, their use of integrated topics, flexibility in use of time and desire to fully immerse children in their own learning.

In England, unlike in many other countries, creativity is no longer afforded a significant profile beyond the early years of education, where, in the revised Early Years Foundation Stage (NLT, 2012), it is acknowledged that, alongside 'playing and exploring' and 'active learning', the third characteristic of effective learning is 'creating and thinking critically'. In Northern Ireland, creativity is included in the 'Thinking skills and personal capabilities framework', which advocates being creative across the curriculum. In Scotland, creativity is built into the experiences and outcomes across the curriculum areas. The Framework for Children's Learning for 3 to 7-year-olds in Wales talks about 'developing their imagination and creativity across the curriculum' (DCELLS, 2008a), although the content area of creative development is limited to art, craft and design, music and creative movement. Nonetheless, creative and critical thinking is also included in the skills framework for 3–19-year-olds (DCELLS, 2008b).

EXPLORING CREATIVITY

With the varied positioning of creativity in UK national curricula, it is crucial for teachers to clarify what creativity means to them in terms of teaching and learning, both in literacy and across the curriculum. Some may need to dispel lingering myths that creativity is an arts-related concept, applicable only to those aspects of literacy that involve literature, drama or poetry, and not to the teaching of literacy skills, for example. Others may need to accept that creativity is not confined to particular children, but is a human potential possessed by all, and one that is open to development.

Creativity, in essence the generation of novel ideas, is possible to exercise in all aspects of life. In problem-solving contexts of a mundane as well as unusual nature, humans can choose to adopt a creative mindset or attitude and trial possible options and ideas. It is useful to distinguish between high creativity and everyday creativity, between 'Big C Creativity' (seen in some of Gardner's (1993) studies of highly creative individuals, for example, Einstein and Freud) and 'little c creativity', which Craft (2000, 2005) suggests focuses on the agency and resourcefulness of ordinary people to innovate and take action. It is the latter, more democratic view of creativity that is adopted in this book, connected to literacy teaching and learning. Boden (2001, 2004) conceptualises creativity as personal and historical; the latter, domain-changing creativity is aligned to Big C creativity, whereas the former is linked to individuals who adopt creative dispositions in everyday contexts. Making original connections in thought, movement and language needs to be recognised as a creative act, just as much as the production of a finished piece of writing or a poetry performance.

Creativity involves the capacity to generate, reason with and critically evaluate novel suppositions or imaginary scenarios. It is about thinking, problem solving, inventing and reinventing, and flexing one's imaginative muscles and critical reflexivity. As such, although an end product is often, though not always, the goal, its nature cannot be predetermined. Creativity is thus a process and state of mind involving the serious play of ideas and possibilities. It involves considerable play, exploration and risk, uncertainty, change and challenge, as well as criticality.

FINDING CREATIVE WAYS FORWARD

If teachers are to adopt innovative ways forward in their English teaching, they need to reconcile the tension between the drive for measurable standards on the one hand and the development of creativity on the other. As children move through school, they quickly learn how the system works and suppress their spontaneous creativity (Sternberg, 1997). Some teachers, too, in seeking to cover the statutory curriculum, curb their own creativity and avoid taking risks and leading explorations in learning. More creative professionals, in combining subject and pedagogical knowledge, consciously leave space for uncertainty and seek both to teach creatively and to teach for creativity. Teaching creatively involves teachers making learning more interesting and effective and using imaginative approaches in the classroom (NACCCE, 1999). Teaching for creativity, by contrast, focuses on developing children's creativity, their capacity to experiment with ideas and information, alone and with others. The two processes are very closely related. As Dezuanni and Jetnikoff (2011: 265) assert, creative pedagogies involve 'imaginative and innovative arrangement of curricula and teaching strategies in school classrooms' to develop children's creativity. This framing is employed within the book.

In examining the nature of creative teaching in a number of primary curriculum contexts, Jeffrey and Woods (2009) suggest that innovation, originality, ownership and control are all associated with creative practice. Other research has affirmed and developed this, showing that creative teachers, both in planning and teaching and in the ethos that they create in the classroom, attribute high value to curiosity and risk taking, to ownership, autonomy and making connections (Cremin, Barnes *et al.*, 2009). They also afford significance to the development of imaginative and unusual ideas in both themselves and their students and foster play and exploration in open-ended contexts (Poddiakov, 2011). Creative teaching should not be placed in opposition to the teaching of essential knowledge, skills and understandings in English, nor does it imply lowered expectations of challenge. Rather, creative teaching involves teaching English in creative contexts that explicitly invite young people to engage imaginatively and that stretch their generative, evaluative and collaborative capacities.

Furthermore, although all good teachers reward originality, Cremin, Barnes *et al.*, (2009) assert that creative ones depend on it to enhance their own well-being and that of the children. They see the development of creativity and originality as a distinguishing mark of their teaching. Perhaps, therefore, the difference between being a good teacher and being a creative teacher is one of emphasis and intention. The creative teacher is one who values the human attribute of creativity in him- or herself and seeks to promote this in others (ibid.). In the process, such teachers encourage children to believe in their creative potential and give them the confidence to try. Furthermore, they seek to foster other creative attributes in the young, such as risk taking, commitment, resilience, independent judgement, intrinsic motivation and curiosity.

Creative literacy teaching is a collaborative enterprise, one that capitalises on the unexpected and enables children to develop their language and literacy in purposeful, relevant and creative contexts that variously involve engagement, instruction, reflection and transformation. Such an approach recognises, as Freire (1985) argued, that 'learning to read and write is an artistic event' and one that needs to connect to children's out-of-school literacy practices. Creative English teaching and teaching for creativity in English aim to enable young people to develop a questioning and reflective stance towards texts and to engage imaginatively, conjuring up new possibilities and evaluating these critically. It is highly motivating and seeks to positively shape children's literate identities in the process.

CORE FEATURES OF A CREATIVE APPROACH

An environment of possibility, in which individual agency and self-determination are fostered and children's ideas and interests are valued, discussed and celebrated, depends upon the presence of a climate of trust, respect and support in the classroom. Creativity can be developed when teachers are confident and secure in both their subject knowledge and their knowledge of creative pedagogical practice; they model the features of creativity *and* develop a culture of creative opportunities.

A creative approach to teaching English encompasses several core features that enable teachers to make informed decisions, both at the level of planning and in the moment-to-moment interactions in the classroom. The elements of creative English practice that are examined throughout the book are introduced here. They include:

1   profiling meaning and purpose;
2   foregrounding potent, affectively engaging texts;
3   fostering play and engagement;
4   harnessing curiosity and profiling agency;
5   encouraging collaboration and making connections;
6   integrating reflection, review, feedback and celebration;
7   taking time to travel and teach skills in context;
8   ensuring the creative involvement of the teacher.

Profile meaning and purpose

Research into effective teachers of literacy shows that effective professionals believe the creation of meaning in literacy is fundamental (Medwell *et al.*, 1998; Wray *et al.*, 2002; Hall, 2013). As a consequence, they highlight the purpose and function of reading and writing in their classrooms. Explicit and focused attention is given to linguistic features, but these are taught in context and practised through meaningful activities, the purposes of which are clearly explained to the children (Myhill *et al.*, 2011). Teachers who are themselves readers and who recognise their reasons for reading different texts and in diverse contexts also tend to foreground reading as a meaningful and purposeful activity in the classroom (Cremin *et al.*, 2014).

The meaning and purpose of literacy learning connects to the outcome sought at the end of the extended learning journey. This may include, for example, a poetry anthology or performance, a newspaper, a website, a PowerPoint presentation, an assembly in which the class's short stories are read, a teach in (where older children teach younger children), letters to individuals or organisations, or a pamphlet/film about the school for new entrants. Young people need to be helped to read, produce and critically evaluate a wide range of texts and engage in English practices that make the world meaningful and imaginatively satisfying to them. Seeking authentic reasons for engaging in literacy activities can help them recognise the value and real-world relevance of literacy. Additionally, in fostering creativity in English, teachers need to be cognisant of individual children's passions, practices, capabilities and personalities, so they can try to ensure the work is meaningful for them.

Foreground potent, affectively engaging texts

Partly as a result of rapid technological advances and the increasing dominance of the image, the nature and form of texts have changed radically, and many are now multimodal. They use sound and music, voice, intonation, stance, gesture and movement, as well as print and image, and exist in many different media, such as a computer screen, film, radio and book. Children bring to reading and writing in school a wealth of multimodal text experiences (Marsh, 2008; Marsh and Bishop, 2014). Their teachers may have experienced a smaller range of textual forms as young readers and writers, but need to recognise that children's creativity is often evidenced in their playful engagement with such contemporary textual forms, and that their passion for popular cultural texts can valuably be harnessed. So, teachers need to connect the literacies of home and school, offering rich textual encounters that bridge the gap between the children's own 'cultural capital' (Bourdieu, 1977) and the culture of school.

Texts play a critical role in creative English teaching, and so teachers' knowledge of children's authors and poets is significant (Cremin, Bearne *et al.*, 2008; Cremin, Mottram *et al.*, 2008), enabling them to select texts for extended study and reading aloud that will evoke an imaginatively vital response. In profiling the learner above the curriculum, creative professionals respond to children's aesthetic and emotional engagement in learning, sharing their own responses to texts and inviting the learners to respond likewise. Children's affective involvement is central to creativity, as it encourages openness and fosters the ability to make personal connections and insights. Teachers seek out potent texts that offer both relevance and potential engagement; they know that fiction, non-fiction and visual texts can inform and expand the horizons of readers and writers, offering rich models, provoking a variety of creative responses and providing a context in which language skills can be taught. As texts are perceived as integral to teaching English creatively and fostering the creativity of young learners, references to high-quality examples of children's literature and other texts are made throughout the book.

Foster play and engagement

The importance of play and deep engagement is widely recognised in fostering creativity; the spontaneous nature of play and its improvisational and generative orientation are critical. A close relationship also exists between the ways in which real-world literacy is used and the nature of play, as both are purposeful and meaningful and offer children choices. Playful endeavours need to be offered throughout the primary phase, perhaps in the context of investigating fictional scenarios, experimenting with different poetic presentations, creating a play-script for performance or examining current issues to debate and discuss.

If the spirit of play and imagination is encouraged, then teachers and learners are more open to new and different opportunities, to trying new routes and paths less well travelled (Fisher and Williams, 2004). Creative English learning is a motivating and highly interactive experience, involving a degree of playfulness and the potential for engagement in multiple contexts. However, as children get older, highly structured activities too often come to the fore, and play and exploration are short-changed. Nonetheless, in studying literature in depth, for example, time for deep immersion and engagement in the theme or genre will need to be provided, as well as dedicated time for play – engaged mental and physical play – with textual patterns, puzzles, conventions, materials and ideas. During this time, children will also experience explicit instruction and tailored teaching. Over time, through activities such as drama and storytelling, art, discussion, drawing and dance, children's outer play encourages the inner play of the imagination, developing their flexibility with ideas and language (Cremin and Maybin, 2013).

Harness curiosity and profile agency

At the core of creativity is a deep sense of curiosity and wonder, a desire to question and ponder; teachers need to model this questioning stance, this openness to possibility and desire to learn. In the context of the literacy classroom, developing opportunities for children to 'possibility think' their way forward is, therefore, crucial (Craft, 2001). This will involve immersing the class in an issue or subject and helping them ask possibility broad questions (Chappell et al., 2008), take risks, be imaginative and playfully explore options and ideas as they work on extended purposeful projects. On the journey, which recent research indicates is often framed as narrative and is driven by questioning and imagination (Cremin, Chappell et al., 2012), knowledge about language and skills will be developed through the children's involvement as readers, writers, speakers and listeners.

Crucial to this exploration will be the development of children's self-determination and agency. Their capacity to work as independent enquirers and creative thinkers will be influenced by the degree to which teachers share the control of the learning agenda (Cremin, Burnard et al., 2006; Craft et al., 2013). Offering elements of choice in reading and writing, in terms of texts to read and the subject matter or form of writing, for example, can help construct literacy curricula that build on learners' interests, as well as their social and cultural capital. Encouraging children to identify their own questions about texts, not just respond to those identified by the teacher, can also increase their involvement, intentionality and agency, but it is not enough. Self-directed learning and the agency of individuals and groups must be carefully planned for, reflected upon and celebrated in order to foster creativity.

Teachers need to be able to stand back and let the children take the lead, supporting them as they take risks, encounter problems and map out their own learning journeys, setting their own goals and agreeing some of their own success criteria in the process. In open-ended contexts, control is more likely to be devolved to children, at least in part, and they are more likely to adapt and extend activities in unexpected ways, adopt different perspectives and construct their own tasks. In this way, innovation and creativity can be fostered. Such an approach resonates with the pupil voice movement (Robinson, 2014) and encourages children to take increased responsibility for their own education.

Encourage collaboration and making connections

The perception of both learning and creativity as collaborative social processes is gaining ground. Although children engage individually, their endeavours are linked to the work of others, and they support one another's thinking and creativity, fostering both individual and collective creativity (Vass, 2004; Craft, Cremin *et al.*, 2012). Creative English teachers seek to foster this and exploit the full range of collaborations available in and beyond the classroom, including, for example, pair work, small-group and whole-class work, as well as partnerships with parents, authors, poets, storytellers, dancers, actors, singers and many others. Children will be involved in generating ideas through interaction and playful exploration, gathering knowledge with and from each other, seeking support from others, evaluating their work and that of others, and transforming their existing understanding through a range of collaborative activities.

Creativity also involves making connections with other areas of learning, with other texts and experiences. Through their own questioning stance, creative teachers actively encourage pupils to make associations and connections, perhaps through connecting to prior learning or making links between subjects and/or across different media for example. Creative teachers make personal connections in the context of literature discussions and share intertextual connections to prompt children to make their own connections. Developing a spirit of enquiry and openness to ideas from different sources, such as people, texts of all kinds, objects and experiences, can help children make lateral and divergent connections. In addition, a range of pedagogical strategies and diverse teaching styles and entry points can be used to enable new connections to be formed in the minds and work of the children.

Integrate reflection, review, feedback and celebration

Creativity not only involves the generation of novel ideas, but also the critical evaluation of them; it involves both selection and judgement, as some ideas are rejected, whereas others may be pursued in more depth. Such evaluative reflection and review need to be effectively modelled by teachers, as they seek to enable youngsters to make insightful self-judgements and to engage in small-group peer review and assessment of their creative endeavours. The creative process may involve rational and non-rational thought and may be fed by daydreaming and intuition (Claxton, 2000), as well as the application of knowledge and skills. So, mapping in moments of reflection and contemplation and encouraging children to incubate their ideas and revisit earlier pieces of writing can, for example, support their development as creative learners.

The ability to give and receive criticism is an essential part of creativity, and so teachers will want to encourage evaluation through supportive and honest feedback, as well as self-reflection and review. This can foster children's metacognitive awareness, which, as Fisher (2013) has shown, contributes to learning. When children are engaged in mindful, negotiated and interactive practices in English, they are more prepared to review their ongoing development work, as well as reflect upon the decisions they have made and the final outcome that has been produced. This relates closely to the autonomy and agency offered and the relevance of the activity in the learner's eyes. Teachers work towards a semi-constant oscillation between engagement and reflection, as learners refine, reshape and improve their work, preparing perhaps for a storytelling festival or a publication deadline.

In addition, creative professionals seize opportunities to share and celebrate children's successes, in part through the actual publication of anthologies of work and festivals or assemblies, for example, but also through informal class sharing of various kinds. Ongoing celebration and focused feedback are also significant; they can help children to reflect upon the creative process, their emerging ideas and unfolding work, and enrich learning.

Take time to travel and teach skills in context

Effective teachers work creatively to balance the teaching of skills, knowledge and understanding, through integrating teaching and learning about the language modes as children undertake extended units of work. Such learning journeys need to be imaginatively engaging, relevant and purposeful, if children's creativity is to be developed. A ten-country European study on creative learning has demonstrated the importance of such extended open adventures, in which children explore and develop knowledge through focused engagement with their work, and review the process and outcomes of their engagement (Jeffrey, 2005, 2006). Additionally, in a United Kingdom Literacy Association (UKLA) project that successfully raised boys' achievements in writing, it was found that taking time to travel enabled the disaffected boy writers to get involved in depth. The use of film and drama to drive the units of work also motivated them, helping raise their levels of commitment and persistence, their independence and motivation, as well as influencing the quality of the work produced (Bearne *et al.*, 2004).

Such extended work is now more common, with opportunities to explore and investigate a particular text type or issue over a period of several weeks, such that grammatical skills, for example, are taught in context (Reedy and Bearne, 2013). This builds in increased time for creative exploration and engagement and also allows emergent issues to be recognised and responded to. This can help teachers trust their instincts and allow them to divert the journey and/or follow the learners' interests, thus creating a more responsive and flexible curriculum. Creative pedagogues, working in partnerships with external specialists, often plan significant holistic projects and tend to have ambitious long-term goals: the production of a film or community play, perhaps (Thomson *et al.*, 2012). In such projects, children are encouraged to initiate activities and direct more of their own work, which can nurture both interest and commitment – potent fuel for a journey of extended exploration (see Chapter 12).

To develop a mastery orientation, whereby children develop self-determination and take ownership of their learning (in contrast to a learned helplessness), they need to feel able to take risks, to try things out and experiment, but, to do this, they need to feel secure and trusted by their teacher (Dweck, 2012). Arguably, they will be helped if they perceive their teacher as a creative individual also.

Ensure the creative involvement of the teacher

In schools where standards in English are high, teachers' passions about English and their own creativity are also valued and given space to develop (Frater, 2001). Creative teachers, as Sternberg (1999) suggests, are creative role models themselves, professionals who continue to be self-motivated learners, value the creative dimensions of their own lives and make connections between their personal responses to experience and their teaching. Such teachers are willing and able to express themselves, even though this involves taking risks and being observed in the process. Wilson and Ball (1997) found that risk taking is a common characteristic of highly successful literacy teachers, not merely in relation to their artistic engagement, but also in their capacity to experiment and remain open to new ideas and strategies that may benefit the learners. Creative teachers plan with specific objectives in mind, but may spontaneously alter the direction of the exploration in response to children's interests and needs.

Through their own imaginative involvement in classroom endeavour, teachers' creative potential can be released, and their confidence, commitment and understanding of the challenge of using literacy for one's own expressive and creative purposes can grow. As artists in their classrooms, telling tales, responding to texts, performing poems, writing and taking roles in drama, teachers are freed from the traditional patterns of classroom interaction and are more personally and affectively involved, using their knowledge and skills, as well as their creativity and experience. The experience and practice of the teacher as artist arguably needs to be reinstated at the heart of teaching literacy. As McWilliam (2008) argues, teachers need to move from being the 'sage on the stage', apparently transmitting knowledge, to becoming 'meddlers in the middle', 'co-learners in the thick of it'. If teachers themselves are imaginatively involved, they are better placed to develop children's creativity, working alongside them in the learning process.

CONCLUSION

Good practice exists when creative and informed professionals respond flexibly to current curricula and develop coherent and imaginative approaches, underpinned by pedagogical and subject knowledge *and* knowledge of individual children. This book seeks to support such practice by offering practical advice and ideas for taking a creative approach to English and showing how knowledge, skills and understanding can be developed through engagement in meaningful and creative contexts. In order to ensure that teachers are able to develop principled practice in teaching English creatively, research and theoretical perspectives are woven throughout. In reflecting upon the combination of practice and theory offered, it is hoped that teachers will appreciate more fully the potential of teaching English creatively and teaching for creativity in English.

FURTHER READING

Craft, A. (2011) *Creativity and Education Futures*. Stoke-on-Trent, UK: Trentham Books.

Cremin, T. (2015) 'Creative teachers and creative teaching', in A. Wilson (ed.), *Creativity in Primary Education* (2nd edn). Exeter, UK: Learning Matters, pp. 33–44.

Cremin, T. and Maybin, J. (2013) 'Language and creativity: Teachers and students', in K. Hall, T. Cremin, B. Comber and L. Moll, *The Wiley Blackwell International Research Handbook of Children's Literacy, Learning and Culture*. Oxford, UK: Wiley Blackwell, pp. 275–90.

Sawyer, R. (ed.) (2011) *Structure and Improvisation in Creative Teaching*. New York: Cambridge.

Thomson, P., Hall, C., Jones, K. and Sefton-Green, J. (2012) *The Signature Pedagogies Project: Final report*. London: Creativity, Culture and Education.

CHAPTER 2

DEVELOPING CREATIVITY THROUGH TALK

Teresa Cremin and David Reedy

INTRODUCTION

When children use language to learn and to communicate in creatively engaging and moti-vating contexts, they experience its powerfully provocative as well as evocative potential. This chapter, alongside the next one on drama, focuses on talk as a highly accessible and potent medium for learning, literacy and personal/social development. Dialogic teaching, the creative nature of talk and the role of the teacher as a model of curiosity and creative engagement are all examined. The chapter also shares practical strategies to develop children's confidence and competence as language artists through oral storytelling (personal and traditional) and in the context of other small-group activities that offer opportunities for engagement and reflection.

In the English NC (DfE, 2013: 3), it is stated that 'pupils' confidence and competence in spoken language and listening skills' need to be 'continually developed'. This encompasses fostering the capacity of young learners to 'explain their understanding of books and other reading, and to prepare their ideas before they write'. Discussion is also seen as critical to developing a secure foundation for learning, and it is stated that children should be taught 'to understand and use the conventions for discussion and debate'. Not dissimilarly, in the Welsh Framework for Literacy (DfES, 2013), the development and presentation of information and ideas through speaking, listening, collaboration and group discussion are statutory. In the Scottish principles and practice document (Education Scotland, 2012), within the Curriculum for Excellence and the Northern Ireland curriculum (DENI, 2011), listening and talking are given equivalence to reading and writing, and there is also recognition that oracy can deepen children's learning and thinking.

PRINCIPLES

Though the weight afforded the spoken word varies in the different UK curricula, all arguably recognise it as a vital foundation for the development of literacy. In their early encounters with language, young children learn to take part and to negotiate meaning, actively solving problems and making sense with and through others. Adults, as their con-versational partners, engage in highly contextualised talk arising out of activities in which they both engage. In their homes, the amount and quality of the dialogue that children experience is highly significant, and the quality of the dialogue in school contexts is, therefore, no less important. As Britton (1970) observed, 'reading and writing float on a sea of talk'; oracy is the basis of much literate behaviour. Talking enables learners to think aloud, formulate their thoughts and opinions, and refine and develop their ideas and understandings through engaging in meaningful dialogue with others. Talk also enables learners to relate new experience to previous knowledge and understanding, and to value their own and others' ideas.

Although talk is a rich resource for learning, it is also a mode of communication, with considerable artistic power and potential. Research into everyday talk affirms that creative language use is not a special feature of some people, but is common to all (Carter, 2004). This research suggests that playful use of language is typically co- produced and is most likely to develop in dialogic and intimate conditions. Through telling stories and taking part in drama, for example, children can experience the potential of the spoken word and enrich their oral artistry. Their creativity, understanding and imagination can also be engaged and fostered through discussion and interaction. So, teachers need to value, appreciate and develop children's spoken language and enable them to learn collaboratively and creatively through interaction.

TALKING AND LEARNING

Arguably, the predominant model of learning in Western societies has been one of information transfer, in which children are seen as empty vessels, passive learners who receive information from their teacher. In this model, learning is viewed as an individual cognitive activity, and teaching centres on individual performance and emphasises personal expression and individual skill development. Research suggests that this transmission model of teaching persists, particularly in the UK and US, where pupils receive information from teachers and are then asked questions to recall this (Alexander, 2000, 2008, 2010; Nystrand, 2006). The Final Report of the Cambridge Primary Review stated:

> Classroom research shows that, in England, teacher–pupil and pupil–pupil talk are under exploited as tools for learning and that their potential for much more than transmission is rarely fulfilled. Talk – at home, in school, among peers – is education at its most potent. It is an aspect of teaching which has arguably the greatest purchase on learning. Yet it is also the most resistant to change.
>
> (Alexander, 2010: 306)

Although teachers intuitively know that learning is often a mutual accomplishment, and that collaboration is a critical way to build intellectual insight and understanding, operationalising this is not always straightforward. Yet many scholars, leaning on the work of Vygotsky (1978), argue for a pedagogy in which talk plays a central role and believe that humans learn through guided participation and the support of more competent others (Wells, 1999; Mercer and Littleton, 2007). Research into development through dialogue proposes that learning is a product of inter-thinking, and that, for a teacher to teach and a learner to learn, they must use talk and joint activity to create a shared communicative space, an 'intermental development zone' (Mercer, 2000; Littleton and Mercer, 2013). In this way, cognitive development has been reviewed as a dialogic process, a transformation of participation.

In classrooms, more attention needs to be paid to the fundamental importance of talk, talk that highlights collaboration, joint knowledge construction and the active engagement of both children and teachers in a community of learners. In such a community, quality oral interaction and full pupil participation play a central role, and children are creatively engaged with their own learning, talking their way forward and making connections as they travel alongside their teachers, whose repertoires of talk matter. Alexander (2000, 2008) argues that five forms of teacher talk should be an integral part of an educator's repertoire, though he sees discussion and particularly dialogue as the most effective in moving thinking on:

■ *Rote*: The drilling of facts, ideas and routines through repetition.
■ *Recitation*: The accumulation of knowledge and understanding through questions designed to test or stimulate recall of what has been previously encountered or to help pupils to work out the answer from clues provided in the question.
■ *Exposition*: Telling pupils what to do, and/or imparting information, and/or explaining facts, principles or procedures.
■ *Discussion*: The exchange of ideas with a view to sharing information, solving problems or making collective decisions.
■ *Dialogue*: Achieving common understanding through structured and cumulative questioning and discussion. There may, or may not, be a right answer but justification and explanation are sought. Pupils' thinking is challenged and so understanding is enhanced. The teacher is likely to share several exchanges with a particular child several times in order to move the thinking on.

(Alexander 2000: 526–7)

Dialogic teaching and learning involve discussion being used as a tool to explore issues and solve problems, fostering a social mode of thinking in order to develop shared knowledge and understanding. In Alexander's (2008) terms, dialogue weaves through the discussion with the teacher (mainly) asking questions and making contributions that are designed, even when they are tentative, to provoke thoughtful responses and to challenge children's thinking, so that justification and explanation are sought, and understanding is enhanced.

The following example of dialogic teaching comes from an extended conversation between a group of 10-year-old girls about Leon Garfield's retelling of Shakespeare's *A Midsummer Night's Dream*. The pupils were familiar with the text and had been asked, in small groups, to prepare a section of it for presentation to the class and be ready to answer questions about their interpretation. After one of the group's performances, the following conversation took place.

Teacher:	Which line from the passage that you prepared do you think was directly quoted from the play?
Pupils 1 and 2:	'The course of true love never did run smooth.'
Teacher:	What do you think that means?
P1:	It means that love never goes how you might plan it.
Teacher:	How do you think that this line is going to tell us about what is going to be happening in the story?

P2:	That nothing is going to go right.
Teacher:	In what way?
P2:	Hermia, Lysander, Demetrius and Helena – their love lives are going to *get all* tangled!
Teacher:	Good. Imagine that you are an agony aunt for a magazine and Helena has written in and told you that Hermia and Lysander love each other, and that she loves Demetrius, but that he also loves Hermia. What would your reply to the Helena be?
P1 and P2:	*Silence – thinking*
Teacher:	It says that Helena is hoping for 'no more than a glance of gratitude and a rag of his comfort'. What do you think that means?
P1:	She's not asking for very much – just a little bit of attention.
Teacher:	Is she looking for a full-blown romance, marriage, house and car?
P2:	No – she just wants him to notice her.
Teacher	So what advice would you give Helena then?
P3:	She could get highlights.
P1:	She should stand up and be a little more confident.
Teacher:	That's good advice.
P3:	She should stand up for herself and not get pushed aside by other people.
P4:	I think she should forget about that and fly off somewhere hot!

The key test for any sequence of classroom conversation must be whether there is evidence of enhanced understanding, of thinking moving forward. In this short extract, the pupils are actively engaged in working together to develop their understanding of the characters' actions and the themes within the play. They add to each other's contributions, and the teacher questions and challenges. Crucially, the first contribution by pupil 3, which at first seems like a throwaway, jokey aside, actually leads to a more subtle interpretation/ understanding on the part of the group about Helena. There is an emerging realisation that Helena does not simply want to have her presence noted, but also desires some emotional engagement. To do so, Helena will need to be more assertive, both physically (stand up) and emotionally (be confident and not pushed around by people). It is significant that pupil 3's second contribution is a more serious and informed response, showing a move forward in her thinking. In addition, pupil 1 adds to her initial response that Helena just needs a little attention, and pupil 4 has listened carefully to all the preceding discussion and finishes it off with a more radical solution.

The teacher's role in this productive conversation is crucial. She initiates and shapes the discourse. She builds the conversation with the pupils, skilfully responding to the content of what they say, and avoids recitation-type talk, so often dominant in English classrooms. The teacher helps the children make connections with their own experience through the suggestion about seeing themselves as an 'agony aunt' and helps them reflect on the dilemma the character Helena finds herself in. After a period of thinking, the pupils collectively make contributions that add to and clarify their own thinking. The teacher affirms this new thinking ('that's good advice'), encouraging the thinking to move forward in a collaborative and collective way. She also varies her responses and listens attentively to the content of the children's utterances. Her statements and questions are structured to provoke thoughtful responses, which in turn provoke further questions. This teacher understands that, although her initial question is important, it is how she responds to what the pupils say as a result that really makes the difference. Their responses are the fulcrum of the conversation (Alexander, 2008).

TEACHERS' ORAL ARTISTRY

Despite the high profile given to dialogic teaching in recent years, the pressure of pace and the desire to cover the curriculum and to raise standards often prompt teachers to short-change their pedagogical principles regarding talk and its role in learning (English *et al.*, 2002; Burns and Myhill, 2004; Coulthas, 2012). However, teachers can modify their talk, and many creative teachers actively seek to model a more speculative, hypothetical and dialogic stance that raises the level of cognitive demand and facilitates children's analytical thinking. These professionals try to use their voices and their imaginations to offer open invitations to learn and negotiate the curriculum content with young learners, whose own voices play a significant role in the learning process. They tend to place the learners above the curriculum and combine this with a positive disposition towards creativity, actively encouraging young people to learn and think for themselves (Craft, 2011). There is evidence that teachers who encourage children to ask questions that puzzle or intrigue them – of the teacher, of each other and of themselves – enable deeper learning to take place (Nystrand, 2006). Such teachers respond to children's feelings and interests, allow them considerable scope to work together, maintain their individual identities/autonomy and foster their capacity to reflect critically (Jeffrey and Woods, 2003). The spoken word plays a significant role in such creative practice, in which teachers seek to allow children real thinking time, model tentativeness and show genuine interest in what the learners have to say. Creative teachers also model language forms that support collaboration and the development of exploratory talk – for example, language structures that support justification ('I think . . . because . . .') and clarification/the eliciting of others' opinions ('What do you think about . . .?', 'I am not sure I understand what you mean . . .').

If teachers develop their own creative potential and value the creative dimensions of their own lives, this can help them extend the children's development as oral language artists and creative language users (Prentice, 2000). The powerful art forms of drama and storytelling both support oral artistry and creativity and demand that teachers are able and willing to express themselves. This involves taking risks and being observed in the process. If teachers are to contribute imaginatively to the construction of confident and curious individuals, their ability to interest and inspire, tell stories and take up roles in drama, using words flexibly and creatively, deserves development (Cremin and Maybin, 2013). In addition, teachers need to be able to bring an author's voice to life evocatively and develop an ear for the colour, movement and drama of the language used by both professional writers and the children themselves. Through inviting their participation and experiential engagement in the process of learning, teachers can help children hear, notice and experience language emotionally, aesthetically and artistically.

FOSTERING CURIOSITY AND AUTONOMY THROUGH COLLABORATIVE GROUP WORK

When teachers and learners embark on a collaborative learning journey that focuses on exploration and playful engagement, the role of curiosity and identifying genuine questions of interest or puzzlement come to the fore. Jeffrey and Craft (2004) describe this as an 'inclusive approach to pedagogy', one that involves posing questions, identifying problems and issues and debating and discussing thinking together. Such questions are the building blocks of dialogic classrooms, in which time is made for discussion and collaboration in whole-class and small-group contexts, right across the curriculum (Alexander, 2000). Research into children's 'possibility thinking' (Craft, McConnon *et al.*, 2012) suggests that teachers who foster this 'what if' frameset make extensive use of large framing questions and employ an explicitly speculative stance in the classroom (Chappell *et al.*, 2008). Possibility thinking, which is seen to be at the heart of creative learning, is driven by curiosity, question posing and question responding (Burnard *et al.*, 2006; Craft, Cremin *et al.*, 2012; Cremin *et al.*, 2013). Teachers' possibility broad questions push children back on their own resources, encouraging knowledge sharing and increased autonomy. When invited to respond to children's problems during such work, such teachers frequently employ reverse questioning, enquiring, for example, 'How could you deal with this problem, do you think? What ideas have *you* got?' (Cremin, Burnard *et al.*, 2006).

In explicitly encouraging children to identify and share their own questions about a text, for example, through thought showers or pair work on what puzzles them, teachers foster children's curiosity and affirm their questions as valid and valuable, demonstrating interest in, and respect for, learners' ideas. As children realise their questions are valued, they begin to ask more, ponder longer and reflect upon other ways to achieve a task or represent their learning. One teacher, employing a 'bookzip' strategy, explained to a group of 8–9-year-olds that the picture book *Farther* by Grahame Baker Smith was zipped up tight and could not be opened (with younger years, teachers sometimes say the lives of book fairies will be endangered if the book is forced open!). Examining the cover, the group voiced multiple questions and comments that reflected their capacity to make creative connections, which offered their teacher an insight into their thinking:

> 'Is that his son?'
> 'Are they both angels?'
> 'They're in heaven I reckon'
> 'Dead'
> 'It's like in space or on the moon, see those rocks?'
> 'It can't be – there are flowers'
> 'Look it says . . . "Then the dream spoke to me and I took up the old wings" – weird'
> 'Cool, they are dead'
> 'Maybe they were angels before, or he was . . .'
> 'They look kind of blank'
> 'Sort of unseeing'
> 'Why are they sitting if they're angels, it doesn't make sense? Angels fly'
> 'Not necessarily'
> 'Maybe the old man is God?'
> 'And the boy Jesus?'
> 'His Father'
> 'No it's Far-ther – there's an r'.

In addition to inciting interest and fostering children's curiosity through book talk, creative teachers set time aside for children to pursue their own enquiries in groups, fostering learner autonomy and giving them responsibility. However, despite children's willingness to engage in small-group activities, they need support in order to work effectively together, using language to generate ideas, solve problems, reason and construct knowledge (Littleton and Mercer, 2013). Programmes such as Thinking Together (Dawes *et al.*, 2004) can be very useful for developing speaking and listening, as can strategies for effective group work. For example:

- *Ground rules*: Create a class poster with ground rules for working in groups. Highlight particular elements in different group tasks through taking photographs of children and incorporating them into the poster. This combination of words and pictures acts as a reminder of what has been agreed.
- *Roles for group members*: Groups decide on roles such as leader, reporter and scribe and review these during the extended activity.
- *Aim, review, question (ARQ)*: Groups monitor their progress to keep on task. Any member or the teacher can play the 'ARQ card' if they feel confused/uncertain of where the group is heading or want to recap what has been agreed.
- *Review time*: Groups are given time to review their work and consider how they are operating; they may also set new targets.

FOSTERING IMAGINATIVE ENGAGEMENT THROUGH STORYTELLING

Too often storytelling is viewed only as an early years practice, and yet *all* children (and adults) have stories to tell: family stories, reminiscences, hopes, warnings, explanations, jokes, televisual tales and tales read, heard and created. Humans use narrative as a way of making sense of the complexity of existence and, as they tell tales, make language choices at the very moment of utterance. So this oral art form can be woven into literacy teaching as a valuable medium to foster creative language use. Oral storytelling builds on children's natural narrative competence, fosters their imaginative engagement in learning and can enrich their confidence. In retelling tales orally, children can develop their verbal artistry and extend their creative capacity, which some find more difficult to develop in writing. As the children's writer David Almond (2001) observed: 'The roots of story are internalised through the circle of reading, writing, telling and listening.'

Personal oral stories deserve a central role in the curriculum. Research has established the developmental significance of storytelling and imaginative play during early childhood (Bruner, 1986; Engel, 2005; Faulkner, 2011) and the importance of autobiography and of individual as well as collective memory in the formation of identity (Rosen, 1988). Through affording space for children to share their personal stories, teachers demonstrate their respect for individuals and offer them the chance to make connections, reflect upon their lives and enhance their confidence and narrative fluency. As children retell chosen anecdotes and incidents from their lives, they make spontaneous choices about vocabulary, style and language, while leaning on the natural writing frame of lived experience. Creating timelines or emotions graphs of significant events in their lives and using these to prompt oral recounts can be valuable on their own, and can prepare the ground for later diary entries or autobiographical extracts. Additionally, making personal story boxes, (using shoe boxes and adding items from home to convey something of themselves, their families and interests) can act as useful prompts. Many tales told will be a combination of remembering/life experience and imagining, as teachers who employ the Helicopter Technique, based on Paley's (1990, 2004) work, have found. This technique involves teachers scribing young children's stories, which are enacted later by the class. The examples of stories (noted below) that were dictated by four 6-year-olds to their teachers highlight the young learners' engagement, rich range of ideas and emerging knowledge of narrative structure. Recent research has shown this approach has considerable potential for developing children's agency; confidence; belonging and identity; communication, language and literacy; and their creativity (Cremin *et al.*, 2013). It showed that the Helicopter Technique was not only motivating, but, crucially, it enabled children to feel safe enough to exercise their own choices as storytellers and story actors, and even to adopt new and self-chosen roles as young story scribes for other children's stories.

> Once upon a time the princess had a sweetie and the greedy wolf came and gobbled up all the sweeties and the princess said 'where did you get all my sweeties?' And the wolf said 'I just want all the sweeties cos I am hungry, cos I don't like rice cos I just like sweeties.' The princess said 'You're not allowed sweeties, it's not good for your teeth. Your teeth will come out.'
>
> (Dictated by Nafisa)

> Once upon a time there was a cheeky princess called Alice; she had a strong imagination and she could do anything with it. Her Aunt Redd was invading after being banished from her hometown. Alice ran with her personal bodyguard through the palace teleport. The personal body guard landed in Paris but Alice landed in London, but they found each other soon. When they came back through the teleport, Alice went through the imagination maze. Now her imagination was strong she killed her Aunt Redd and she never returned.
>
> (Dictated by Eddie)

> Once upon a time there was a dinosaur and once upon a time there was a girl. And every animals came to eat all the people and then there was a dinosaur eating another dinosaur. Then it was night and the snow come and it was cold and the dinosaur was freezing. And then the dinosaur eat and eat and then grow up. And then he gonna fight with the peoples and eat the peoples. And then the dinosaur eat the girl.
>
> (Dictated by Saif)

Traditional tales, myths and legends also deserve a prominent role in a creative approach to literacy teaching. Originally moulded for the ear, those with a strong oral orientation still retain considerable repetition, rhythm and sometimes rhyme, which make them easier for children to recall. If teachers tell, as well as read, traditional tales and offer opportunities for children to develop as storytellers, then, over time, they will come to employ strong narrative structures and use rich and memorable language in their tales. The process of preparing to tell a tale to others is not a memory test, however, but an opportunity to share the soul of the story, leaning on the narrative structure and enticing listeners to imagine and respond. Oral storytellers are language artists, who make full use of their voice and experiment with pause, pace and intonation, as well as gesture and facial expressions (Grainger, 1997). Tellers choose how to share the essence of the story, using skills to assist their telling that suit the tenor and temperature of the tale. Through retelling

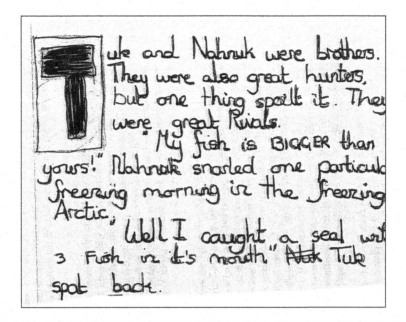

Figure 2.1 Two story beginnings

tales, children experience the fluency, flow and feel of their words and can try out their own and others' tunes and receive a response. It is worth paying particular attention to traditional story beginnings as supportive scaffolds. These can be collected, displayed, imitated and innovated with when telling or writing tales. The examples in Figure 2.1 reflect the influence of the oral in the written, capture the readers' interest and reveal a sense of each teller's fluency and flow.

Support for remembering story structures

In preparing for a storytelling festival or story-sharing event with another class, at the end of an extended learning journey, various strategies can be used to help children remember the structure and events in their chosen tale, albeit they may improvise around these elements:

■ *The three seeds of story*: These represent the beginning, middle and end of the tale. Pictures are drawn on paper seeds of different sizes to deconstruct a tale (or plan a new one), and are then watered in the retelling by the storyteller's words.

▨ *Story mountains*: These paper mountains reflect the trajectories of stories and are particularly useful for climactic stories. Symbols, pictures or words that represent key events in the tale are drawn on different parts of the mountain range.

▨ *Skeletal summaries*: These key-word summaries are listed on the body of a skeleton drawing. Significant phrases from the story can be included to aid recall. See Figure 2.2.

▨ *Story plates*: Key elements of the tale are drawn to act as structural prompts for retelling see Figure 2.3.

▨ *Emotions graphs*: These involve recording, on a graph, a character's journey though the narrative. The vertical axis represents the emotions of the character, from low to high; the horizontal axis represents the timeline of the tale.

There are a range of organisational strategies to support retelling tales or parts of them to story partners or in groups. These help to embed the narrative in the mind and foster fluency and confidence:

▨ *Storytelling pairs*: In A and B pairs, tellers retell their tale to their listening partner, taking turns.

▨ *Whole-class story circle*: As a class, perhaps using a story icon, retell the tale, but avoid taking pressurising turns around the circle.

▨ *Rainbow regroup*: Tell part of a tale, invite groups to predict the next part and give each member a colour in order to form new groups; in these, each child retells their own group's ending to the others.

▨ *Story conferences*: These are opportunities for children to retell a tale/part of one, in preparation for an event, to a small group that offers support and feedback to the teller.

Over time, the creative experience of oral storytelling and revoicing known tales can have a marked impact on children's literacy learning and their creative capacity to transform texts (Fox, 1993a, 1993b; Grainger *et al.*, 2005; Cremin *et al.*, 2013). Reading traditional tales can also enrich children's repertoires and the structures and language upon which they draw. Leaning on powerful storytellers in this genre, such as Kevin Crossley Holland, Mary Medlicott and Fiona French, can be enriching, as can playing with parodies, such as the recent and delicious *Good Little Wolf*, by Nadia Shireen and the older, but very powerful and ironic, *Squids will be Squids*, by Jan Scieszka and Lane Smith. Being playful, a group of 10-year-olds produced their own broadsheet, *The Daily Crime* (see Figure 2.4 for the front-cover spread) based on traditional tales and parodies thereof.

REFLECTING UPON TALK

Children can benefit from considering the role of talk in learning and their role as members of groups, building understanding through collaborating together. They need opportunities to verbalise what they know and what they have learned, and to share their discoveries with each other, evaluating their own and each other's thinking and contributions in constructive ways. Their understanding of group interaction and their ability to monitor, select and reflect upon their use of language are crucial to the success of group

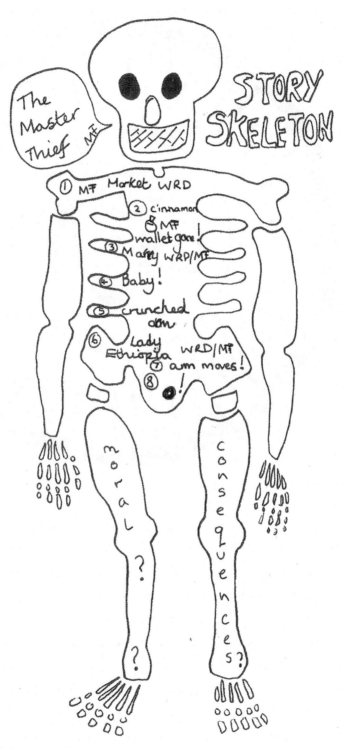

■ **Figure 2.2** A story skeleton

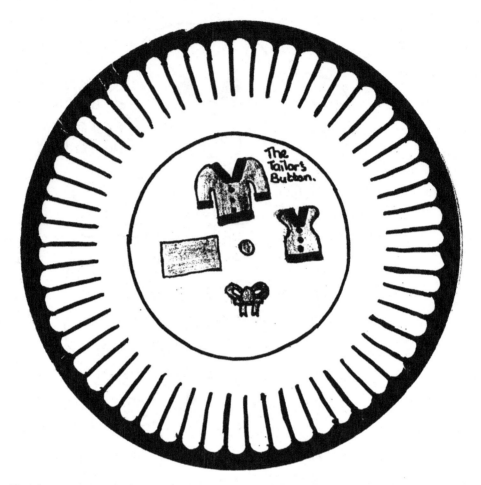

■ **Figure 2.3** A story plate

work (Mercer and Littleton, 2007). Alongside developing ground rules for talk, strategies such as the following help raise the profile of talk:

■ *Talk detective work*: Individuals take it in turns to be a talk detective and listen to a group at work, making notes and commenting on their interaction afterwards.
■ *Reporters*: Individuals take it in turns to create a summary of their group's work and then review this with their group, to see if they represented the discussion fairly.
■ *Recording group talk*: Groups listen to short taped extracts of their collaborative work and comment on their own and each other's contributions.
■ *Identifying good talkers and listeners*: Children discuss those they see as skilled talkers and listeners (within and beyond school) and consider their characteristics.

In seeking to widen children's understanding of how talk is used in society, teachers can make use of different technologies, using drama to recreate and review such language use. Talk within Parliament, radio programmes, documentaries, chat shows, reality shows,

THE DAILY CRIME

THE FAMILY COMPANY

Issue 56

2/4/1942 Monday

2 DOWN 1 TO GO

On the 16th of August, 1942, Wallace Wolf, A.K.A The Big, Bad Wolf, slaughtered 2 pigs, and ate them. He is currently being prosecuted for cannibalism, trespass, and vandalism.

We have got an exclusive interview with a murderer and a survivor. In the late afternoon of Wednesday a wolf was seen committing the atrocious crime of pig slaughter. Two pigs were killed in his merciless killings. The third lives to tell the gory tale: " I heard my second brother shouting for help as his house fell down, of course at the time I wasn't very worried, because I knew the idiot had built his house out of sticks and sticks can't be that heavy, can they? I was just phoning the fire brigade when I heard the wolf coming up to my door.

quickly phoned the police and told them of my situation."

Next we talk to the wolf himself: "This a big misunderstanding", he quoted, "all I wanted was a cup of sugar for my dear, dear granny. This is a total setup to bad mouth me and the wider wolf community. I only blew down the house with a sneeze, I mean, what kind of idiot makes a house out straw and sticks! And they were dead before the house fell down. I was simply eating what I found on the floor. I think of them as cheeseburgers, lying there, asking to be eaten. So you see I'm innocent, 100% innocent". Unfortunately wolf was cut off from us there as his visitors time at the prison was over.

So who's side are you on? The so called innocent wolf, or the grieving pigs.

Reported by Will Carus and Mat Hill

Other broadsheets

- *THE DAILY DING DONG*
- *THE FAIRY LAND HOME BUYER*
- *Mother 'Hubbard's*

Magical Mischief!

Today Miss Cindersmella is being charged for fiddling with fate. She is probably going to spend the rest of her life in a cellar.

Last night cindersmella, 43, was tried for messing about with fate. Aided by her fairy god mother she made sure she could meet Prince Casserole. She succeeded in this part of her plan, but then Prince Casserole slapped her in the face with a wet herring. Soon after 24:00 came and she had to leave the ball. Prince Casserole's brother followed her and found out her true identity. He immediately phoned the police and told them that a tramp had snuck in. When questioned Cindersmella admitted all.

Inside this issue:

The Dodgy Teacher	1
Simpson's Invade	2
The Funnys	3
Birthday Boy	4
Weather	4
News	5
Sports	6

■ **Figure 2.4** Front cover of *The Daily Crime*, a group newspaper adverts and a wealth of other oral texts can all be used in the classroom, to offer real-world relevance and help children reflect upon how people use language for different purposes, in different situations and social groups. For example, the language and oral skills of TV presenters on children's shows when making a craft item could be analysed and discussed, and then emulated as an improvised oral procedural text.

In addition, teachers will wish to assess children's growing confidence and competence as talkers and listeners and gather information from a range of contexts that can be summarised to make judgements about the progress of each child. Focusing on a couple of children each week to ensure systematic coverage of the whole class and building opportunities for assessing talk across the curriculum can help as teachers identify and review targets with and for children.

CONCLUSION

The value of the spoken word is important to recognise and develop in the classroom. Talk can enrich children's confidence and competence as effective language users and support their development as creative thinkers who employ their imaginations to find ways forward in collaboration with others. As language artists in the primary classroom, creative teachers are freed from the traditional patterns of classroom interaction and are arguably more personally and affectively involved. Such professionals capitalise upon dialogic teaching and remain alert to children's playful use of language, building on this and affording opportunities to learn through talk and reflect upon it. As they stretch their own use of language, as storytellers, problem solvers and different characters in drama, teachers model the capacity to question, generate and evaluate their ideas and support development of children's creative language use.

FURTHER READING

Alexander, R. (2008) *Towards Dialogic Teaching: Rethinking classroom talk* (4th edn). Cambridge, UK: Dialogos.

Carter, R. (2004) *Language and Creativity: The art of common talk*. London: Routledge.

Cremin, T. and Maybin, J. (2013) 'Language and creativity: Teachers and students', in K. Hall, T. Cremin, B. Comber and L. Moll, *The Wiley Blackwell International Research Handbook of Children's Literacy, Learning and Culture*. Oxford, UK: Wiley Blackwell, pp. 275–90.

Littleton, K. and Mercer, N. (2013) *Interthinking: Putting talk to work*. London: Routledge.

CHILDREN'S BOOKS

Baker Smith, G. (2011) *Farther*. Dorking, UK: Templar.

Foreman, M. (2002) *Dinosaur Time*. London: Walker.

Grindley, S. (ed.) (1997) *Breaking the Spell*. London: Kingfisher.

Rosen, M. (1995) *South, North, East, West*. London: Walker.

Scieszka, J. (1998) *Squids will be Squids*. New York: Viking.

Shireen, N. (2013) *Good Little Wolf*. London: Jonathan Cape.

DEVELOPING CREATIVITY THROUGH DRAMA

Teresa Cremin

INTRODUCTION

Drama, the art form of social encounters, offers children the chance to engage creatively in fictional-world-making play. Such play, whether in the role-play area or in classroom drama, involves making and shaping worlds, investigating issues within them and returning to the real world with more understanding and insight. The key features of creative literacy practice are evident in improvisational drama: it fosters play, collaborative engagement and reflection, is often based on a powerful text and harnesses children's curiosity and agency. Neelands (2011), who conceptualises drama as creative learning, explains that improvisation is itself a creative activity, because it requires teachers and learners to imagine themselves and the world differently, making spontaneous decisions and responding to the unexpected.

In the English NC (DfE, 2013: 4), it is stated that, 'pupils should be enabled to participate in and gain knowledge, skills and understanding associated with the artistic practice of drama', and that they should be able to 'adopt, create and sustain a range of roles, responding appropriately to others in role'. Additionally, it is expected that they will have opportunities to improvise and to respond to drama and theatre performances, as well as write their own play-scripts. In the Welsh (DfES, 2013) and Scottish curricula (Education Scotland, 2012), drama is not explicitly mentioned, although, in the latter, in the experiences and outcomes listed for listening and talking, it is stated that children should encounter a wide range of ways in which they 'can be creative', and that they should engage in 'imaginary situations'. In the Northern Ireland Curriculum (DENI, 2011), children are expected to 'take part in a range of drama activities to support activity based learning across the curriculum', and to improvise based on 'experience, imagination, literature, media and/or curricular topics'.

PRINCIPLES

Drama is imaginatively and intellectually demanding, a highly motivating tool for learning. It encompasses a very wide selection of practices, ranging from free play on the playground to more formal theatre trips (see Figure 3.1). Most of the activities noted, such as improvising with puppets and performances in assemblies, trigger children's imaginative

Informal   Formal

A Continuum of Primary Drama

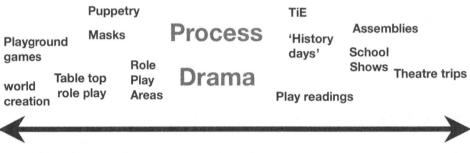

■ **Figure 3.1** The primary drama continuum

involvement and involve an act of pretence. However, the most valuable form of drama at this phase is improvisational classroom drama. This involves children in exploring issues in role and improvising alongside their Teacher In Role (TIR), building a work in the process. It is commonly referred to as process drama or structured improvisation (Greenwood, 2009), although the structures are not those of a written script. Oral language is an important component of this symbolic and dramatic play, in which, through the use of the TIR and other drama conventions, alternative ideas and perspectives are voiced. Classroom drama can help children dig down into the substrata of texts, increase their involvement and insight, and enhance their related written work, often undertaken in role.

Improvisational drama explores the unknown and tends to eschew acting out what has already been decided; this does not mean acting is not involved, however: acting 'as if' one is someone else is essential, and 'thinking in role', rather than 'performing a role', is foregrounded. For example, rather than a performing a play of *Goldilocks and the Three Bears*, children may be engaged in investigating the consequences of Goldilocks' wilful behaviour, through a court scene perhaps, or in her bedroom back home, when her mother seeks to know where she has been. Improvisational drama challenges children to imaginatively make, share, and respond to each others' ideas, collaboratively co-authoring new narratives through the use of a number of drama conventions and reflection upon the unfolding work. It encompasses considerable spontaneity and playfulness.

Creative teachers often use drama in literacy time as part of shared reading or as preparation for shared and independent writing. They also offer children extended drama sessions: longer dramatic explorations, based on literature or linked to a cross-curricular focus. Drama makes use of a range of conventions (see Figure 3.2), which can be combined and adapted to suit the dramatic exploration. Teachers need to develop the widest possible repertoire of drama conventions, also employing metaphors and symbols, objects or icons as signifiers. Perhaps the most significant convention, however, is that of TIR. McWilliam

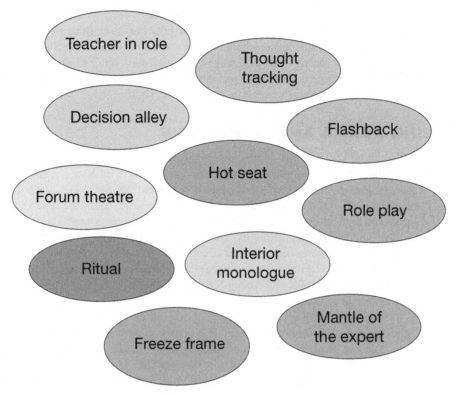

■ **Figure 3.2** Drama conventions

(2008) suggests that teachers who foster creativity are neither the 'sage on the stage' nor the 'guide on the side', but are more actively involved as co-constructors of meaning and are 'meddlers in the middle'. This aptly describes TIRs in drama, as they participate and extend children's creative learning.

DRAMA AND LEARNING

Rooted in social interaction, drama is a powerful way to help children relate positively to each other, experience negotiation, and gain confidence and self-esteem, as well as confront ethical principles, personal values and moral codes of conduct (Freebody, 2010). Drama also offers rich opportunities for imaginative development through the creation of a questioning stance and the exploration of different possibilities and perspectives (Cremin, Goouch *et al.*, 2006). In each drama, children will be learning about the chosen content – the life of Mary Seacole or the evacuees in World War II, for example – and should be able to develop, use and refine their knowledge and understanding of this area. Recent research indicates that children view drama as highly motivating and believe they are able to gain a deeper understanding of knowledge as a result of this 'vivid method of learning' (Chan, 2009: 201). Children are drawn, not just to the content or plot, however, but also to the dramatic forms and conventions that allow them to explore meaning and express their ideas. They can learn to select, shape and transform these conventions for their own purposes and become more adept at discussing them, employing an increasingly critical language to describe and evaluate drama. Crucially too, as learning in drama arises out of the experience alongside the children's personal and social reflection upon it, drama enhances their reflective and evaluative capacities and ability to make connections. The key areas of learning in drama include: the imagination, personal and social issues, literacy, reflection, the content of the drama, and the form itself.

LINKING DRAMA AND LITERATURE

Although no script is in evidence in improvisational drama, literature is often used as a structural or thematic support, and shared fictitious worlds are created through the imaginations of both children and teacher (Taylor and Warner, 2006). Such drama focuses on the process of meaning making, has no immediate audience and is spontaneous, unpredictable and emergent. It frequently creates motivating contexts in which reading, writing and speaking and listening are natural responses to the various social dilemmas encountered. It also invites children to exchange ideas and experiment with alternative perspectives, and it raises questions rather than answers them. Significantly, it leaves room for ambiguity and challenges young learners to cope with open-ended scenarios and live with uncertainty (Grainger, 2003).

When literature is used to trigger classroom drama, fictional moments need to be carefully chosen to ensure they involve a degree of tension, doubt or misunderstanding. Many such moments will be present in the text; others can be evoked through examining unmentioned conversations, nightmares, premonitions, a character's conflicting thoughts on a particular issue, and/or earlier or later problematic events that connect to the present situation. Fiction is packed with unresolved conflicts to choose from, and non-fiction also contains contested issues to construct, investigate and examine. When selecting potentially rich moments, it is important to consider:

■   What tense moments in the text would help reveal more about the theme, the characters, their motivation and relationships?
■   What possible scenarios might occur as a consequence of, or as a precursor to, the current difficulty that could usefully be brought to life?
■   What drama conventions could be employed at these moments to open up the text?
■   How much of the text needs to be revisited/read aloud immediately prior to the drama, to contextualise the action?

For example, in planning a drama around the picture book *Giant* by Juliet and Charles Snape, in the context of a unit of work on the environment, teachers could select a number of moments within the tale to explore using different drama conventions. In this tale, the Mountain Giant realises that the humans take her for granted, and the combined effects of pollution and erosion wear away her desire to remain on the Earth. Teachers could read the story aloud, stopping intermittently along the way to examine issues through drama. The moments of dramatic exploration could include:

■   examining the front cover with the title removed and, in pairs, generating possibilities based on the visuals;
■   discussing these and making connections to other texts and tales;

- reading the beginning and, in small groups, creating sound collages and visual representations of the Mountain Giant when she realises that the humans have not cared for her;
- creating a decision alley as Giant walks into the ocean to leave and considers her options. Should she leave or has Lia, the young girl, persuaded her to stay?
- inviting half the class to represent the humans and half her forebears, the giants of the sea and sky, each seeking to persuade Giant to join them. What are their arguments? How persuasive can they be?
- creating small-group improvisations at the end of the tale, of one of the following or their own idea: a TV news items about the disappearance of the Mountain; the myth about how Giant and her relatives first came to dwell upon the Earth; the consequences for the community 10 years after the event;
- generating written communications about the incident; these might include: plans for a documentary, a letter from Lia to Giant found by her grandchildren years later, the myth of the mountain Giant, the autocues of the news report, a play-script or a newspaper article (see Figure 3.3 for 10-year-old Mark's example, which indicates his involvement and strong sense of voice).

A wide range of picture fiction texts can be used to support drama in this way, with teachers reading some of the text and then stopping to open up the tale for the children to inhabit in role. Often, the text will be left behind, as a new narrative based around the children's interests emerges, built upon the shoulders of the old. Examples of quality texts that work powerfully in drama planned in this way include: *Quetta*, *Memorial* and *The Watertower* by Gary Crew, *Death in a Nut* by Eric Maddern, *The Wolves in the Walls* by Neil Gaiman, *Encounter* by Jane Yolen and *The Promise* by Nicola Davies. Creative teachers will find their own favourites that offer a degree of tension and ambiguity, interest and challenge.

TEACHER IN ROLE

The TIR is key to developing the educational potential of drama. This does not involve teachers in performing, but in imagining and acting as if they are someone else, taking on this role and participating with the children from this perspective. Teachers model the commitment and belief involved, uniting the class and engaging them in collaborative world-making play. Through this role, teachers help shape the imagined experience, negotiating this with the learners, and support, extend and challenge their thinking from inside the fictional context. The TIR can also help children consider the consequences of their actions. In the motivating world of drama, children often reflect the commitment and involvement that their TIR demonstrates. Rather than always adopting high-status roles, teachers can experiment with a variety of equal- and/or low-status roles, which create new opportunities. They can take up oppositional roles, roles of those who have been affected by the children's actions or roles as messengers, shadows and storytellers. The spontaneous, improvisational nature of these roles can create productive tensions that need to be resolved.

When not in role, teachers can offer children opportunities to reflect upon and evaluate the drama, discussing the emerging situation and making connections. This pattern of oscillating between full involvement in the role and then separation from the role – as

EVENING HERALD

'Mountain village'
Debate the future

Following the recent spectacular disappearance of the mountain 'Giant', members of Littertown on the Ouse, have been holding urgent meetings to debate their future. Villagers are devastated that 'Giant' has left, wrenching up trees and plants and part of the river bed. A rare breed of badgers is also missing, presumably they fled as the Giant demolished their sets. Old Mr hogwart, who lived on the edge of the mountain, is now forced to take lodgings in a nearby town. The council are seeking permanent accomodation for him somewhere safe and peaceful.

All the village are worried and frantic to know whether the Giant will come back. if she doesn't their grazing land will be gone forever with there orchards and their crop." What have we done to deserve this?" exclaimed Mr Derby, a local councillor. Others felt that it was their fault, and said "we made it happen – we polluted her with insecticides and litter –

WE MUST CHANGE our ways on pay the price

J. Snape

■ **Figure 3.3** A newspaper article

decisions are discussed and options are considered and reflected upon – is a core characteristic of improvisational classroom drama. It deepens children's commitment and involvement and extends their learning about the issues being explored. TIR has been found to be highly effective in engaging students in creative learning (Sæbø, 2009).

DRAMA AND SPEAKING AND LISTENING

As extended classroom drama is oriented towards investigating problems and opening up issues, talk is an essential part of its currency. Drama creates imaginative and motivating contexts that are often experienced as real and that provoke a variety of oral responses. In the context of improvising a decision alley or planning, discussing and evaluating a freeze-frame, for example, children spontaneously talk and listen to one another's ideas and often need to negotiate and make decisions together. So, a number of forms of talk are used, as well as gestures, facial expressions and movements to convey meaning. In drama, children adapt their speech for different purposes and audiences, using language styles and registers appropriate to both their role and the imaginary scenario. The opportunity to reflect upon these language choices can contribute to a growing command over the spoken word. Feelings, intuitions and a playful imagination come to the fore in drama, enabling both purposeful and creative language to be generated and a wider than usual range of vocabulary. The emotional engagement that drama triggers also influences the children's spoken contributions, which may be freer than in more conventional or formal classroom contexts.

Different drama conventions create different demands and prompt particular kinds of talk. For example, a class of 8–9-year-olds investigating *The Minpins* by Roald Dahl might be involved in the following activities:

■ creating interior monologues and the desperate thoughts of young Billy, who, trapped indoors, dreams of venturing into the forest – *using reflective introspective talk*;
■ role-playing the conversation between Billy and his mother – *using persuasive talk* (see below for an example, created by Sam and Kaz, aged 9); this could also be improvised with TIR as Billy and the class as mum:

> Mum please can I go out, it's so hot in here – please?
> Then take your jumper off and I'll open the window a little.
> But I want to go out, I'm bored.
> Then read a book and before you ask – no you can't go on your playstation.
> Oh mum, the forest looks so exciting – I wouldn't go far, honest.
> I told you before it's not safe.
> Why, what's in there? What are you afraid of?
> I'm not afraid, but we don't know who'll be out there and I've told you before about strangers.
> In school Simon said 'Strangers don't come out 'til after dark'.
> What rubbish that boy talks. Woods are not safe places.
> I promise I won't talk to any strangers.
> You are not going and that's that. And if you carry on arguing with me young man you'll be grounded.
> Oh mum you're *so* unfair.

▨ whispering into Billy's ear in role as the devil – *using descriptive talk* to tempt and interest him in the Forest of Sin (see Figure 3.4 for an example of a note from the devil);

▨ Voicing Billy's thoughts in role in a decision alley as he approaches the door and has to decide whether to slip out against his mother's wishes – *using discursive reflective inner talk*;

▨ creating a freeze-frame of Billy encountering someone or something in the Forest of Sin – *using generative talk* to share ideas and then negotiating to decide on one, and discussing as a group how best to convey this.

> Come on little Billy, come and join me in here. You lead a dull life, in here there are playstations and gameboys, chocolate dripping off the trees and sweets growing from the ground. Do you like marshmallows? Their taste is sweet and soft, they melt on your tongue. Come on little Billy come and join me. Open the window and climb into a new world.
>
> Darren

▨ **Figure 3.4** Writing in role

These activities and forms of talk merely relate to the first few pages of the text, before Billy has even met the Minpins! If an extended drama based on this introduction is developed, then the class might decide on the creature/person Billy met and explore the consequences of this with their TIR. Oral improvisational work can also be based on non-fiction texts; for example, children could create their own persuasive adverts to be filmed and reviewed, make news broadcasts about real-world events, past or present, and improvise documentaries about cross-curricular issues, with scientists, world experts and local people's views being sought. In each context, the type of talk used will be different.

DRAMA AND READING

Drama offers a valuable context for enriching inference and deduction; it prompts textual interrogation and helps bring narratives to life. In drama, an 'aesthetic' reading of the text is created, in which the focus is on the insights and satisfaction gained from the textual encounter (Rosenblatt, 1978). During drama, children employ a number of strategies that are also central to reading, including: prediction, image construction, making imaginative connections, co-authoring the text, developing empathy and engaging emotionally and reflectively (Grainger, 1998). Drama can help children become more effective at reading both text and subtext and can extend their understanding of characters' motives, behaviour and possible histories.

If drama conventions are employed in shared reading, then more may be revealed about the characters, narrative events and themes. For example, in *The Time it Took Tom* by Nick Sharratt, the class can – in role as mum – speak out loud simultaneously, when she enters the sitting room after Tom has painted it red! This will help generate more details about her reaction. Tom's views and his response to his mum could also be created through role-play, in pairs or with half the class adopting one role and half the other. Observing the physical positions adopted and freezing the action to add the inner thoughts of these characters can also support inference and deduction.

Reading part of a text and then using a drama convention to explore the implied character relationships can also aid comprehension. For example, in the beginning of *Holes* by Louis Sachar, Stanley Yelnats is sent to Camp Green Lake, a youth penitentiary in the desert, for a crime he did not commit. Not all the boys and staff there welcome him. The class could be invited to collaboratively create a sculpture of Stanley, Mr Sir, Mr Pendanski and some of the boys he has just met (such as Magnet, Zero and Armpit) at supper one night – this is one way to construct and explore their relationships. The children's suggestions about the positioning of the characters, their body postures and facial expressions will need to be defended with reference to the text. In addition, Stanley's or other characters' thoughts at this first meal could be voiced in interior monologues, to explore their relationships in more detail.

In exploring a non-fiction theme, drama can help extend children's reading of the context, text and subtext. For example, a number of contrasting images could be constructed of the rainforest through freeze-frames. In creating these as photographs taken from multiple perspectives for a book on the subject, subtitles and paragraphs could be added to highlight the diverse positions and standpoints held. This will draw upon the children's understanding of the issues and motivate their comprehension of each other's representations.

DRAMA AND WRITING

Drama provides meaningful contexts for writing, both individual and collaborative. In-role work can lead to emotive writing from different stances and perspectives, and can make a real contribution to children's development as writers. Through orally rehearsing and refining ideas for writing and sharing these with one another, children can enrich their written work, adding both passion and pace to their prose. Both qualitative (Crumpler and Schneider, 2002) and quantitative studies (Fleming *et al.*, 2004) demonstrate that, if drama is used in literacy sessions and in extended units of literacy work, it can make a significant contribution to children's writing. In the former, the focus will be on using drama to help generate and sculpt a particular genre of writing; in the latter, the drama, not the writing, will take precedence, and teachers will 'seize the moment to write' in response to the imagined context (Cremin, Goouch *et al.*, 2006). Both approaches are valuable and are explored further in the following sections.

Drama and writing: a genre-specific approach in literacy time

When drama is used as a prompt in shared writing, to support the writing of a specific genre for example, then thoughtful bridges need to be built between the actual drama conventions used and the form of writing desired. Although several conventions may be used to percolate ideas and involve children, the final convention employed needs to link closely to the chosen genre. In this way, the last improvised scenario acts as a kind of dress rehearsal for writing and an oral writing frame. This has been described as a 'genre specific' approach to combining drama and writing (Cremin, Burnard *et al.*, 2006). Suggested links between different drama conventions and different genres are noted in Figure 3.5.

For example, in Jacqueline Wilson's *Cliffhanger*, young Tim makes it clear he does not wish to go on an adventure holiday. His father, however, is determined that he should go, to strengthen his physique and character, whereas his mum is worried for her beloved son. A family row ensues. If this is initially improvised in threes, the class can then engage in thinking out loud in role as Tim, pondering his options, his parents' views and his own fears. In this way, the children will be prepared to undertake diary writing in reflective mode, as the interior monologue convention is, in oral form, close to the first person narrative writing found in diary recounts.

In non-fiction shared writing, if the class is exploring the genre of instructional texts, for example, children can lean upon TV programmes such as *Blue Peter* or *Art Attack* and work in role as presenting teams, demonstrating how to make cheese nachos or Christmas crackers. Watching programmes to observe the oral genre in action can help children analyse the structure and purpose of such presentations and highlight options. Their eventual improvisations can be watched and evaluated for ease of communication and interest. Alternatively, the TIR could demonstrate an instructional text in the style of one of the TV presenters, while the class makes notes and writes up the instructions for the programme's website. This operates as a formative assessment activity, as it helps to identify what the class knows about the structure, organisation and language features of procedural texts. For more examples of drama and fiction/non-fiction writing links, see Chapters 6 and 7.

Recount	Storytelling in role TV interview recounting an event
Diary	Thought tracking/interior monologue Telephone conversation
Report	Freeze-frame Hot-seating
Poetry	Group sculpture on theme Ritual
Instructions	Group improvisation Freeze-frames of process
Story structure	Freeze-frame significant events as a storyboard Improvised flashback/flash-forward
Explanation	Documentary improvisation by a scientist/ historian, etc.
Dialogues	Role-play Interviews
Notes/minutes	Hot-seating in role Formal meetings
Persuasive/discursive	Decision alley Formal meetings
Advertisement	Group improvisation – spontaneous or planned Freeze-frames brought to life
Play script	Role-play in pairs for conversation Small group play-making

■ **Figure 3.5** Making connections between drama and specific genres of writing

Drama and writing: seizing the moment to write during extended drama

When classroom or process drama is integrated into an extended unit of work in literacy and in cross-curricular contexts, it can energise the children's imaginative engagement and help sustain their sense of focus and interest. It can also operate as a supportive scaffold for writing and help young writers develop what they want to say, find their position and perspective, and prepare them to commit this to paper or screen. In process drama, literature is often used as a catalyst, and a range of drama conventions are employed to explore the ideas, issues and themes in the narrative. Although a lesson plan with learning intentions will exist, teachers will be responding to the interests of the children and venturing into the unknown.

When teachers engage as artists alongside children in the tense scenarios being investigated, they learn to trust themselves and the children and recognise opportunities to seize the moment and write. In employing a 'seize the moment' approach to drama and writing (Cremin, Goouch *et al.*, 2006), teachers need to remain open to possibilities as the drama unfolds, living with the uncertainty of what might happen next and discerning when purposeful writing might be fruitful. In involving children in the often conflict-driven, open-ended contexts that are typical of extended classroom drama, teachers offer children considerable choice in terms of perspective, purpose and form in writing; this fosters their commitment and concentration and frequently results in high-quality writing.

Improvisational classroom drama has the potential to contribute markedly to composition and effect in writing and helps children create writing that captures the reader's interest and attention. It is critical, however, that time is taken to journey, and that the drama is foregrounded, not any particular form of writing. This will ensure that, at a moment of dramatic tension, when the emotional engagement of all involved is assured and the perspectives of many have been examined, the teacher can 'seize the moment' to write. At such moments, children's writing seems to flow from the imagined context with relative ease and is frequently full of 'stance and scenario' (Bruner, 1984: 98), reflecting their engagement in the issues and showing considerable attention to detail.

FOSTERING IMAGINATIVE ENGAGEMENT IN ROLE-PLAY AREAS

Role-play areas are a kind of microcosm of classroom drama. The imaginary contexts of such areas enable children to converse, create and draw on their experience, knowledge and understanding of the world to make meaning. In order to develop children's agency and ownership of learning, creative teachers negotiate possible options for role-play areas with them. Role-play areas are frequently established in early years classrooms, but inventive teachers of older learners also make good use of them, creating police stations, Egyptian archaeological digs and Victorian workhouses, for example, and offering children opportunities to use their knowledge and understanding in other areas of the curriculum (Cremin, McDonald *et al.*, 2009). Role-play areas fall into three types, in which there is some degree of overlap. These include:

▦ real-world settings, e.g. doctor's surgery, the garden centre, post office or café;
▦ imaginary/fantasy settings, e.g. a cave, a forest, an enchanted land, on the moon, under the sea;
▦ fictional settings, e.g. Katie Morag's post office from Marie Heiderwick's series, Mr Majeika's classroom from the series by Humphrey Carpenter, Mr Grindle's lighthouse from Rhonda and David Armitage's series.

In addition, children's popular cultural interests can be valuably built upon, as they are highly motivating; so, for example, Bob the Builder's yard or the Wombles' world could be created, or the perennial café could be created as a McDonald's or Pizza Hut, in response to request. What is essential, therefore, is that teachers know their children's passion for particular popular cultural texts, as many young learners enjoy the same narrative in different modes. In a recent project, the teachers found that, when they connected their role-play areas to the children's interests, the young learners' confidence grew (Cremin *et al.*, 2015). This highlights the importance of teachers recognising the relationship between home and school learning (Alper, 2013).

There is a tendency for real-world settings to dominate school role-play areas, but more fictionally oriented and open-ended imaginary/fantasy areas allow children to engage in more imaginative play, building on the foundation of known stories, making connections between tales and allowing characters from well-known narratives to inhabit the area. Children who are more used to the imitative play found in real-world areas may, at first, find the demands of more open-ended areas very challenging and may need more support from the TIR. See Figure 3.6 for an example of a piece of writing that emerged spontaneously from a greenhouse role-play area based on the *Percy the Park Keeper* books by Nick Butterworth. Child-initiated, this invitation to Percy from the fox drew on Callum's knowledge of the stories and provoked an interesting dilemma for Percy. Later the same day, when this had been discussed, the class engaged in improvisational classroom drama and held fox's party, which Percy and many animals attended.

In exploring connections between role-play areas and fictional texts, as well as role-play and extended classroom drama, children can expand their understanding of different settings, make intertextual links and use literacy and language purposefully in imaginary contexts. It is, therefore, useful for teachers to read related tales, so that they can be revisited, re-enacted and recreated imaginatively, and for teachers to provide related literacy resources. For example, if the area is a desert island, texts such as undersea maps, diagrams of shipwrecks, fiction and non-fiction books, a captain's log, a ship-to-shore radio, bottles for messages and sand can all help. Planning involves considering the key drama trio of the place, the people and the predicaments, alongside considering potential literacy opportunities. See Figure 3.7 for planning both a castle as a tourist venue role-play area and a café, and Cremin, McDonald *et al.* (2009) for more ideas.

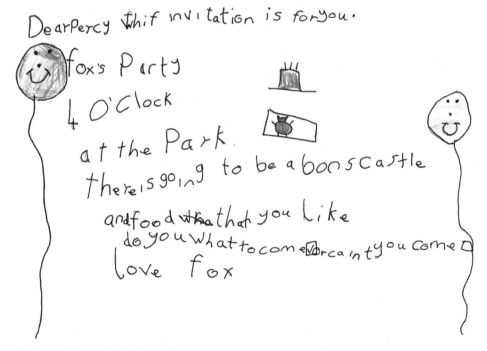

■ **Figure 3.6** An invitation to Percy

A CAFÉ

▨ PLACE and resources

Tables and chairs and stools, cloths and
napkins
Cutlery, cruet sets, menu holders, a till
Kitchen area, stove, cooking materials

▨ PEOPLE, living/working and visiting

Waitresses and waiters
Chefs and managers
Cleaners and customers
Health/food inspectors and delivery
people
Plumbers and electricians
Telephone engineers and vermin control
personnel

▨ PREDICAMENTS and TIR options

Chef is sick but children's themed
birthday party is due to begin
Health inspector finds mouse droppings
Electricity officer visits – imminent power
cut
Complaining customers
Phone call announces celebrity arriving
Menus not arrived in time for the grand
opening

▨ READING/WRITING opportunities

Menus, notepads for food orders
Receipts, cheques, letter-headed paper,
money, computer
Telephone and notepad
Miss Wobble the Waitress (Alan Ahlberg)
This is the Bear and the Bad Little Girl
(Sarah Hayes)
Cookery books and party texts
Promotional materials for today's
specials
Adverts/ posters for the café

A FOREST

▨ PLACE and resources

Crepe paper hangings, tree trunks for
sitting on
Branches, twigs and leaves, paper
campfire

▨ PEOPLE, living/working and visiting

Tourists and walkers
Birdwatchers and wildlife specialists
Children on school outing and families
camping
Fictional characters: Three Bears and
Goldilocks, Hansel and Gretel, The
Animals from Farthing Wood, Harry
Potter characters
Forestry management workers
Arboretum inspectors, local farmers, fire
brigade

▨ PREDICAMENTS and TIR options

Campfire gets out of hand
Walker lost, mobile broken
Trapdoor found in tree
Countryside commissioner visits
Forestry worker has accident
Poacher seen stealing eggs
Gate left open and cows stray
Someone stranded up a tree

▨ READING/WRITING opportunities

Countryside code posters
Maps with walks
Secret message found in tree
Notices on gates
Book on flora and fauna of forests
Arboretum guide about trees
Camper's diary
Forestry worker's report

▨ **Figure 3.7** Planning for role-play areas

Physically co-creating the area helps to build interest and involvement, as does visiting a vet's surgery or estate agent's, for example, prior to constructing one. However, although planning how to create the area and collecting resources are important, considering the people who might live, work or visit the area and the difficulties they might encounter is much more important. Without a real sense of possible characters and their problems, the children's socio-dramatic play will lack imaginative involvement. Planning possible people and their predicaments also offers multiple TIR options. The TIR, TAs or children from older classes can offer valuable models of the various scenarios generated and can engage in using reading and writing in the process.

In these small worlds, children lean on the support of the environment and are challenged by their TIR as they use language to imagine and create roles and experiences. Although allowing children to initiate their socio-dramatic play is important, and over-zealous TIR interventions are to be avoided, the presence of an adult can enhance role-play. Observation is essential, so that an appropriate moment to play alongside the children or to intervene with a challenge in role can be identified. In addition to adopting high-status roles, such as the king of a castle or the manager of Toys R Us, for example, teachers and TAs can adopt equal or low-status roles, to create new opportunities for learning. They can also develop the literate potential of the area through TIR, requesting advice and a map of the ocean when visiting an undersea cave as a mermaid from foreign seas, for example. The teacher will need to act spontaneously, but can consider possible roles, perhaps offering new knowledge of difficulties ahead, such as warning tales of sharks and sightings of humans investigating a shipwreck. The improvisational qualities of TIR work can create productive tensions and challenge children to resolve these problems through their play.

As with all creative learning, reflection and feedback are essential; children need to be given the chance to share the imaginary scenarios and difficulties they encounter and their responses. Sometimes guided and challenged by their TIR, they will be improvising and imagining as a small group in the area and will benefit from sharing the resultant narratives with the class. This can help develop their pleasure in role-play and enrich the ideas and possibilities on which other groups can draw.

CONCLUSION

The multimodal art form of drama, which draws on the 'dramatic literacies' (Nicholson, 2000) of facial expression, body language, intonation, gesture, mime, movement and space, has the potential to create motivating contexts for powerful literacy learning. Creative literacy teachers plan opportunities to link drama and literacy and let each enrich the other; they also work flexibly, responding to children's interests and letting them lead as they imagine unknown territory together and learn from living in another space and time alongside them. Both in literacy time and in extended classroom drama sessions right across the curriculum, drama offers purposeful contexts for reading, writing, speaking and listening. It is an essential pedagogic tool in a creative teacher's repertoire.

FURTHER READING

Cremin, T. and McDonald, R. (2012) 'Drama: A creative pedagogic tool', in D. Wyse and R. Jones (2012), *Creative Teaching*. London: Routledge, pp. 183–97.

Cremin, T., Goouch, K., Blakemore, L., Goff, E. and McDonald, R. (2006) 'Connecting drama and writing: Seizing the moment to write', *Research in Drama in Education*, 11(3): 273–91.

Edmiston, B. (2013) *Transforming Teaching and Learning With Active and Dramatic Approaches: Engaging students across the curriculum*. New York: Routledge.

Greenwood, J. (2009) 'Drama education in New Zealand: A coming of age?', *Research in Drama Education: The Journal of Applied Theatre and Performance*, 14(2): 245–60.

John, R., Kempe, A. and Baldwin, P. (2012) *Inspiring Writing Through Drama: Creative approaches to teaching ages 7–16*. London: Continuum.

CHILDREN'S BOOKS

Butterworth, N. (2001) *Percy the Park Keeper Collection*. Godalming, UK: Ted Smart.

Crew, G. (1994) *The Watertower*. Flinders Park, Australia: Era.

Crew, G. (1999) *The Memorial*. Sydney, Australia: Lothian.

Crew, G. (2002) *Quetta*. Flinders Park, Australia: Era.

Crossley Holland, K. (1997) *The Green Children*. Oxford, UK: Oxford University Press.

Davies, N. (2013) *The Promise*. London: Walker.

Dahl, R. and Benson, P. (1993) *The Minpins*. London: Puffin.

Gaiman, N. and Mckean, D. (2003) *The Wolves in the Walls*. London: Bloomsbury.

Maddern, E. and Hess, P. (2007) *Death in a Nut*. London: Frances Lincoln.

Sachar, L. (2000) *Holes*. London: Bloomsbury.

Sharratt, N. (2000) *The Time it Took Tom*. London: Scholastic.

Snape, J. and Snape, C. (1999) *Giant*. London: Walker.

Wilson, J. (1995) *Cliffhanger*. London: Corgi.

CHAPTER 4

CREATIVELY ENGAGING READERS IN THE EARLY PRIMARY YEARS

Henrietta Dombey

INTRODUCTION

Teaching children to read is neither a trivial matter nor just a technical task. For both children and their teachers, it is probably the most momentous achievement of the early school years. So, primary professionals should approach it thoughtfully and creatively. This chapter focuses on teaching reading creatively to 5–7-year-olds and looks at how teachers can support the questioning stance of young learners, helping them to apply this both to lifting the words off the page and also to making sense of what they read. In addition, it reflects on teachers as readers, on enriching children's responses to reading and encouraging their independence.

The first two aims set out for English in the NC (DfE, 2013: 3), that all pupils in the early years of primary education should 'read easily, fluently and with good understanding', and that they should 'develop the habit of reading widely and often, for both pleasure and information', need to colour all teachers do in the name of teaching reading. In the Northern Ireland Curriculum (DENI, 2011: 1), it is expected children will 'read, and be read to from a wide selection of poetry and prose; read with some independence for enjoyment and information; and read, explore, understand and make use of a range of traditional and digital texts'. To achieve these laudable aims, which are echoed in the Scottish and Welsh curricula, teachers need to understand the complex process of literacy learning and be imaginative in their approach to both children and the task of teaching them to read. A 'tick box' approach will not produce fluent, perceptive and committed readers, nor will the rigid separation of word identification from comprehension.

Learning to read, particularly in English, is difficult for most children. Teachers need to constantly demonstrate that it is not just a series of arbitrary tasks that children need to do to please the teacher, but a communication system that is worth the effort. Teaching reading well means tapping into the energetic desires of children to make sense of the world and to connect with the people in it. So, although it is often useful to focus on one aspect (such as particular spelling patterns or story structure), this does not mean that this complex endeavour should be segmented into its component parts, with each of these addressed in turn and in isolation from the others. A narrow conception of learning to read as primarily concerned with learning phonics may conflict with the idea of reading that children bring to school and restrict their understanding of what reading has to offer.

PRINCIPLES

Children have to learn how to make the black marks speak – out loud at first, and later in their heads. However, the English language, with its complex spelling, makes lifting the words from the page much more difficult than it is in other languages, such as Italian or Finnish, that are fortunate in having more regular spelling systems. So, if children are to persist, teachers need to make reading and learning to read both pleasurable and creatively engaging. Unfortunately, England's primary schools are less successful at building positive attitudes to reading than those in most other comparable countries (Mullis *et al.*, 2012a), and this has an impact on children's decoding proficiency and their readiness to make the most of the written word. If teachers are to help children understand themselves and the world around them in complex ways, then reading must be made a creatively engaging activity for them, one that they will choose to do outside school, as well as inside it.

Becoming familiar with the language of written texts is an essential part of this early learning, for written language is very different from spoken language. It tends to be more tightly constructed, both at the level of the sentence and over large stretches of text. This is true for texts ranging from shopping lists to novels and is certainly true of texts written for young children. Extensive written texts also tend to use a wider range of vocabulary. So, if they are to become effective and enthusiastic readers, children need to become familiar with the language of books, to experience making sense of the world through this language, and to take pleasure in its power. Children need to taste the fruits and experience the rewards of learning to read if they are to invest the necessary energy, commitment and focused attention that are required.

'Learning to read is fundamentally a task of learning how to orchestrate knowledge in a skillful manner' (Bussis *et al.*, 1985: 113). To achieve this orchestration requires both creative teaching and creative learning. However, it is certainly not the case that anything goes: all teaching acts should be shaped by principles arising from knowledge and understanding about how children learn most richly. In reading, these include the following:

▨ *Learning to read, write and talk are interdependent.* As the NC (DfE, 2013) states, 'Spoken language underpins the development of reading and writing'. There is substantial evidence to support this view (e.g. Clark, 1976), and talk can also be enriched by reading as is evident when a more experienced reader mis-pronounces a word encountered in print. Similarly, it is clear that what children read influences their writing, and writing can also make them more aware of how authors make choices and structure the texts they read. So, teachers need both to plan specific activities that encompass reading, writing and talk, and also to work to make the schoolday a ceaseless interplay of language in all its modes.

▨ *Reading is an active, creative process from the earliest stages.* In order to make sense of the text in front of them, children need to make creative use of both their knowledge of letters and spelling patterns and also their knowledge of other texts and the wider world. Making imaginative links to their own experiences and engaging as active constructors of meaning are important from the earliest stages.

▨ *A rich experience of stories and poems has a central role to play.* While it is essential that children learn how to read non-fiction texts, it must be acknowledged that poetry and stories have a particular power. Through literature, we all experience other ways of looking at the world and can savour the heightened use of language. Through poetry, children can take pleasure in the patterns and rhythms and the evocative power of memorable language. In re-reading their favourites, they gain practice in decoding words and making deeper meanings from them. Narrative enables us to give shape and meaning to experience and can inspire and excite, giving children a powerful incentive to read and offering deep satisfaction. This is essential if children are to persist and engage with the large quantity of text that is necessary if they are to become effective readers. It is particularly important for those who start school with a limited experience of being read to (Lefebre *et al.*, 2011).

■ *The experience of hearing stories has particular importance.* For decades, it has been established that listening to stories enriches children's literacy learning in powerful ways (Bus *et al.*, 1995). Creative teachers read aloud frequently, offering children a rich experience of narrative and providing common points of reference.

■ *The texts that children experience out of school are significant.* Text pervades children's out-of-school lives. Most learn early to 'read' signs such as McDonald's and the labels on the coffee jar and their favourite sweets. Eye movement studies have shown that children attend even more closely to the words in such 'environmental print' than they do to the words in stories (Neumann *et al.*, 2014). Teachers also need to find out about their preferences and the techno-literacy practices in their homes and communities, their 'funds of knowledge' (Moll *et al.*, 1992), in order actively to build on these in school, while also introducing them to other texts that extend their grasp of the world. Young children's experience of text may be largely digital: they come to school with a breadth of experience of such texts, many of which involve written language (Carrington and Robinson, 2009; McPake *et al.*, 2013).

■ *Play provides a vitally important context for young children's literacy learning.* Play of different sorts (role-playing the teacher, fantasy role play, play in the home corner) can give children the opportunity to rehearse and integrate what they have learned about literacy at home and at school, and also to extend their literate behaviour (Wohlwend, 2011). Play can provide a 'third space', where children can bring different 'funds of knowledge' into conversation with one another (Levy, 2008).

■ *Assessment of children's experience, strengths, needs and interests is central.* Numerous research projects show that successful early teaching of reading always takes account of individual learners' literacy skills and experiences (Pressley *et al.*, 2001; Taylor and Pearson, 2002).

These principles connect to the conception of creative practice permeating this book. Their implications are explored in the sections below. Adopting a creative approach to early reading involves engaging in a variety of classroom experiences, including, as national curricula across the UK emphasise, the teaching of both letter–sound relationships and comprehension. However, a creative approach means more than this: it is also concerned to foster children's imaginative engagement in meaning making that matters to them.

TEACHING PHONICS CREATIVELY

There may be a temptation to view the teaching of phonics as the antithesis of creative teaching, as an exhaustive and exhausting drilling in phonic rules. Certainly, the statutory requirements for children aged 5–6 years in England look daunting (DfE, 2013: 10).

However, phonics can be conceived of and taught as a creative enterprise. Such teaching needs to be set in the context of a rich and rewarding experience of written text. Given the vagaries of English spelling, children need a commitment to the language and meanings of written text, if they are to make phonics work for them. Research evidence that has stood the test of time shows that the most effective phonics teaching places it in the context of making meaning from text (Medwell *et al.*, 1998; for a review, see Hall, 2013). Recent research into eye movements has also shown that more effective learners, even children taught by a strictly phonic approach, aim to make sense of what they read and should be encouraged to do so (Brown *et al.*, 2012).

Books such as *Tanka Tanka Skunk* by Steve Webb, *Wriggle Piggy Toes* by John Agard and many by Julia Donaldson, Dr Seuss and others can make this learning meaningful and fun-filled. Such enticing and highly patterned books enable children to participate in playing with the sounds of words as they read and make meaning. Treating children as active learners makes the process more enjoyable for both teachers and children. So, although phonics teaching needs structure, it is also necessary to appeal to children's inventiveness and make use of their interest in language play. Useful guiding structures are provided by *Letters and Sounds* (DfES, 2007), which sets out a sequence for teaching the correspondences between spoken and written English that operate at the level of the phoneme. It also includes activities for teachers and teaching assistants to use to implement this teaching. However, a number of these are fairly rule-bound, with little appeal to children's inventiveness, and need to be supplemented with activities of a more engaging and open-ended nature. Playing with magnetic letters can involve children in inventing nonsense words and their meanings, the most interesting of which can be displayed on the classroom wall.

Collaboratively constructed class alphabet books or friezes can give children a greater sense of possession of their own learning than commercial ones. This is especially true if children's own interests and experiences are drawn upon in the creation of the book or frieze. Popular culture print – names and catch phrases from TV shows the children know, in the print format they are used to at home – can be useful, with the children being invited to match these with the same words in the classroom format (Vera, 2011).

Rhyme and analogy have a key role to play when someone is learning to read English spelling. It is not infallible, but rhyme is often a better guide to a word's pronunciation than synthetic phonics on its own, providing a more direct route to decoding than sounding and blending each phoneme. So, drawing an analogy with a familiar word such as 'ball' is more helpful to a child trying to work out an unknown word such as 'fall' than sounding it out letter by letter. Young children need experience of playing with language through rhyme and alliteration (Bradley and Bryant, 1983) and instruction in onset and rhyme (Goswami, 1999). Songs, rhymes and tongue twisters can all develop children's phonological awareness and are extensively used by creative teachers who seek to adopt a playful approach to language, highlighting pattern, sound and rhythm. In addition to introducing children to memorable examples of language play in books such *Chicky Chicky Chook Chook* by Cathy MacLennan, and playground rhymes and chants, teachers can help children construct their own nonsense rhymes and play their own phonic games. This could include 'silly registers', where the teacher adds a rhyming epithet to children's names, or creating alternative variations to 'Two Little Dicky Birds' and other rhymes.

Many children have reliable phonic knowledge but do not always put it to use in reading. They need extensive demonstrations of how this is done and opportunities to do it themselves in supported situations. Perhaps the most creative aspect of teaching phonics involves teachers in seizing unexpected opportunities to draw children's attention to letters, words and sounds, as they seek to make learning to read a positive and engaging experience.

Children who experience some difficulty in phonics learning may be significantly helped by well-designed computer-assisted reading interventions. One such is GraphoGame (http://info.graphogame.com), developed at the University of Jyväskylä in Finland and adapted for English in two versions, one based on phonemes and one on rhymes. Six- and 7-year-olds in England, who spent a total of 11 hours over 12 weeks playing GraphoGame, made considerably greater improvements in their reading than classmates who did not have this opportunity (Kyle *et al.*, 2013). The rhyme version was particularly effective.

READING AND LEARNING

Outside school, young children like to read jokes, magazines, comics, fiction, TV books and magazines, signs, poetry and websites (Marsh, 2011; Clark, 2013). Many children show a preference for multimodal screen texts (Nestlé Family Monitor, 2003). Children as young as 5 demonstrate sophisticated expertise in on-screen reading, influenced by experience gained at home through friends and family. Extensive use of DVDs also appears to contribute to children's early awareness of screen conventions (Bearne *et al.*, 2007). So, classrooms need to be hospitable to a wide range of texts, reflecting the range available in twenty-first-century digital homes. The texts teachers choose for inclusion should all have something interesting to say and be capable of opening new doors, as well as making connections between home and school. Encouraging children and parents to add to the class collection can make the classroom a lively meeting place for the children's different out-of-school experiences and help children develop an integrated understanding of what literacy is about and how it works (Rogers and Elias, 2012).

However, stories and poems in books still have a potent role to play in teaching children to read: nothing else offers such a rich experience of language, such an infectious demonstration of its powers. Reading stories and poems aloud in an inclusive and involving way makes this language available to children and is an essential daily practice throughout primary school. Creative practitioners draw extensively from literature and invite children to engage in other worlds and imagine other possibilities through sharing a wealth of powerful narratives and poetry with them (Gamble and Yates, 2008).

Some children come to school having experienced over a thousand story readings, many of which will have been tuned to their particular interests and experiences by people who mean a lot to them. As well as enlarging their sense of the world and how people live in it, this daily encounter with the language of written text widens their vocabularies, extends their command of sentence structures and gives them a sense of the shapes of stories and poems (Purcell-Gates, 1988). So, these children approach the business of learning to read with a strong sense of the rewards it can yield and also a familiarity with books and the language of stories. They know the kinds of thing books say and the sort of language through which they are said. Put this together with phonic knowledge, and they can move forward with assurance.

However, others will have considerably less experience of books on arrival in school. So, teachers need both to value the print with which children are familiar (e.g. environmental print, household labels, TV guides and DVD covers) and also to initiate them quickly into the pleasure of hearing stories and poems read aloud. Teachers may choose to start with alluring, wordless texts that involve high drama and encourage the reader to turn the page. When such 'reading' is established, teachers will want to read books that reverberate – texts that speak to the children and bear considerable re-reading, ensuring that the experience of listening is an active one. However, such reading aloud needs to be fully interactive. Through joining in, speculating on what might happen next and checking to see if this is the case, children can identify with the characters and situations and make connections to their own lives in the process. This is possible well before the start of primary school, as the following example demonstrates.

It is towards the end of the summer term in a nursery class where only one child has been read to at home before school. However, since the start of the school year, the 3- and 4-year-olds have been involved in active exploration of picture books through a daily 'story time'. They have learned to predict what will happen on the next page and to check carefully to see whether they are right. Today, however, Lee is wriggling, as his teacher, Nicky, is reading a carefully chosen text for the first time – Leo Lionni's *Fish is Fish*, a story of friendship between a minnow and a tadpole. Lee is successfully re-engaged as Nicky comments:

'Fancy that, Lee, fancy waking up in the morning to find you'd grown two little legs in the night!' A few pages later, the minnow, having leapt out of the water in imitation of his friend, lies stranded on the bank.

'He began to die' reads Nicky.

'But the frog might push him back!' shouts out Lee.

Instead of asking him not to call out, Nicky responds, 'D'you think he might? Let's find out and see'.

This sort of approach to reading has a value that endures throughout the primary school. The texts will change, but the teacher's open invitation to the children to join their teacher and the author in constructing meaning should ensure that reading is a truly creative activity, both when children are engaged in shared reading and when they are reading independently. Part of the significance of a story is always that it might have been otherwise. In Pat Hutchins' *Rosie's Walk*, for example, each time Rosie the hen sets off on her odyssey around the farm, her life is at risk, as she is unknowingly being followed by a fox. The enduring pleasure of the text lies in the tension between the possible, as presented in the pictures, and the actual, as presented in the verbal text. Texts such as this and the work of picture-fiction creators such as John Prater, Colin McNaughton, Jeanne Willis, Emily Gravett, Lauren Child and Philippe Dupasquier, for example, offer considerable imaginative scope. Novels, too, offer similar pleasurable tensions and rich possibilities for readers to imagine, create visuals in the mind's eye, ask questions and engage affectively.

Shared reading of Big Books, whether in paper or electronic format, gives an unrivalled opportunity for children to combine their growing knowledge of the language of books and how stories work with their developing skill in word identification, and to make meaning together. 'Home-made' posters of poems provide similar opportunities. Books with a simple repetitive text, such as *We're Going on a Bear Hunt* by Michael Rosen, *Mrs Wishy Washy* by Joy Cowley and Quentin Blake's *All Join In*, bear repeated re-reading. And children can be helped to identify key words such as 'mud' with the aid of their phonic knowledge, as well as some of the more common 'tricky words', such as 'the' and 'to'. The aim should be to ensure that reading the text is not a laborious exercise in word identification, but a quest for pleasurable meaning in which word identification contributes to the process, rather than distracting from it.

Repetition has an important role to play. Hearing the story for a second or third time gives children the opportunity to deepen their understanding and, where a Big Book is involved, to recognise more of the words. Re-reading favourite stories is also hugely helpful in developing fluency.

TALK AND CREATIVE ENGAGEMENT

Children need to establish connections between their own experience and the texts they encounter in school. Life-to-text and text-to-life connections enhance the significance of both. 'Is your bedroom like that?' asked a nursery teacher, as she showed the children the forest growing in Max's bedroom in Maurice Sendak's *Where the Wild Things Are*. Leaving space for children to think, connect and voice their thoughts is a crucial element of creative practice. Teachers' questions and comments can guide children to identify their own connections, but, in addition, the voicing of children's own questions and puzzlements needs to be actively encouraged.

Moving around in an imaginary world can greatly enhance children's pleasure in text. If the role-play area is turned into the Three Bears' kitchen, the 'Zoopermarket' from Nick Sharratt's book or a magical castle, children can get right inside the story. More informally, hats or masks for outdoor play may help young learners re-enact the week's key book. Props of all kinds, as well as puppets and storybags, can also support retellings, and, in improvised classroom drama, children can explore gaps in the story and deepen their understanding of the particular text and their larger awareness of the possibility of texts in general. Powerful texts provide rich spaces for all forms of improvisation. For more ideas on developing children's creativity in role-play areas and through drama based on fiction, see Chapter 3.

The most important talk happens as teachers read and explore powerful stories with children. The meanings of written texts can only be fully realised through active engagement, through connections with first-hand experience, identification with the characters, wonder at their circumstances or moral judgement about their actions. Making story time the site of such open explorations is a rich and thoroughly enjoyable way of initiating children into reading for significant meaning. By engaging in this process together, children can support one another and so learn more than they could on their own (Vygotsky, 1978; Mercer and Littleton, 2007). To do this, children need to listen to and build on each other's contributions. This means that teachers need to take a less-dominant role in the process than they usually do. They need to listen to and respect children's comments and questions, creating an atmosphere in which all observations are welcome, provided they enrich the process of making sense of the text. Teachers can repeat or expand a pertinent observation in a way that invites other contributions. 'What does anyone else think?' asked his teacher, when Charlie, aged 5, interpreted one of the early pages in *Farmer Duck* by Martin Waddell as indicating a flood. This prompted close examination of the picture and consideration of the story so far, in an interchange in which three other children made overt contributions, leading another to make an apt prediction.

Teachers have privileged access to printed text, but it can be highly productive to relinquish an all-knowing role, handing it over to the children to decide whether a particular prediction was right and encouraging them to use the evidence of both words and pictures. Once the children have a purchase on phonics, it can even be useful for teachers to make carefully chosen errors in their Big Book reading, provided they are confident that a child will correct them. For example, when a teacher of 4–5-year-olds read, 'No, said his mum', Freddy, in outraged tones, corrected her, saying, 'Look, it's got a "the" in it, so it says "mother", not "mum"'. The teacher acknowledged her error and reminded herself out loud how important it is to look at all the letters.

TEACHERS AS READERS

Teachers' attitudes to reading and their knowledge about children's literature and other texts can markedly influence their capacity to teach reading creatively, their ability to engage learners in extended units of work based on texts, and their ability to foster independent reading for pleasure. Unfortunately, many primary professionals feel less than confident in this area and tend to rely on the books they enjoyed as children (Cremin, Bearne *et al.*, 2008; Cremin, Mottram *et al.*, 2008). In a survey of 1,200 teachers, UKLA found there was evidence that teachers relied on a narrow canon of children's authors and, in particular, had very limited repertoires of poetry and picture fiction (ibid.).

In relation to picture books, when asked to name six picture-fiction creators, only 10 per cent of the teachers could do so, and a worrying 38 per cent named only two or one. Remarkably, 24 per cent named none at all (Cremin, Mottram *et al.*, 2008). The highest number of mentions by far was for Quentin Blake (423), and four others were mentioned more than a hundred times: Anthony Browne (175), Shirley Hughes (123), Mick Inkpen (121) and Alan Ahlberg (146). Some of these picture-book makers were also named in the 'authors' list. There were also 302 specifically named books whose authors were seemingly not known or could not be recalled while the teachers were completing the questionnaire. These included, for example, multiple mentions of various Martin Waddell and Jez Alborough titles. However, without knowing the authors, teachers cannot seek out more of their books, or recommend the writer or illustrator to children.

So, many teachers are not in a position to encourage children to branch out and taste the powerful texts produced by a wide range of authors, nor to teach as creatively as they could with the invaluable support of contemporary writers and illustrators. To widen their repertoires, teachers can use a number of strategies, including regularly visiting the local library with the class, working with librarians and other teachers to share texts, reading Saturday review sections in newspapers and browsing in bookshops. There are also a number of excellent printed guides and websites to help teachers extend their knowledge of good books for children. These include:

■ Gamble and Yates' *Exploring Children's Literature* (2008) is packed with productive ideas.

■ *BookPower Year 1* (Bunting, 2009) and *BookPower Year 2* (Bunting *et al.*, 2010) are publications that put literature firmly at the heart of literacy teaching. Both contain suggestions for programmes of literacy teaching and learning, based on children's texts of high quality, 'chosen because they will stir children's ideas and feelings and involve them in discussion' (www.clpe.org.uk/publication/2).

■ *Books for Keeps* (www.booksforkeeps.co.uk) is a magazine, packed with book reviews and recommendations and published six times a year.

▨ The Book Trust (www.booktrusted.co.uk/books) is a free-access website that constantly updates its recommendations.

▨ Write Away (www.writeaway.org.uk) is a free-access website with information on new books.

▨ Seven Stories, the centre for children's books in Newcastle upon Tyne, has a good recommendations area on its free-access website (www.sevenstories.org.uk).

Most teachers do some reading for pleasure. By alternating adult fiction with books written for children, they can extend their knowledge. This may rekindle some of the pleasures of childhood reading and will help teachers to share new books more effectively with children, to tempt them into new texts and guide their choices. It is also certain to make the process of exploring literature in class more varied and enjoyable for all concerned. This approach is supported by research evidence. In a careful and wide-ranging survey, Medwell *et al.* (1998) found that knowledge of children's literature was one of the key features distinguishing the most effective literacy teachers from their less effective colleagues.

RESPONDING TO READING

Learning to read, as outlined above, is about learning to orchestrate knowledge on a number of different levels, from word, to sentence, to whole text. It is a complex process, but, in the most successful classrooms, children encounter engaging texts and learn how to put their technical knowledge to use in making sense of them (Hall, 2013). Reading in these classrooms always involves response, both the reader's response to the words and the teacher's response to the reader's attempt to make sense of them. To develop active, engaged readers who approach reading with enthusiasm, carry it out effectively and relate what they read to what they have learned elsewhere, both kinds of response are crucial.

So, whenever teachers model reading, they need to model a response to the text, whether it is 'That sounds tasty!' to the dinner menu, or 'I'm not sure I would wish for that!' to one of desires expressed by the *Fish Who Could Wish* by John Bush and Korky Paul. Whenever children read to teachers, their responses should be invited. Sometimes, predictions may be appropriate; sometimes, it may make more sense to ask for genuine clarification, as I did of my 7-year-old daughter: 'I don't understand. Is Robin Hood outside the castle trying to get in, or inside trying to get out?' Frequently, it may be to make connections with the children's own experience: 'Have you played a game like that?' Teachers voicing their own responses can elicit responses from children and prompt questions, which are central to learner engagement in the activity of making meaning.

There is a danger that responding to text orally is not perceived as a legitimate literacy activity, because it doesn't look like work. But it serves three essential purposes. Through refocusing the reading on meaning, it promotes comprehension in all its complexity. Through helping children make personal sense of texts, it makes reading more enjoyable and fosters the positive attitudes that children in England lack. Through encouraging reflection on such matters as moral issues and the writer's skill, it enables children to become more discerning readers. So, responding to text is a central part of learning to read, not an optional extra.

Formative assessment of children's reading requires a rather different kind of response. Effective teaching is always informed by continuous assessment of how the children are doing, against identified learning goals and targets. This involves watching what they do and talking with them. Many teachers use notebooks to make brief, concrete, dated observations about each child's reading. These might include comments on a spelling pattern the child is finding problematic or surprisingly easy, the child's need to slow down and look at words more carefully, or to speed up and focus more on their meaning. Effective teachers also note how a child copes with complex sentence structures, their readiness to read for pleasure, their persistence in doing so and their newly acquired interest in a particular author. The richer teachers' conceptions of reading are, the more creative their responses are likely to be to individual children. Such day-to-day observations help teachers decide when to wait, when to intervene and what to point a child towards. This knowledge is useful in whole-class, small-group or one-to-one contexts. It is helpful to go through the notebook systematically once a week or so.

Children need both to hear their teachers' reflections on their progress and to make their own observations. They need to be helped to appreciate and articulate their strengths and areas in need of attention. This can be formalised in jointly agreed target setting that takes into account the importance of engaging with and responding to texts. An agreed response target might, for example, be 'find three books that I would want to read again and recommend these to others'. There should be a time when the child's progress towards this is reviewed.

FOSTERING CHILDREN'S INDEPENDENCE AS READERS

In a sense, all the activities mentioned above are about fostering independence. From the nursery on, however, children also need time when they read self-chosen books, individually or in twos or threes. At first, they may just turn the pages, commenting on the pictures. As they become familiar with the language of books, they will start to 'talk their way through' them, drawing on their knowledge of how stories work. Children in all age groups choose their texts and read them for pleasure: it's not the time to urge a child to choose a 'harder' book. Re-reading a much-loved text can have a number of positive effects.

Although younger children cannot be expected to be silent, as they have to talk to think, teachers tend to aim for a quiet hum and model the process by reading themselves, or use the time to work with an individual or group. Many teachers working with 6–7-year-olds introduce quiet reading with a daily 10-minute session, expanding this by degrees, across a year, to 30 minutes or so. Teachers also often include a short plenary, in which readers can share enjoyable incidents or pictures. However, effective teachers of reading don't use reading as a filler activity for children who finish other tasks early, as this does nothing to encourage concentration. Instead they offer word searches or maths puzzles.

A system of taking books home, some to be read by the child and some by the parent, helps strengthen connections between home and school and fosters independence. It has repeatedly been shown to be effective in improving children's reading, in research summarised in DCSF (2008). Here again, choice matters. The more familiar teachers are with children's books, and the better they know the children, the more they will be able to guide their choices effectively, first of all by the selection of books available in the classroom, second, by whole-class 'taster' sessions of these books, and, third, by individual recommendations. A number of other activities can actively foster children's growing independence as readers, some of which are noted below:

■ *Offer guidelines in making choices*: 'Look at the cover. Is this an author/illustrator you know? What do you think it might be about? Read the blurb on the back. Still interested? Read the first page and see if you want to turn over' can be useful advice. The books teachers read aloud, however, may have the biggest influence on children's choices.

■ *Offer a diverse range of texts*: Create boxes with comics and magazines, joke and poetry collections and non-fiction books on subjects that interest the children. Offer these for quiet reading and to take home.

■ *Involve children in book ordering*: It is important to involve the children in selecting new books, perhaps thorough voting for favourite authors, or examining websites and publishers' catalogues.

■ *Create a class library/ book area*: Class libraries and book areas should be both orderly and highly appealing. Boxes are easier to riffle through than shelves and can be arranged by topic and moved around to keep the display fresh. Comfortable book areas, which the children help to plan and create, can make reading more inviting, as can book displays and comments encouraging children to try new authors and titles.

■ *Promote book ownership*: It is hardly surprising that possessing books is connected to reading proficiency. Developing a parent- and child-friendly way of selling books increases the potential for commitment to reading. A school bookshop run by parents, with savings cards available and stock from a local bookshop on a sale-or-return basis, can make a real difference, as can publishers' book clubs. For other possibilities, see Lockwood (2008).

■ *Join the national Young Readers' Progamme*: This enables children to choose up to three free books a year to take home and keep. The programme draws on the expertise of local teachers and librarians. To find out more, see www.literacytrust.org.uk/yrp

■ *Connect to the local library*: Signing children up as members and taking them on visits can help, as can inviting the librarian to visit and share new titles, and encouraging them to register on the Summer Reading Challenge. See http://summer readingchallenge.org.uk

■ *Organise a book-swap day*: Everyone, teachers and parents included, brings a book to exchange for a book ticket, the books are spread out in the hall, and classes visit to choose different books. Class books swaps are also worthwhile.

■ *Organise a book week*: This needs to be planned well in advance and should preferably include the involvement of a children's author. The benefits of a well-organised book week are enormous in terms of raising the profile of reading.

■ *Shadow a children's book award*: Buying or borrowing the shortlist of the Kate Greenaway award or the UKLA book award for children's books can help introduce new books and engage the children in the process of text selection.

CONCLUSION

Teaching young children to read can be a tiresome and frustrating business, if a rigid phonics programme dominates and if reading instruction is not concerned with reader engagement. However, if teachers treat it as a joint voyage of creative exploration, in and out of the spelling patterns of English, as they travel through stories and poems, sharing inventions, wonder and laughter along the way, it can be a source of pleasure and satisfaction for teacher and taught. And the children are much more likely to become committed, engaged, imaginative and successful readers.

FURTHER READING

Brown, J., Kim, K. and O'Brien Ramirez, K. (2012) 'What a teacher hears, what a reader sees: Eye movements from a phonics-taught second grader', *Journal of Early Childhood Literacy*, 12(2): 202–22.

Bussis, A.M., Chittenden, E.A., Amarel, M. and Klausner, E. (1985) *Inquiry into Meaning: An investigation of learning to read*. Hillsdale, NJ: Lawrence Erlbaum.

Hall, K. (2013) 'Effective literacy teaching in the early years of school: A review of the evidence', in J. Larson and J. Marsh, *The Sage Handbook of Early Childhood Literacy* (2nd edn). London: Sage, pp. 523–40.

Kyle, F., Kujala, J., Richardson, U., Lyytinen, H. and Goswami, U. (2013) 'Assessing the effectiveness of two theoretically motivated computer-assisted reading interventions in the United Kingdom', *Reading Research Quarterly*, 48(1): 61–76.

Lockwood, M. (2008) *Promoting Reading for Pleasure in the Primary School*. London: Sage.

CHILDREN'S BOOKS

Agard, J. and Bent, J. (2008) *Wriggle Piggy Toes*. London: Frances Lincoln.

Blake, Q. (1998) *All Join In*. London: Red Fox.

Bush, J. and Paul, K. (1998) *The Fish Who Could Wish*. Oxford. +Kindle.

Clark, M. (1976) *Young Fluent Readers: What can they teach us?* London: Heinemann Educational Books.

Cowley, J. and Fuller, E. (1980) *Mrs Wishy-Washy*. Auckland, NZ: Shortland.

Dunbar, J. and Ayto, R. (1998) *Baby Bird*. London: Walker.

Hutchins, P. (1970) *Rosie's Walk*. London: Penguin, Puffin.

Lionni, L. (1974) *Fish is Fish*. London: Random House.

MacLennan, C. (2008) *Chicky Chicky Chook Chook*. London: Boxer.

Martin, B. and Carle, E. (1995) *Brown Bear, Brown Bear, What Do You See?* London: Penguin, Puffin.

Rosen, M. (1989) *We're Going on a Bear Hunt*. London: Walker.

Sendak, M. (1970) *Where the Wild Things Are*. London: Penguin, Puffin.

Sharratt, N. (1995) *I went to the Zoopermarket*. London: Scholastic.

Waddell, M. and Oxenbury, H. (1991) *Farmer Duck*. London: Walker.

Webb, S. (2003) *Tanka Tanka Skunk*. London: Random House.

CHAPTER 5

CREATIVELY ENGAGING READERS IN THE LATER PRIMARY YEARS

Teresa Cremin

INTRODUCTION

Once children have learned to read, the continuing challenge for teachers is to help them become engaged, enthusiastic and fluent readers who understand the pleasures and value of reading, and who choose to read beyond the demands of the curriculum. Helping children develop into such readers requires more than simply giving them opportunities to read longer and increasingly complex texts, although such experiences are important. This chapter focuses on teaching reading creatively to 7–11-year-olds; the primary focus is on supporting deeper engagement with texts through creative approaches that build a reflective reading culture within the classroom, develop children's understanding of the texts they read and encourage personal responses, including critical readings. It also looks at how teachers can support children as they develop and expand their reading preferences and highlights the importance of teachers' own experiences and knowledge of children's books in building communities of readers.

National curricula across the UK include the requirement to help readers develop a love of literature through widespread reading for enjoyment. For example, the English NC (DfE, 2013: 3) aims to ensure that pupils 'develop the habit of reading widely and often, for both pleasure and information'; the Northern Ireland NC (DENI, 2011) states that, in the later primary years, pupils should 'engage in sustained, independent and silent reading for enjoyment and information'. These statutory orders and those in Wales and Scotland also suggest an acknowledgement of the importance of the reader developing personal preferences and responses to reading and developing their capacity to understand, analyse and evaluate texts. In a creative classroom, as well as through independent, private reading, these elements should be developed by experience of reading as a social activity, where readers share their responses and experiences within a community of readers.

PRINCIPLES

Creative teachers of reading who teach to promote children's engagement with and response to texts, and who seek to build reading fluency at this age, use pedagogical practices underpinned by a number of principles. These include:

- valuing reading and reflection;
- knowing that understanding (comprehending) texts is critical to engagement, enjoyment and learning;
- providing potent and engaging texts;
- recognising the importance of talk around and in response to texts;
- building a reading culture within the classroom (including reading aloud to children);
- encouraging independent reading and personal choice (including texts from children's twenty-first-century culture);
- offering clear modelling through their own reading experiences, responses and expertise;
- giving supportive feedback and suggestions for further development.

Various factors have been identified as important in teaching reading. Based on an extensive research review, Pressley (quoted in Harrison, 2002: 16) listed those factors he regarded as 'research proven' in the teaching of reading. Removing the use of decoding skills from his list as being largely used in the early reading stages, the list contains the following: encourage extensive reading; do explicit work on sight vocabulary; teach the use of context cues and monitoring meaning; teach vocabulary; encourage readers to ask their own 'Why?' questions of a text; teach self-regulated comprehension strategies (for example, activating prior knowledge, visualisation, summarising); encourage reciprocal teaching (teacher modelling of strategies and scaffolding for independence); and encourage transactional strategies (an approach based on readers exploring texts with their peers and their teacher).

The teaching approaches of reciprocal teaching and exploring texts with peers and teachers that Pressley (ibid.) identifies are central to the collaborative, reflective and supportive ethos found in creative and playful classrooms. However, the specific teaching strategies he mentions, such as teaching comprehension strategies and vocabulary, need to be embedded and contextualised in the extensive reading of exciting and affecting texts (Cremin *et al.*, 2014). This is because becoming a fluent reader does not just mean getter quicker and more accurate at automatic word recognition and recognising an increasing number of words. Although fluent reading – being 'the ability to read with comprehension, accuracy, speed and appropriate expression (prosody)' (Johns and Berglund, 2006: 3) – involves using cognitive skills, becoming an engaged and motivated fluent reader means much more than this.

Children who are not engaged and motivated to read do not benefit from reading teaching (Wigfield *et al.*, 2004; Krashen, 2011). Becoming an engaged and motivated reader has social, emotional and cultural dimensions and involves the reader in seeing a purpose for reading. This is supported by children positioning themselves as a reader within a social, collaborative community, with shared practices and expectations. It also involves readers in responding to the feeling and emotions in texts. Sensitive and creative teachers of reading seek to create a community of readers within their classrooms, a context in which children's diverse cultural capital and home literacies are acknowledged, and creativity, speculation, experimentation, play, risk taking and reflection on reading are all encouraged.

READING AND LEARNING

Reading is a central tool of learning and one that underpins learning across the curriculum. In order to learn from reading, readers must engage with the text they are reading in a way that ensures that what they read connects with what they know and stays in their minds afterwards; that is, readers need to read actively, making links with what is already known and expanding or adjusting schema to include the new information (Rumelhart, 1985; Wray and Lewis, 1997). However, readers come to texts with many different purposes – they may want to identify specific information, get a sense of what it was like to live in a particular time, entertain themselves, and so on. Rosenblatt (1985) distinguishes between two different kinds of reading: efferent and aesthetic. In efferent reading, the reader's attention is centred on what should be retained after the reading, such as information to be acquired or a process to be followed. In aesthetic reading, readers focus on what they are living through during the reading and pay attention to ideas, characters, images and so forth. Of course, either kind of response is possible to most texts, depending on the reader's stance. Creative teachers of reading seek to maintain a balance between these two kinds of response in literacy sessions and across the curriculum, for example, seeing the aesthetic potential within information texts, as well as using them for information gathering and textual analysis. (See Chapter 10 for discussion of non-fiction texts.)

A study of World War II at KS2, for example, will involve reading information books on the topic, watching film materials, exploring written and visual artefacts such as ration cards and posters, and searching the Internet for relevant websites, which need multimodal literacies to be read. These reading events offer opportunities for efferent transactions and – in creative classrooms – aesthetic transactions. A ration card, for example, could be viewed as an information source, but it could also prompt discussion, drama and role-play about queuing for supplies, the desire for rare foodstuff and the struggle to feed a family. In planning to work creatively, teachers need to consider their purposes for examining texts, as they will prompt different stances.

Learning about this period should also involve reading narrative, poetry and first-person accounts. These offer rich opportunities for the reader to engage with the emotions, sights, sounds and smells experienced. Emotionally engaging stories about this period include, for example, the novels: *Goodnight Mr Tom* by Michele Magorian, *Line of Fire: Diary of an unknown soldier*, translated by Sarah Ardizzone, *Once* by Morris Gleitzman and the picture fiction books: *War Boy* by Michael Foreman, *My War Diary* by Marcia Williams, and *Rose Blanche* by Christophe Gallanz, edited by Ian McEwan. Each of these offers powerful opportunities for readers to be involved in aesthetic transactions with the text. Creative teachers often offer a summary of several novels and then negotiate with their class which of these might become the core book for their extended unit of work, which will also encompass writing. As Clark (2013) has shown, young people who read above the level expected for their age also write above the expected level, and the inverse is also evidenced. Reading challenging texts to children and fostering independent reading remain important in the later primary years. Creative teachers will also recommend texts to readers, perhaps seeking to stretch the oldest primary children's understanding about war through suggesting Mal Peet's *Life: An exploded diagram* (set in the time of the Cold War) or Jason Wallace's *Out of the Shadows* (about a newly independent Zimbabwe), during a unit on war.

TALK AND PLAYFUL ENGAGEMENT

Through talking about texts, learners come to articulate and share their thoughts, feelings and ideas, and listen to those of others. Talking about and questioning a text enable children to share their understanding and puzzlements. Hearing the ideas of others may deepen their understanding and offer new insights, as social enquiry promotes metacognition and reflection. Creative teachers encourage curiosity and ownership of the learning process, enabling focused conversation to enrich comprehension and the development of empathy. As Maybin (2013: 65) argues, 'imagination and creativity, emotional and moral engagement and humour and fun are all intrinsically important aspects of children's responses to fictional texts'. Through book discussion circles, book groups, book buzz sessions, book swaps, book recommendation slots, *X Factor*-style book awards, guided reading and so on, creative teachers of reading develop an ethos where response to texts is taken as the norm in the classroom. They encourage and support talk by asking open-ended, higher-order questions and spend considerable time encouraging children to ask these too. Their questions and enquiries, their interests and confusions can lead to discussions around texts, supported by their teachers, who help them make connections both to their lives and to the text. The 'Tell me' approach (Chambers, 1993) and the use of literature circles offer examples of how such discussions can be organised and guided. See Chapter 8 for more details.

Spending time on a powerful, affecting book can enhance the quality of the talk, as discussion becomes more informed and complex over time. If this is picture fiction, it can be revisited, and new insights can be discovered. Highly potent examples that trigger discussion include *The Wolves in the Walls* by Neil Gaiman, *Black Dog* by Pinfold, and *Belonging* and *Mirror* by Jennie Baker (both of these Baker texts have no words, but prompt curiosity and conversation). Gathering collections of books that explore particular themes enables contrast to be made and diversity to be recognised. For example, books that explore bereavement and loss, such as the novels *A Monster Calls* by Patrick Ness and *My Sister Lives on the Mantelpiece* by Annabel Pitcher, or the picture texts *The Scar* by Claire Moundlic and *The Heart and the Bottle* by Oliver Jeffers, offer rich material for reflection, when sensitively read and discussed.

Focusing on a single novel too can also enable teachers to teach reading skills in context. A creative teacher used the class novel, *King of the Cloud Forest* by Michael Morpurgo, with 10–11-year-olds over several weeks, to encourage aesthetic responses and talk and teach comprehension skills in context. The result was a high level of motivation, understanding and engagement. The text is full of action, emotion and dilemmas and offered plenty of opportunities for discussion and drama, encouraging personal and critical responses and building understanding through creative activities to develop empathy, inference and deduction. It linked to the theme of mountains, being studied elsewhere in the curriculum. The class was used to working on a class novel over a period of weeks, with the teacher reading aloud, alongside reading in independent and guided contexts. Reading journals, in which the class recorded comments, questions and drawings, were also kept (see Chapter 8 for more details).

Modelled by the teacher, the class developed an ethos of discussion and listened supportively to others' ideas during extensive book talk. The children were encouraged to reflect, both on their growing understanding of the story, and on *how* this had happened. Encouraging the children to be metacognitive – to think about how they had learned, as well as what they had learned – is part of the process of creating reflective readers (Kelley and Clausen-Grace, 2007).

To foster close attention to the text and deduction, and to teach visualisation as a skill that can enhance understanding, the children made a map of the compound after reading the first chapter. This involved careful re-reading and deduction and helped children 'see'

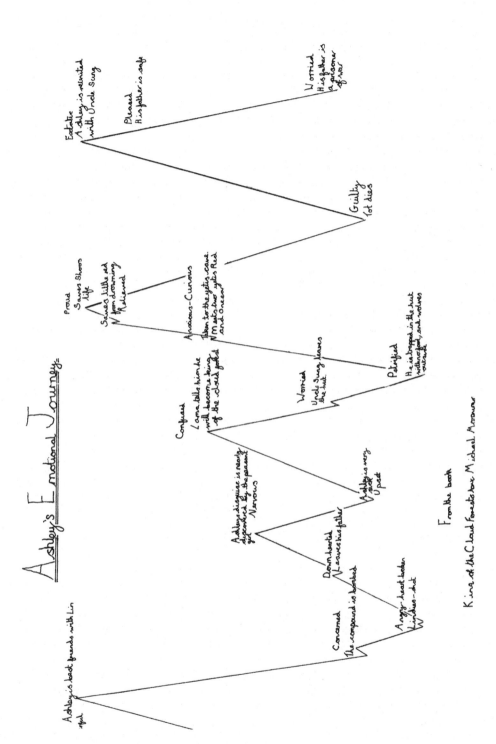

Figure 5.1 An emotions graph to reflect Ashley's journey

the setting, as well as read about it, enabling their teacher to assess their comprehension of the story so far, and enabling them to make connections to map-making/scale plans in geography and mathematics. Throughout, they noticed how the descriptions of the mountain environment and its weather gave richness to their studies in geography.

A compare-and-contrast activity was used to illuminate the relationship between the main character and his best friend. Children noted that, over time, the main character began to question what his father told him. This led to drama and an intense debate about tolerance, with the class drawing on their own lives for examples. The respectful ethos being developed, where talk and risk taking were encouraged, meant that one child felt able to reveal that his parents had divorced because of different beliefs. This aspect of the story touched on a deeply personal experience and enabled the child to examine it.

Freeze-frames, drama and hot-seating were used throughout to consider cause and effect and develop empathy, and the boy's decision whether or not to leave was explored in a conscience alley. Critical and alternative viewpoints were encouraged. After drama activities, children sometimes completed a 'think, feel, say' grid from a chosen character's perspective.

The class also reflected on the characters' changing emotions. Key points were noted on a board using post-it® notes, and groups arranged these on an emotions chart, which triggered further discussion. Finally, emotions graphs were made that involved identifying effective vocabulary in this purposeful, contextualised context (see Figure 5.1). The teacher felt that the quality and amount of talk about the text increased 'phenomenally' over this unit of work, and the children's comprehension improved as they explored the text orally, visually, aurally and kinaesthetically. This active, creative and collaborative approach had an impact on the readers' enthusiasm and enjoyment of the text, and several of them went on to buy their own copy.

TEACHERS AS READERS

One significant omission from Pressley's list of factors noted earlier is the teachers' attitude to reading and their knowledge and experience as readers. Studies of effective teachers of literacy show they are knowledgeable about children's literature and teach reading in context (Medwell et al., 1998; Hall, 2013). However, it is questionable whether primary professionals have sufficiently enriched repertoires to foster reader development (Cremin, Bearne et al., 2008; Cremin, Mottram et al., 2008), and studies show teachers can constrain and limit children's reader identities (Hall, 2012). Nonetheless, research studies highlight an apparent continuity between Reading Teachers – teachers who read and readers who teach (Commeyras et al., 2003) – and children as engaged and self-motivated readers. Such teachers model being readers and share their reading lives and strategies in order to build genuinely reciprocal reading relationships that support young readers. They share explorations of texts with children, model the speculation, questions and responses that happen as they read and hook children into reading by reading books aloud, giving less-able readers access to books they could not read independently. Reading Teachers are well enough informed to introduce children to new writers and genres and to select complex, potent books for extended study.

Aware of their own reading preferences, habits, behaviours and strategies, Reading Teachers capitalise upon their own awareness of the social nature of reading, recognise the significance of readers' rights and identities, and successfully influence both children's engagement as readers and the pleasure they derive from it (Cremin *et al.*, 2014). They do not seek to foster imitation – a do-as-I-do frameset – rather they:

> work[ed] to recognise diversity and difference. They encouraged children to develop their own preferences and practices as readers; readers who could choose what to read, and, where possible within the school day, when and where to read. In sharing their own identities as readers, the Reading Teachers came to consider the ways in which they framed and positioned young readers in school, and sought to offer new forms of participation and engagement.
>
> (Cremin *et al.*, 2014: 153)

As a consequence of teachers repositioning themselves as readers in classrooms and teaching 'from a reader's point of view', as one teacher described it (Cremin *et al.*, 2014: 86), new reader relationships and networks developed between teachers and children and children and children. The role of 'texts in common' (which had been read aloud and/or swapped) was evident, providing a focus for conversations and making connections. The teachers shared their reading identities, interests and preferences with children, who in turn were invited to reflect upon their own reading histories and habits, their likes and dislikes.

Activities that reflect a Reading Teacher stance should be mapped into classroom practice on a regular basis, so that insights about reading are not just offered to certain individuals (e.g. the most able/interested readers), but to the whole class. Such activities involve the teacher initially, and then the class, talking about the experience of being a reader and reflecting on their reading practices. They could include the following:

1 *Bringing in texts from childhood*: This might also involve visiting an early years classroom to borrow their collection for an afternoon of pleasure, re-reading and related activities.

2 *Exploring and creating reading histories*: This could involve noting the wide range of texts encountered, and the people and places involved. Visuals from the Internet could enable PowerPoints of these histories to be made, and actual copies could be sourced from classrooms of younger children.

3 *Exploring reading diversity*: This could involve doing a 24-hour read, where all reading undertaken across 24 hours is collected and displayed – individually or as a class.

4 *Focusing on readers rights*: This could connect to Daniel Pennac's (2006) *The Rights of the Reader*, wonderfully illustrated by Quentin Blake (see the Walker website to download this) and might include examining the right to be silent, the right not to finish, the right to skip pages and so forth.

5 *Focusing on space, place and time for reading*: This could involve teachers sharing where and when they like to read – at home, in the community, at work, on holiday – and discussing whether the place influences the choice of reading material. Photos and displays could be created.

RESPONDING TO READING

Children's personal and critical responses to a text are supported through the kinds of teaching outlined earlier. Creative teachers seek to enable children to become readers who ask questions of texts and use each other and their understanding of the world to make multiple interpretations and personal connections. Such readers are enticed and prepared to imagine, to inhabit and to interrogate what they read and, as a consequence, learn to appreciate and understand the texts they read on several levels. Response to text can involve talk, drama, art, dance, photography, writing and use of multiple media to convey emerging meanings. Any discussion prompts and questions that teachers use need to focus on engagement and response first, leading to interpretation and consideration second. This will help to ensure that the pleasure principle is retained, and reading fiction engages children as enquirers and problem-solvers. Teachers can also engage learners in discussion through Chatterbooks clubs, which, facilitated by The Reading Agency (TRA), can be run in schools, or by encouraging them to join the Summer Reading Challenge, again run by the TRA, in local libraries, though schools too can get involved in order to avoid the summer dip in reading performance. See Chapters 4 and 8 for more details of response activities. Developing children's response to increasingly complex texts across the years is not an optional extra, but an essential element of fostering reflective, creative and critical young readers.

Formative assessment of a child's reading and their responses is also an essential element. This goes well beyond just 'hearing a child read' and putting a tick or comment in a record book. It includes oral feedback and might include self-assessment, peer assessment, such as reading-partner comment books, and parents' comments and observations. Encouraging children to self-assess and compare this with teacher assessment provides areas for discussion, and any gaps between the two can help identify next steps. Assessment of reading should also publicly acknowledge and celebrate reading success and endeavour, be it via a Mexican wave, a 'happy teacher' postcard sent home, a certificate in assembly or a book award.

Involving children in reading assessment is valuable, as the following example demonstrates. Simon was a fluent reader, in the sense that he was reading at an age-appropriate level. His automatic word recognition skills were good, and he seemed to enjoy reading, but he read aloud in a monotone. His teacher taped him reading aloud, played it back to him and asked him what he thought. He was quick to identify that, 'I read in a boring voice', and agreed a target with his teacher, 'to read with expression and pace'. His teacher ensured he had lots of opportunities to hear fluent, expressive reading, including hearing her read aloud to the class, listening to story CDs, watching stories enacted on screen and being matched with a reading partner who modelled fluent reading. She gave him the chance to re-read familiar texts, to reduce some of the cognitive demand, build familiarity and deepen understanding of stories. She planned activities where he would have a purpose for using expressive reading in context, such as reading play-scripts, taking part in choral poetry readings with actions, creating 'radio broadcasts' such as commentating on a playground football match, recording stories for younger children and so on. Simon often had an audience and, having listened to his own, recorded performances, he discussed his progress with his teacher. His improved oral reading was celebrated by his performance of an action poem in assembly, one that he performed with expression and passion.

Increasingly, children like Simon are being assessed against targets linked to specific learning goals/objectives, making the criteria for assessment clear and giving feedback against the target (Black *et al.*, 2003; Clarke, 2005). Such an approach aims to help a child see where they are in their learning and how to move forward. Specific feedback such as this is important, but teachers must guard against teaching to the target and criteria in such a way that they limit the range of possible ways of learning and demonstrating that learning.

A child's target of 'I can recognise how characters are presented in different ways and show this using evidence from the book' could be taught and demonstrated in many ways: through discussion, role-playing characters and drawing or making puppets of the characters. It could also involve enacting a scene, through identifying 'show not tell' passages and talking about what they mean, and making character fact files, character pockets and so forth. Teachers must also be alert to the potential danger that, in focusing on one or two targets, they miss other significant evidence of learning. A child may demonstrate an understanding of simile in their reading, even though that is not their target.

In creative classrooms, teachers will balance the focused nature of targets with a commitment to an engaging, playful and wide-ranging exploration of texts that foster skilled, assured and independent reading.

FOSTERING CHILDREN'S INDEPENDENCE AS READERS

International evidence tends to suggest that a worrying number of young people report that they do not like reading (OECD, 2010; Mullis *et al.*, 2012b). In the 2011 Progress in International Reading Literacy Study, which assesses 10–11-year-olds' reading behaviour, attitudes and attainment in over fifty countries and nation-states across the world, although enjoyment in and motivation for reading had improved slightly for English children, 20 per cent responded that they did not like reading, compared with an international average of 15 per cent (Twist *et al.*, 2012). British teenagers also continue to report reading for pleasure much less than their peers in other countries, and an increasing number report never reading for pleasure and view it as a waste of time (OECD, 2010).

In a UK-based survey undertaken by Clark (2013), which involved nearly 35,000 young people from 8 to 17 years, although roughly half reported enjoying reading, fewer reported reading on a daily basis than in previous National Literacy Trust surveys, and, more worryingly still, attitudes to reading had become more negative. Additionally, the proportion of 8–11-year-olds who read for pleasure and who read daily had dropped very significantly, compared with earlier surveys. Over a fifth of children and young people reported rarely or never reading in their own time, and nearly a third agreed with the statement, 'I only read when I have to' (Clark, 2013). Nor is it the case that these young people are turning to digital texts, as, with the exception of text messages, reading across most formats (including, e.g., magazines, comics, websites and emails) was shown to have fallen between 2005 and 2013 (Clark and Foster, 2005; Clark, 2013).

In this context, fostering reading for pleasure and nurturing children who can and do choose to read are particularly critical. In order to do so, teachers need to find out more about children's everyday lives and reading practices and broaden their understanding of the wide range of texts that children choose to read in their homes and communities. One strategy, developed from Cliff Hodges's work (2010), to find out about children's reading practices beyond school is to create reading rivers, through collage or PowerPoint or in any medium. Omar's reading river (see Figure 5.2) indicates the breadth of his reading and the pleasure he finds in searching the Internet for possible bargains, as well as reviews of YouTube videos. He is also involved in reading on social networking sites and is aware his mother likes magazines and newspapers, as well as perusing the TV guide. With new knowledge of children's current reading practices, teachers can honour and validate these in school and potentially broaden children's conceptions of what reading encompasses.

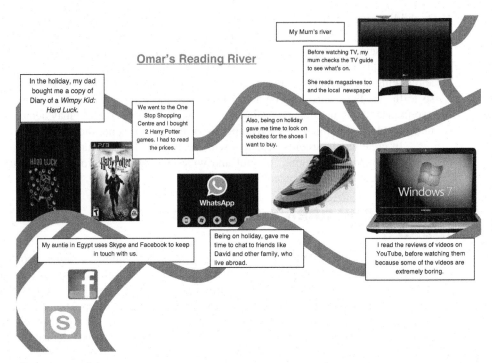

Figure 5.2 Omar's reading river

In order to develop as independent readers and recognise themselves as readers in diverse contexts, children need:

■ to understand the pleasures and purposes of reading, so they can see what is in it for them;

■ opportunities to read individually and independently, as well as in shared and group contexts;

■ access to high-quality, motivating materials;

■ opportunities to choose their own reading materials and explore their own preferences;

■ experiences and support that encourage them to widen their range, persevere and try new things;

■ opportunities to become members of a community of engaged readers.

Although events such as World Book Day and Book Week can raise the profile of reading, they cannot, as stand-alone events, permanently influence the reading culture of the school. In order to foster independent, volitional reading, a classroom reading-for-pleasure pedagogy is essential, alongside and as part of reading instruction and wider reading events and opportunities (e.g bookshops, trips to the local library). A reading-for-pleasure pedagogy involves four core elements: a rich reading environment, varied read-aloud programmes, substantial space for book talk and book recommendations, and the provision of quality time for independent, choice-led reading (Cremin *et al.*, 2014). These pedagogic practices can help to build reading communities in the classrooms of teachers who share a wide and encompassing conceptualisation of reading and do not see it merely as the elements defined within, and assessed by, the NC. Much, however, will depend on the manner in which they are offered and developed. For example, to what extent are the children themselves involved in deciding what their teacher is going to read aloud? Is space built in for children to make suggestions and requests? To what extent is reading time enforced as a silent period? Who decides? What reading materials are available to read in this context? Must children read their assigned colour-coded or reading-scheme book?

Children need to select their own reading materials to develop their independence as readers with preferences. As well as a free choice of books provided by the school, creative teachers encourage children to read materials from their life outside school, be it books, comics, magazines, hobby texts, collectors' cards or instruction manuals. Teachers include such texts in their teaching sessions to give them value and status and to engage interest. They also encourage children to share their choices with each other and suggest related items that might extend children's choices. Schools can set up regular orders for comics such as *Shout* and *The Simpsons*, magazines such as *The Young National Geographic* and newspapers such as *First News* and, in so doing, help to motivate young readers. Teachers also invite children to share their ideas about creating comfortable classroom spaces to relax in while reading. Negotiating new ways of responding to children's needs as readers and honouring their choices (while also introducing them to new writers) are important, if communities of readers are to be built.

Through the creation of such communities, characterised by reciprocity and interaction, increased independence and pleasure can be developed (Cremin, Mottram *et al.*, 2009, 2014). Such communities arguably encompass:

- a shared concept of what it means to be a reader in the twenty-first century;
- considerable teacher and child knowledge of children's literature and other texts;
- pedagogic practices which acknowledge and develop diverse reader identities;
- new social spaces that encourage choice and child ownership of their own reading for pleasure;
- spontaneous 'inside-text talk' on the part of all participants;
- a shift in the locus of control that fosters reader agency and independence.

(Cremin *et al.*, 2014: 155)

FOSTERING IMAGINATIVE ENGAGEMENT: EXTENDED EXPLORATIONS

Creative teachers of reading find imaginative ways to journey inside a book on extended explorations, as outlined throughout this book. For example, several teachers using the book *Dragonology: The complete book of dragons*, by Dr Ernest Drake, shared their ideas and found a myriad of ways of firing children's imaginations and heightening engagement.

In one class, children received a letter telling them that their application to take the secret and ancient Society of Dragonologists Course 'Working With Dragons' had been accepted (see Figure 5.3). Each morning thereafter, the class repeated the oath of the Dragonologist Society, and their teacher 'found' an old school report that showed that the most famous dragonologist, the 'author' of the book, had attended school nearby (see Figure 5.4). The report gave them evidence about his interests and skills that led to some informed and engaging hot-seating.

S.A.S.D.

SASD
Wyvern Way
London

Dear Student,

I am delighted to inform you that your application to take
the Secret and Ancient Society of Dragonologists course
'WORKING WITH DRAGONS' has been accepted.

You may now consider yourself a fully fledged
Dragonology student. Upon signing the *Oath of
Dragonology*, you are entitled to honorary junior
membership of the SASD.

Yours in Dragonology,

Earnest Drake
(President)

■ **Figure 5.3** The invitation to join the Ancient Society of Dragonologists

On another occasion, the teacher created a nest of stones and rocks in the middle of the classroom. Inside were thirty dragon eggs waiting to hatch. Candles were burning and music was playing as the children entered the classroom. The teacher spoke of the tangible sense of awe and wonder present. How long would it take for them to hatch? What care would a baby dragon need? The book might provide the answers.

Other children watched a video their teacher had filmed in advance. Face to camera, in documentary style and using formal language, she confessed to being a secret dragonologist and showed them sites in a nearby forest where she claimed there was evidence of dragon occupation. Thus, a dead tree had been killed by the heat of the dragon's breath, broken branches showed the dragon's flight path, a large heap of brushwood was the remains of a dragon's nest and so on. Still on camera, she told them that they would be visiting the forest the following week to undertake their own search for evidence. What other signs might there be? Would they recognise them?

A real purpose for reading was established in these classrooms, imaginations were fired, and the motivation to read was high. For several weeks, the children read books about dragons, found a wealth of stories and myths about dragons, role-played dragons, created a dragon's den in their classrooms, and produced live and exclusive TV news reports, as well as newspaper articles. The writing that arose from this engaged reading was, unsurprisingly, of consistently high quality. The teachers' creative approach inspired intense levels of imaginative engagement.

Celtic Preparatory School

Progress report on Earnest Drake   Age 10 yrs 11 months   Form 6H   Term 18 48

SUBJECTS	REMARKS	Examination	Effort	Teacher initials
READING	*A keen reader but spends too much time reading about dragons, fairy tales, myths and legends. Needs to widen his interests.*	98%	B	*MH*
WRITING	Earnest is a very capable writer. I am pleased to hear he keeps a journal of the wild life he has observed. He must NOT use the margins of his exercise book to draw dragons	92%	A	MH
ARITHMETIC	Earnest could do better if he applied himself. He spends a great deal of time daydreaming rather than getting on with his sums.	63%	C	CP
HISTORY	Has a strong interest in history, but needs to be more critical in distinguishing facts from fiction. Must realise that myths are NOT facts.	56%	B	GF
GEOGRAPHY	*V. good. Knows all principal rivers, mountain ranges, climates of Great Britain and Europe etc. One would think he was a great traveller.*	**95%**	A	**WK**
NATURAL SCIENCES	Has an excellent knowledge of fauna and flora and exceptional field work skills for a boy of his age.	99%	A	AE
CONDUCT Good ATTENDANCE one absence PUNCTUALITY Good			
GENERAL COMMENTS: Earnest has the ability to go far if he concentrates on practical, everyday knowledge rather than ancient myths and stories. HEADMASTER			

■ **Figure 5.4** Ernest Drake's school report

CONCLUSION

If teachers wish children to become lifelong, committed readers, then they must bring passion and excitement into the teaching of reading and teach reading creatively, as well as teaching for creativity. Building communities of engaged readers in school will mean creating new spaces for children and teachers to participate in, shared talk about reading and readers' lives, recognition and valuing of diversity in reading preferences and practices, the teaching of reading skills in motivating contexts and more choice in independent reading. In such communities teachers will be providing imaginative ways into reading and creative activities to explore texts of all kinds.

FURTHER READING

Cremin, T., Mottram, M., Collins, F., Powell, S. and Safford, K. (2014) *Building Communities of Engaged Readers: Reading for pleasure*. London: Routledge.

Gamble, N. and Yates, S. (2008) *Exploring Children's Literature* (2nd edn). London: Sage.

Hall, L.A. (2012) 'Rewriting identities: Creating spaces for students and teachers to challenge the norms of what it means to be a reader in school', *Journal of Adolescent and Adult Literacy*, 55: 368–73.

Lockwood, M. (2008) *Promoting Reading for Pleasure in the Primary School*. London: Sage.

CHILDREN'S BOOKS

Baker, J. (2008) *Belonging*. London: Walker.

Baker, J. (2010) *Mirror*. London: Walker.

Barroux, (2014) *Line of Fire: Diary of an Unknown Soldier* (trans. Sarah Ardizzone). London: Phoenix Yard.

Foreman, M. (1989) *War Boy*. London: Pavilion.

Gaiman, N. and McKean, D. (2003) *The Wolves in the Walls*. London: Bloomsbury.

Gallaz, C., McEwan, I. (ed.) and Innocenti, R. (1985) *Rose Blanche*. London: Jonathan Cape.

Gleitzman, M. (2006) *Once*. London: Puffin.

Jeffers, O. (2010) *The Heart and the Bottle*. London: HarperCollins.

Magorian, M. (1998) *Goodnight Mr Tom*. London: Longman.

Morpurgo, M. (2006) *King of the Cloud Forest* (new edn). London: Egmont Books.

Moundlic, C. (2011) *The Scar*. London: Walker.

Ness, P. (2012) *A Monster Calls* (from an original idea by Siobhan Dowd). London: Walker.

Peet, M. (2011) *Life: An exploded diagram*. London: Walker.

Pinfold, L. (2011) *Black Dog*. Dorking, UK: Templar.

Pitcher, A. (2011) *My Sister lives on the Mantelpiece*. London: Indigo.

Steer, D.A. (ed.) (2003) *Dragonology: The complete book of dragons*. Dorking, UK: Templar.

Wallace, J. (2010) *Out of the Shadows*. London: Andersen.

Williams, M. (2008) *My War Diary*. London: Walker.

CHAPTER

6

CREATIVELY ENGAGING WRITERS IN THE EARLY PRIMARY YEARS

Teresa Cremin

INTRODUCTION

Young children need to be offered the time and space to use different forms of writing in imaginatively engaging contexts, in which their early attempts at mark making are recognised as acts of communication and their words and meanings are valued. As Vygotsky (1978: 118) suggested, 'an intrinsic need should be aroused in them, and writing should be incorporated into a task that is necessary and relevant for life'. When writing to express themselves, to communicate information of personal significance, to reflect upon their lives and voice their views, children should be affectively and cognitively engaged as young authors, not as scribes. This chapter focuses upon teaching early writing creatively, focusing primarily on developing the compositional skills of young writers aged 5–7 years. It highlights, in particular, the role of improvisation in early writing, the importance of play and imaginative engagement, the value of teaching grammar, appropriately and in context, and the teacher's role as model writer. In addition, the importance of fostering young writers' authorial agency and independence is examined.

All the national curricula in the UK encompass both transcriptional and compositional aspects of writing, though these are only separated out in this way within the English NC (DfE, 2013). Transcription focuses on spelling and handwriting, whereas composition is more relevant to fostering the creative voice of the young child, both on page and screen, and is thus the core focus of this chapter. In Northern Ireland (DENI, 2011), attention is paid within the language and literacy curriculum to talking about and planning with 5–7-year-olds, in order that they are 'writing without prompting, making their own decisions about form and content', and writing expressively for a variety of purposes and audiences. The Scottish principles and practice document (Education Scotland, 2012) encompasses creating texts as a core strand but affords less detail on reasons for writing. The Welsh Framework (DfES, 2013) foregrounds this more, recognising that writing involves recording and exploring one's thoughts, feelings and opinions; communicating with others; and expressing ideas through the power of language. However, all these curricula acknowledge writing as an act of meaning making and communication.

PRINCIPLES

To develop creatively as writers, children need extensive experience of texts, tailored teaching of the appropriate skills, the opportunity to be imaginatively engaged in open-ended, interactive contexts and the chance to make choices and write for real purposes. Key principles in early writing include: recognising and building upon children's existing and often implicit knowledge about language, providing a print-rich environment and offering opportunities to write in playful contexts. The combination of the teacher's invitation to engage and imagine and the professional use of observation and fine-tuned intervention can help move children's learning forward (Geekie *et al.*, 1999). Although the new Early Years Foundation Stage (DfE, 2014) in England is somewhat focused upon developing children's readiness for school, it is still crucial that a play-based, observation-focused approach to early language is fostered, and that early mark-making and writing take place within meaningful and engaging activities. However, with the downward pressure from the readiness agenda, not all teachers feel confident enough to contextualise early writing in play-based contexts.

Children in the early years make no distinction between drawing, painting, modelling or writing as means of recording and exploring their experiences, and need to be offered opportunities to mark-make in a range of playful contexts using 'what is to hand' (Kress, 1997). Through experimenting with different materials, they draw on their knowledge and experience of different literacy practices and begin to gain control over writing, expanding their theories of how the writing system works in the process. In supporting emergent writers, teachers encourage children to make independent attempts at communicating and focus on their intentions as writers. Knowledge of the range of literacy practices in which children engage in their homes is essential to enable teachers to build upon their diverse literacy resources and cultural capital and to recognise the influence of the digital literacies that young children have access to at home. Creative teachers encourage children to connect their own 'school of knowing' with the 'school of expressing' (Malaguzzi, 1998), making use of words, images, objects and sounds, as well as their own bodies, to help them compose.

In classrooms where teachers make use of the Helicopter Technique (teachers scribe children's stories, which are later enacted), children are helped to learn about writing and the link between the spoken and the written word. They may also spontaneously imitate the teacher's role and scribe other children's stories or write or draw their own. Research in this area indicates the technique offers strong support for apprenticing young writers, as writing each other's stories and making books to write stories are likely to emerge naturally in classrooms using the technique, and blank story books may be needed in which children can write their own or others' narratives during free play (Cremin *et al.*, 2013). In these, children aged 3–7 years ascribed meaning to their mark-making, used long strings of letters or lines, and experimented with the written word. One of 6-year-old Isabelle's tales (see Figure 6.1) was a comforting and thought-provoking story of the little bird that shivered in the nest as the tree branches were blowing, though he knew he was safe because his mother was with him. In this text, found inside her class's book, Isabelle underlined a number of words, a Helicopter Technique convention to indicate the nouns for later enactment. Although she has not achieved this entirely, it is clear she is beginning to understand the convention. She was observed later taking the role of the little bird when her classmates acted it out on the 'stage' (see Chapter 3 for an account of this approach, or visit the MakeBelieve Arts website: www.makebelievearts.co.uk).

one windy
day The
Tris brunchis
wer
and a LITLe
berd
Siverd in
his nest
but mummy
wos bside him

Figure 6.1 Isabelle's tale of the little bird

Developing children's positive attitudes to writing and confidence in their ability to 'write' independently is crucial, and so teachers need to offer such spaces for volition, choice and self-determination in writing. Creative teachers, convinced of the importance of developing individual child writers, rather than just teaching the skills of writing, acknowledge that writing involves both the emotions and the intellect and plan accordingly. They seek to offer a motivating and creatively engaging curriculum in which writing for a range of purposes and audiences is commonplace and in which the skills of writing are both taught and applied. Such teachers try to balance the development of children's technical competence alongside their ability to express ideas and communicate confidently, with voice and verve. The concept of voice, 'like a fingerprint, reveals identity' (Andrews, 1989: 21) and comes to represent, 'the concept of individuality, the uniqueness of the individual writer, who draws upon their own experience, knowledge, attitudes and engagement' (Grainger *et al.*, 2005: 196).

In celebrating children's unusual ideas, noticing their playful use of spoken language, and affirming their growing independence as writers who have something to say and the means to convey this, teachers can help children construct positive dispositions towards creativity, individuality and difference in writing. For, although young writers need to learn about the different types of text and spelling and punctuation conventions, for example, they also need to develop an understanding of the purpose and pleasure to be found in writing and the impact of their work on others. Research also highlights that automaticity in handwriting is significant in facilitating composition and deserves increased attention as part of a creative approach (Medwell *et al.*, 2007).

READING, WRITING AND LEARNING

Reading offers young learners different models of language, and, if texts are actively inhabited, explored, read and discussed, children appropriate such language into their own repertoires. Speaking and listening, reading and writing are interdependent language modes and need to be taught as such, to enable each mode to enrich the others. When teachers immerse children in powerful literature and other texts and explore these in playful contexts on extended learning journeys, then a range of purposeful reasons for writing emerge. In Chapter 7, Figure 7.1 shows an extended process of teaching literacy for planning these and mapping in purposeful writing.

Shared reading feeds and enriches shared writing. Teaching about language and organisational features of texts, aligned with opportunities to work on sustained pieces of parallel writing in guided-group contexts, helps children become aware of the way in which authors choose to organise, structure and manipulate language to achieve effects. With support, children can transfer this knowledge and understanding into their own work (Corden, 2000). Shared writing encompasses teacher modelling, as well as scribing the children's suggestions in joint composition. Guided writing, the next step towards independent writing, involves children leaning on the model created and more independently drafting, revising and editing their work. Guided writing allows teachers to offer small-group-focused support, whereas shared writing is whole-class oriented. In both, teachers may choose to use a writing frame to help scaffold the children's writing. Frames are skeletal outlines that offer a series of prompts of starters, connectives and phrases suitable for particular text types (Wray and Lewis, 1997). They can be very valuable to help embed the structure of different text types, although they should be viewed as flexible templates according to the purpose and audience of the writing.

Potent literature has a marked influence upon young writers, particularly when teachers take the time to explore the whole text and focus on the dilemmas of the characters, the issues arising and the themes. In one class of 6–7-year-olds, the teacher, seeking to challenge traditional assumptions about wolves as the evil characters in children's stories, sought to read a range of texts and created several 'roles on the wall', giant outlines of the various wolves, and, through drama and role-play, investigated the particular characteristics of individual wolves. Many tales were told and read, including Little Red Riding Hood, The Three Little Pigs, Pascal Biet's *A Cultivated Wolf*, Michael Morpurgo's *The Last Wolf*, Helen Creswell's *Sophie and the Sea Wolf* and Emily Gravett's *Wolves*. The main focus, however, was on *Little Wolf's Book of Badness* by Ian Whybrow, the first in a series of books that examine Little Wolf's adventures. In this one, the young wolf travels to Cunning College for Brute Beasts, where he is meant to become a big bad wolf. The book is comprised of his letters home to his parents. Work on the book involved turning the role-play area into Beastshire and the 'Frettnin Forest' and other work in role, as well as creating 'rules of badness' and examining Little Wolf's spelling problems. The book and the wider work around it involved the children actively and imaginatively, which was demonstrated in their writing. In Figure 6.2, Philip's letter, written in role as Little Wolf, shows how this young author has leant upon some of the text's features, such as the letter format, the deliberate misspellings and the ink stains. However, in addition, Philip playfully adds new rules and makes good use of a number of punctuation conventions, such as parentheses and exclamation marks, which are also used by Whybrow. The former had not been discussed by the class, but so many of them used such brackets in their letters home that the teacher was prompted to focus on this punctuation feature, celebrating the skill of these young writers who had noticed and imitated this appropriately.

Children play with the possibilities of texts that they encounter and make use of these in their compositions, often combining both text and image, as Philip does in this context (Bearne and Wolstencroft, 2007). Although the communicative practices to which they are apprenticed at home include many traditional forms, these exist side by side with new practices that blend different media. So, in school, teachers need to recognise and build upon children's cultural experiences and the plethora of digital literacy practices (which may involve, e.g., computer games, Wii, video/DVD and TV), as well as their more traditional experiences of books and writing materials (Marsh, 2004, 2008). National curricula differ in the extent to which they recognise this diverse range of communicative practices, England's English curriculum appears to ignore the visual/digital, whereas the curricula in Wales and Scotland sensibly expect children in the early primary years to create simple texts on paper and on screen that combine words, images and sounds, encouraging them to select presentational features to suit their particular writing purposes. Nonetheless, teachers in England can still capitalise upon possibilities, and all professionals can lean on contemporary films or television, making explicit links between visual texts and written outcomes, and teaching the language of media structures to support writing.

Clearly, children need support to master digital as well as non-digital spaces for communication, through perhaps working with accessible iPad apps (Kucirkova, 2013). One such is *Our Story*,[1] an open-ended app with which children can create their own story in pictures, photographs, sounds/voice and/or written text. Their multimodal stories can be played direct from the iPad or shared with the class through the interactive whiteboard

Figure 6.2 Little Wolf's letter home from the Adventure Academy

and can also be sent home using Dropbox or iTunes. Classroom work has shown that this app supports young learners in drafting and reshaping their story creations, enabling them to give their stories a real voice, literally and metaphorically (Kucirkova *et al.*, 2014). See Chapter 11 for a fuller discussion of using visual and multimodal texts.

TALK AND PLAYFUL ENGAGEMENT

Speaking and listening contribute significantly to learning, and so ensuring a wealth of opportunities exist for children to talk before, during and after they write offers real support to young writers. The relationship between talk and writing has been demonstrated in a number of studies, many of which focus on developing boys' writing (Essex County Council, 2003; Bearne and Grainger, 2004). These indicate the importance of talk, interaction and creative engagement in developing young writers' motivation, interest, commitment and achievement.

Play, which is essentially improvisational in nature, can give rise to many reasons for writing, as well as help generate the content of the communication. Young learners can use different resources, such as sand and water, paint and modelling clay, their bodies, as well as pencils and paper, with which to represent their meaning making. When children engage playfully, they imagine possibilities, manipulate materials and objects and talk, draw and create meaning. In playing around with such materials and ideas in action, children begin to ask questions, as well as play with words, their intonation and possible meanings. The Talk to Text project (Fisher *et al.*, 2010) focused on the early years, sought to support the oral rehearsal of written texts and introduced strategies such as invisible writing and the magic pencil, which imaginatively engaged the learners and enabled them to 'write aloud' as they composed sentences. Through participating in playful motivating contexts, children can develop their creative capacity to experiment with language, interpretation and meaning. Their visual and bodily play and the exploration of multiple modes of communication enrich this capacity. Although the serious play of writing is framed by rules or conventions, these are purposefully employed and experimented with in the context of creatively engaging playful experiences. 'The roots of writing lie in the other forms of symbolising (drawing, modelling, play, drama) that children engage in before they come to the abstract symbolic system of writing' (Barrs, 1988: 114).

Through the imaginative use of talk and by bringing texts to life in a variety of playful ways, children try out, absorb and transform others' voices and begin to trust and stretch their own; this can enrich the voice of the child (Bakhtin, 1986). In the extended process of composition, children use talk opportunities to voice their own and others' views and feelings within the imaginative experience. In such contexts, talk is used to reconstruct events, share ideas and generate new insights. As tellers of tales, for example, they may initially imitate and lean on known tales, but will gradually move to innovate and invent their own tales, leaning on the narrative repertoire they have established through retelling tales and reading. In effect, they internalise the form and structure of known narratives and borrow elements of the memorable language too, widening their written vocabulary in the process. They may, for example, borrow the repetitive language patterns in traditional tales, appeal rhetorically to the reader, or borrow and adapt story beginnings they have heard and used orally, as the following extracts from a class of 6–7-year-olds' tales indicate:

> He travelled over many tall mountains, through many long valleys and across many rivers until he reached the River of Hope and a very little river it was too.
>
> And then Moonkaia whispered 'It's me your brother'. Sunkia looked up at him and could hardly believe her eyes. Was it really him?
>
> The little man stamped his feet so hard, Stamp Stamp Stamp and he banged his fists, Bang Bang Bang and he shouted 'No, No No!'. Can you hear him shouting?

> Many golden suns and many silver moons ago there lived a tiny fairy who
> loved to dance. She so loved to dance so much that . . .
>
> In the time before men and women had begun to live on the earth, when the
> skies were always blue, there lived a strange creature who . . .

Children at play, Vygotsky argued, often travel further and, in such contexts, act as
if they are 'a head taller than themselves' (1978: 103). Through playfully engaging with
stories, information, physical resources and each other, motivated young thinkers often
move almost seamlessly into writing and, in the process, are able to draw upon the source
and substance of their improvised and imaginatively motivating play.

TEACHING GRAMMAR CREATIVELY AND IN CONTEXT

In England, the new NC (DfE, 2014) includes requirements to teach specific knowledge
about grammar and associated terminology to young writers. For example, 5- and 6-year-
olds are expected to be able to use terminology such as 'word, sentence, singular, plural,
question mark and exclamation mark', and 6- and 7-year-olds are expected to be able
to use 'verb, tense (past/present), adjective, noun, suffix, command, question, statement,
explanation, and apostrophe'. Faced with these, teachers will be asking themselves questions
such as, why is it important to teach these grammatical features explicitly, and how
can it be done creatively? In response, Reedy and Bearne assert: 'Good writing is what
works to do the job the writer wants. And studying how language works – grammar –
should help young writers to say what they want to say as effectively as they can' (Reedy
and Bearne, 2013: 4).

Drawing on the available research, these scholars outline a clear process for teaching
grammar, REDM (see Figure 7.1 in Chapter 7). This starts with reading and investigation
of the specific language feature (R), followed by explicit teaching and explanation (E). It
then moves into creative ways of discussion and experimentation (D), which enable young
learners to make more informed writing choices. The context teachers create using this
process should ensure the activity is purposeful in making meaning (M), as well as engaging
and playful. For example, within the context of writing a narrative, a teacher wanted to
develop children's understanding of how their choice of verbs could have a significant
effect on meaning. At the beginning of a sequence of work, she asked the children to
consider the sentence, 'The boy went down the road.' She then underlined the word 'went'
and asked the learners to suggest alternative verbs that would fit in that slot. The children,
in twos and threes, generated alternatives, including: walked, ran, sprinted, crawled, hopped,
crept, tiptoed, skipped and trudged.

Following a negotiated demonstration of how the teacher should move if she was
tiptoeing, skipping and trudging across the class, for instance, there was a discussion
about the information implied within the verbs about the way the character moved and
felt. This activity was repeated, with small groups generating verbs and taking it in turns
to demonstrate these through role-play. In this way, the children began to understand how
the choice of verbs was a powerful way of helping the reader to gain a deeper understanding
of both action and mood and were able to apply and actively use this terminology. They
then decided which verbs should be displayed and referred to these when drafting their
subsequent stories, to help them make the meaning they wanted to achieve.

Other examples of teaching grammar in context are offered in Reedy and Bearne (2013), including a case study of 6- and 7-year-olds where the REDM process was used to teach explicitly about adjectives. Based on this, Kennedy (2014) explores a unit of work based on the picture book *Naughty Bus*, by Jan and Jerry Oke. The intention here was to help develop the children's choices in narrative, and the outcome was a Naughty Bus adventure set in the school grounds. The children had many opportunities to write creatively within the unit, and the explicit teaching of adjectives was integrated into the teaching sequence. After reading the story and engaging with the character of the Naughty Bus, the children were helped to explore more- and less-appropriate adjectives for it. The teacher prepared a basket of cards, each with an adjective written upon it, and this was passed around for each child to pick out an adjective and consider whether it described the bus. They then had to justify their opinion, using their knowledge of the text and character; for example, one boy noted, 'Naughty Bus is cheeky because he zooms past the toys.' The teacher followed this by modelling how to choose adjectives when writing descriptive passages and encouraged the children to visit the independent writing area and use their

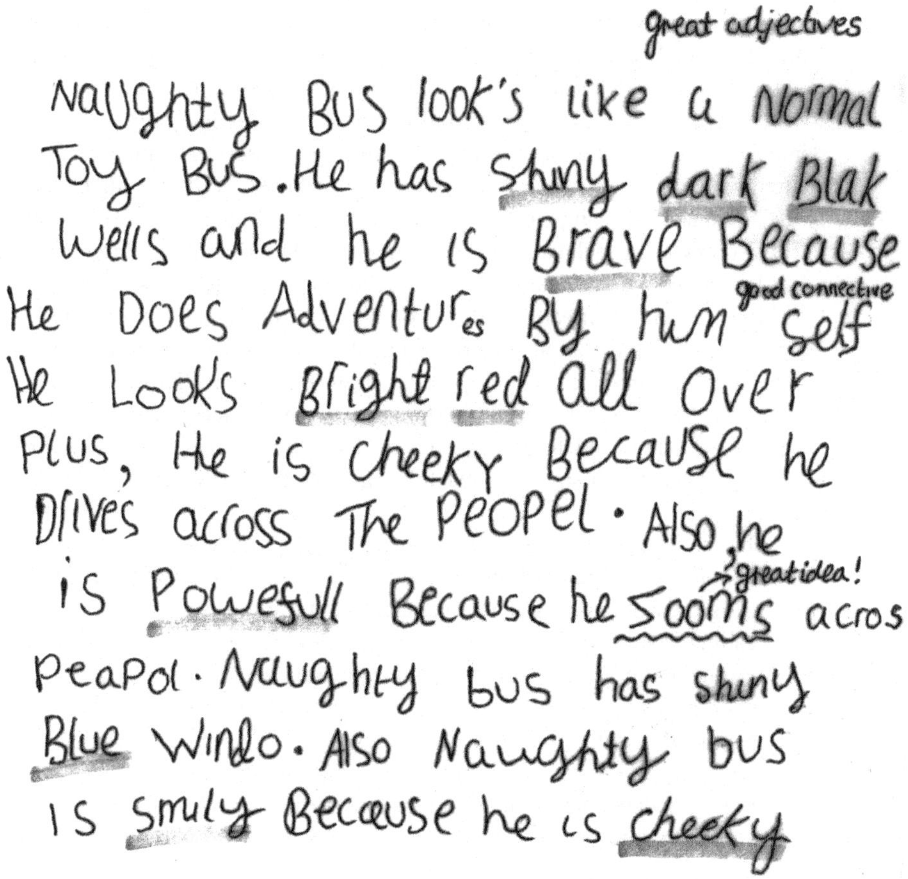

> great adjectives
>
> Naughty Bus look's like a Normal Toy Bus. He has shiny dark Blak Wells and he is Brave Because He Does Adventures By him self *(good connective)* He Looks Bright red all over Plus, He is cheeky Because he Drives across The Peopel · Also he is Powesull Because he Sooms *(great idea!)* acros Peapol · Naughty bus has shiny Blue Windo · Also Naughty bus is smily Because he is cheeky

■ **Figure 6.3** Description of the main character after teacher modelling ideas to write about this theme. Figure 6.3 shows how Syed applied this grammatical knowledge in his independent writing.

Later, the teacher consolidated the children's understanding through further writing activities, including an authentic poetry-writing experience based on a short bus ride. Because the children had previous experience of developing noun phrases, they were more confident in the choices they made.

Ultimately, this is why teachers teach children about grammar. It is important that young readers and writers know how language is organised, so that they can make their own informed, creative choices to make meaning themselves. The terminology is important because it enables teachers and children to have a shared vocabulary – a metalanguage to support development.

TEACHERS AS WRITERS

If children are to take part in the creative processes of exploring and experimenting, and selecting and evaluating their ideas for writing, teachers need to work artistically, offering sustained opportunities for composing and engaging themselves as writers in the classroom. This involves teachers in interpreting the curriculum requirements imaginatively and learning through composing; it also involves modelling writing and demonstrating to children that their own teachers are writers in the real world. Do children see their teachers writing for themselves, or only for instructional or pedagogic purposes? It is valuable to demonstrate to children that writing is a common feature of human life, and that adults write for a variety of purposes too. As Frater (2001) observed, too much writing in school is undertaken for the purpose of learning to write and practising writing skills; too little has real purpose and relevance to the writer or fosters their playfulness and creativity.

Research suggests that there may be advantages to teachers engaging as writers in the classroom (Grainger *et al.*, 2005; Yeo, 2007; Cremin, 2008; Cremin and Myhill, 2012). When teachers write alongside children and learn about writing from an insider's perspective, this evidence suggests they recognise for themselves the significance of talk and creative engagement in writing, the influence of choice and the writers' relationship to the subject matter, and that they perceive value in identifying a clear audience and purpose in writing. There are many ways teachers can take part as writers in school, including:

- sharing what they write at home – the forms, purposes and audiences;
- demonstrating spontaneous modelling – thinking aloud as they compose;
- using their drafts – for class evaluation and response;
- leading shared writing sessions – engaging in whole-class composition;
- writing alongside children – working towards the same goals;
- being a genuine response partner – listening to and responding to others' writing, as well as sharing their own;
- publishing alongside children and teaching assistants;
- writing independently in school – in their own writing journal/during writing workshop time.

In the early years, teachers need to commit time to engaging authentically as writers and modelling different forms, as well as writing alongside the young learners. Through sharing their own writing and modelling possible ways to express ideas, teachers can enhance children's creativity. For more advice on teachers as writers, see Chapter 7.

RESPONDING TO WRITING

Writing in the early years is a highly social process, and classrooms need to reflect this, not only in the generation of ideas, but also in response to them. Children need to be both encouraged and enabled to read and respond to their own and each other's writing, as well as their teachers'. Additionally, this will involve teachers in reading children's developing work back to them, for, as Barrs and Cork (2001) indicate, this can reveal the pattern and texture of the writing and heighten the child's awareness of what they are trying to communicate. To be fully aware of what they have written, the young writer needs to hear it and listen to it. Connecting to research, teachers may encourage children to 'say it – write it' (Fisher *et al.*, 2010) as they compose, but often, re-reading writing at the point of composition is not taught, and teachers tend to read and respond to finished work. Reading aloud children's unfolding work is also important. It is important that children are taught to read aloud and later sub-vocalise as they compose, as such monitoring allows them to hear the tunes and rhythms of their work and increases their syntactic awareness.

Teachers' positive responses to young children's written attempts at communicating meaning are crucial; their knowledge of the history of a child's text and its multiple origins can contribute to this response, but demands that teachers make full use of their awareness of the child's interests and social and cultural background (Pahl, 2007). One of the most effective forms of feedback is to provide focused oral and written feedback that helps children recognise the next steps they need to take, and how they might take them, and, in the process, focuses on celebrating their achievements during an extended learning journey, as well as at the end of it. (See Chapter 7 for a response framework.)

In sharing learning goals and deciding how far the writer has fulfilled their intentions, teachers help young authors consider their work and begin the process of self-assessment and evaluation, which will be further extended later in primary school. Teachers will wish to assess children's progression as writers by examining a range of writing from different contexts, but, if they focus on the surface features of language – the marks on the page – at the expense of responding to the deep structure of language – the meaning (Smith, 1982) – then young writers will themselves learn to focus on the unimportant minutiae, at the expense of developing a sense of themselves as authors with something to say.

FOSTERING CHILDREN'S AUTONOMY AS WRITERS

In order to foster increased independence as writers, creative teachers encourage children to communicate through writing and mark-making in myriad ways: through the use of a writing table with a range of resources, for example (Bhojwani *et al.*, 2009), and through offering choice in writing journals and writers' workshops. Modelling the use of the writing table and sharing examples of texts, as well as offering ways for children's writing to be posted, passed on or shared with their chosen audience, are important. Audiences increase the salience of the writing. See Figure 6.4 for an example of a note brought in for the home-writing display by a 5-year-old; her message indicates she understands writing's communicative intent and has used it for her own purposes.

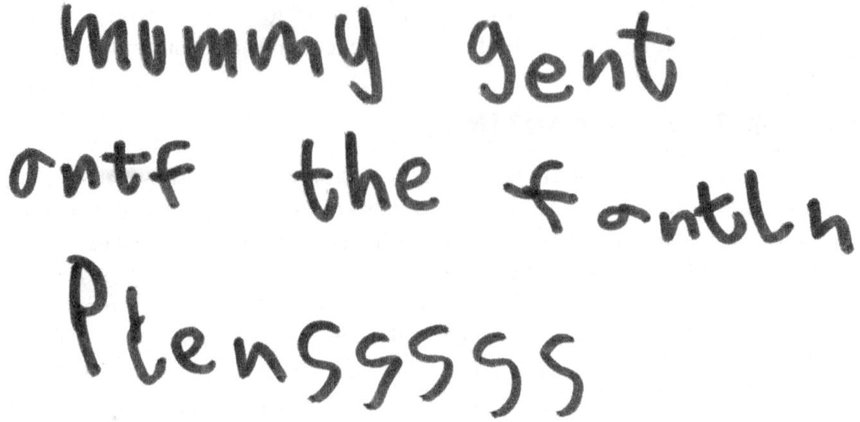

mummy gent
ontf the fantln
Plensssss

■ **Figure 6.4** A message on the home-writing display

Audiences can include parents and grandparents, friends, book characters, the teacher, headteacher, visitors and even soft toys that become imaginary characters in the classroom. Teachers can also establish a class postbox and routinely empty this, writing to children and receiving letters, notes and cards from them, as well as encouraging children to communicate with one another. See Figure 6.5 for an example of 6-year-old Lucy's self-initiated letter to thank her parents for helping raise money for the class's Skylarks appeal. Practice that focuses on identifying real reasons to write can ensure a better balance between the teaching of writing and the actual production and creative use of it.

In addition, many teachers establish writing journals or run writing workshops, in which children make choices about what to write (see Chapter 7 for more details on establishing writing journals). Opportunities also need to be seized for children to write for real in response to religious and secular events, and school events in response to their interests. For example, when teaching instructional texts, teachers can invite children to identify areas of interest and expertise and then create useful instructions that the young writers could give to someone to use. In one class of 6–7-year-olds, the instructional texts produced included, for example: how to change a baby's nappy, how to ride a bicycle, how to look after various small animals, how to cheer mummy up, how to climb a tree, how to play snap and how to get your own breakfast. In offering content choice in this context, helping the children connect to their lives and identify a clear audience for their writing, the teacher gave purpose and relevance to the work and supported the development of the children's autonomy as writers. There are a range of activities that can support choice and create real reasons for writing, including the following.

Activities to support choice and reasons for writing

■ *A writing table/area*: This can offer a wealth of resources, cards, post-it notes, paper of different sizes and colours, envelopes, notepads, notelets, labels, mini books, iPads and writing/colouring implements. See Figure 6.6 for 5-year-old Elliott's writing, triggered by the thunder he had heard in the night.

Daer mummy and Daddy
Thankyou for helping
Skylarks Appeal raised £28.63
Send money to R.S.P.B.
Evrybody worked hard and
reAlly enJoyed buying
and selling The cakes
Love Lucy

Figure 6.5 Lucy's letter to her parents, posted in the school postbox

▒ *A postbox*: This can encourage diverse communication across year groups or in class. Birthday invitations and thank-you cards can also go through this postal system, emptied as 'the Friday post'.

▒ *A class home-writing board*: Owned by the children, this can display children's home writing and might also include cut-outs brought in from magazines, comics, junk mail, catalogues and environmental print.

▒ *A graffiti wall*: This is a brick wall, created with paper bricks, and children can write messages, poems, sayings or information for others, straight on to the wall.

▒ *Registers*: Children's registers are created for free-choice/golden-time activities, and signing is expected.

▒ *The teacher's Notebook of Surprises/Reminders*: Teachers keep a precious notebook in which children can write reminders, messages and notes, or share information with them. This may prompt replies.

▒ *Diaries*: A class diary can be modelled over a week, and tiny folded-paper diaries can be offered for the weekend and/or added to the writing table.

▒ *Mini newspapers*: Through creating instant newspapers to take home, children choose the content and can highlight personal, school and/or pretend news.

▒ *Letters/information to parents*: Children are encouraged to write to their parents about events in school and issues they care about, as information updates.

▒ *Playing with notices*: Invite the class to collect, copy and display notices from their environment – for example, 'Keep off the grass' or 'Do not feed the animals' – and experiment with replacing some of the words.

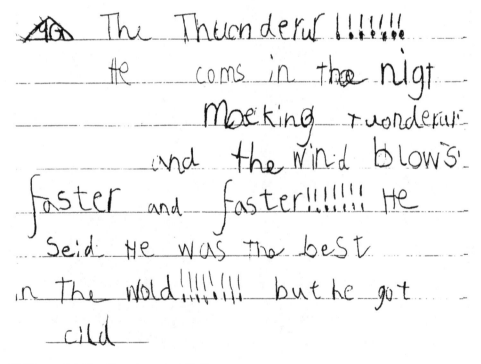

■ **Figure 6.6** The Thunderer, by Elliott

FOSTERING IMAGINATIVE ENGAGEMENT: WRITING IN ROLE

When children write in role in extended drama sessions in which they are other people, in another place and time with life problems to be solved, their writing retains a sense of this other person and often has a strong sense of voice and verve (Grainger *et al.*, 2005; Cremin and McDonald, 2012). This is, in part, because dramatic improvisation is focused on the divergence of ideas through play: verbal, physical and mental play with ideas and options; it represents a rich and supportive resource for young writers. The opportunity to generate, explore and share options through improvisation appears to expand the flow of ideas available and thus supports the development of children's ideational fluency, helping them make unusual associations and connections and select particularly evocative language as they compose (Cremin, Goouch *et al.*, 2006). As they are improvising in drama, children are thinking, feeling, visualising and creating multiple possibilities, and, in their related writing, they are often able to make this thinking visible. Their imaginative engagement in the tense scenarios of classroom drama appears to help them form and transform experience and effectively communicate their own and each other's ideas in writing.

Research findings indicate that the adoption of multiple-role perspectives in extended classroom drama can contribute to the quality of writing (Cremin, Goouch *et al.*, 2006). For example, in one class of 6–7-year-olds, during a cross-curricular exploration about the sea, the teacher used several books to trigger extended dramas (e.g. Kathy Henderson's *The Little Boat*, Elisabeth Beresford's *The Smallest Whale* and David Weisner's *Flotsam*). In the dramas, the class travelled to distant lands, lived underwater as water sprites, rescued a beached whale and met and became different people/water creatures. During their drama based on *Flotsam*, a wordless picture book in which a boy finds an underwater camera (the film in which reveals an extraordinary world under the ocean), the class were shrunk via the use of fairy dust (sea salt) and a magic spell, to enable them to travel inside the camera. Their under-sea adventures involved meeting mer-folk whose homes were being destroyed by human pollution, and sheltering from real children messing around in the rock pool where the miniature class was hiding. The children returned to the real world, were enlarged again and brainstormed the possible actions they could take to stop others polluting the ocean. Letters were written, posters were designed, and news items were broadcast. Many of the children chose to write in role from the perspective of someone they had been in the drama: Gabriella wrote in role as a starfish to herself in class, and Ethan wrote as the Mer-king, affirming the agreements made. Their different perspectives demonstrate the importance of allowing children to choose.

Dear friends,

Thank you for visiting our land. We are depending on you to stop the troubles. Please do not let us down or forget us. All the families of the kingdom of Neptune are hoping you will win. Adults can be difficult to change. Good luck.

The Mer-king

PS. Come and visit us again to tell us the good news.

Dear Gabriella,

I liked meeting you under the sea. I hope you will be able to get rid of the oil that sits above us like a black cloud. I HATE it. I am glad I was able to help hide you in the anemones. Children often mess up the rock pools and steal my friends. It is scary when their fingers come down to grab you. You must tell them to stop it. NOW!

with love from your friend,

Sammy the starfish.

The different views expressed by these two children, the length of their written communication and the speed with which it was composed suggest that writing in role during a drama may be particularly accessible to children, because of the immediacy of the imagined context. When children write in role, this can help them use the vividly imagined details of the setting, characters or events they constructed in action. For additional ideas on developing writing in drama, see Cremin *et al.* (2008).

Teachers can encourage writing in role in a number of different drama contexts, including the following:

- *Extended drama sessions*: Classroom improvisational drama involves travelling to and from other worlds, countries and times and perhaps writing and drawing during this, or afterwards. This may involve sending postcards home, writing letters to characters or retelling the adventures experienced as news reports.
- *Drama in literacy time*: Drama conventions can be used as part of shared writing to prompt in-role work and develop an understanding of the characters and plot.
- *Imaginary friends*: Such a character, in the form of a stuffed bear, doll or mannequin may be found hiding in the classroom, bearing a message or request. Over time, children write to them and receive replies, perhaps taking them home too and making diary entries in role.
- *The role-play area*: Through modelling the use of literacy materials in the area, teachers prompt children to write in appropriate ways, for example in the captain's log, or the mechanic's repair book.
- *Tabletop role-play*: Children draw on a covered tabletop and create their own world, with objects and small-world play toys. This may involve oral or written storytelling and writing in role.
- *Puppets shows*: Making paper-bag or cloth puppets can encourage children to make plays to share, to write scripts or produce theatre programmes.
- *Story cauldrons*: Create a story cauldron, in which one child dresses as a witch/wizard and the class adds story features, such as characters, settings, possible problems, different beginnings and so on. Children stir the cauldron to make their own/class/ group stories, which they retell, perhaps as fairies or goblins.
- *Fictional story boxes*: Themed shoe boxes, lined and decorated with small toys and objects inside, can prompt small-world story creation and in-role writing – for example, dinosaur world, space, under the sea, the world of the fairies, Bob the Builder's yard, Nick Junior's world.
- *Story sacks*: Sacks that include a core text and small puppets, toys or objects that connect to the tale can encourage play, retelling from the point of view of one of the characters, and the production of new stories and sequels.

CONCLUSION

When children are given space, time and appropriate resources to engage playfully and imaginatively, and are allowed to attend to what interests them and bring their own unique life experiences into the classroom, then their motivation increases, and writing is undertaken as part of a meaningful, creative endeavour, not as a separate task or a school activity to master and practise. Writing that emerges in such contexts has a stronger sense of the writer's voice and rings with authenticity and conviction. Through engagement in creative contexts, and through instruction and support in shared and guided writing, as well as though focused feedback and response, children make progress as writers – writers who have something to say and the means and desire to convey their message effectively and creatively.

NOTE

1   *Our Story* was developed at the Open University, UK, and is freely available from Apple store (http://itunes.apple.com/gb/app/our-story/id436758256?mt=8) or from the Google market for Android devices http://play.google.com/store/apps/details?id=uk.ac.open.ourstory&hl=en).

FURTHER READING

Fisher, R., Jones, S., Larkin, S. and Myhill, D. (2010) *Using Talk to Support Writing*. London: Sage.

Kennedy, R. (2014) 'Being authors: Grammar exploration', *English 4–11*, 50: 2–4.

Kucirkova, N., Willans, D. and Cremin, T. (2014) 'Spot the dog! Spot the difference', *English 4–11*, Summer edn: 11–14.

Pahl, K. (2009) 'Interactions, intersections and improvisations: Studying the multimodal texts and classroom talk of six- to seven-year olds', *Journal of Early Childhood Literacy*, 9(2): 188–210.

Marsh, J. (2008) 'Productive pedagogies: Play creativity and digital cultures in the classroom', in R. Willet, M. Robinson and J. Marsh (eds), *Play, Creativity and Digital Cultures*. New York/Abingdon, UK: RoutledgeFalmer, pp. 200–18.

CHILDREN'S BOOKS

Beresford, E. (1996) *The Smallest Whale*. Dublin: O'Brien.

Biet, P. (1999) *A Cultivated Wolf*. London: Siphano.

Creswell, H. and Cockroft, J. (1997) *Sophie and the Sea Wolf*. London: Hodder.

Gravett, E. (2006) *Wolves*. London: Macmillan.

Henderson, K. (1997) *The Little Boat*. London: Walker.

Morpurgo, M. and Foreman, M. (2002) *The Last Wolf*. London: Corgi.

Oke, J. and Oke, J. (2004) *The Naughty Bus*. Buddleigh Salterton, UK: Little Knowall.

Weisner, D. (2006) *Flotsam*. New York: Houghton Mifflin.

Whybrow, I. (1996) *Little Wolf's Book of Badness*. London: Collins.

CREATIVELY ENGAGING WRITERS IN THE LATER PRIMARY YEARS

Teresa Cremin and David Reedy

INTRODUCTION

Almost all writing can be approached creatively, and, in order to do so, teachers need to create contexts and opportunities for writers 'to explore the possibilities of ideas and the possibilities of language to express those ideas' (Cremin and Myhill, 2012: 24). Teacher expertise and direct instruction are, of course, needed, but so is child choice, ownership and decision-making, such that, over time, child writers develop their capacity to take risks in writing, to shape their writing in ways that satisfy them and to reflect upon the reasons for their writing choices. However, accountability cultures tend to incline teachers and young writers to remain within the boundaries defined by assessment structures, and this is likely to limit children's authorial agency and creative engagement.

Independent writers are not only able to make informed choices about form, audience and purpose; they also have something to say worth saying, and the voice and verve to express themselves effectively. This chapter focuses upon engaging older writers and teaching writing creatively to 7–11-year-olds. It examines the artistic process of composing, the teaching of grammar in meaningful contexts, the significance of autonomy and teachers' engagement as writers.

In the English NC (DfE, 2013) for older primary writers, it is recognised that the range of 'real purposes and audience' with which they engage as writers 'should underpin the decisions about the form the writing should take, such as a narrative, an explanation or a description'. Additionally, practices such as thinking aloud to explore and collect ideas, drafting, and re-reading to check their meaning is clear are seen to be essential support for composing, which is the core focus of this chapter. The other UK curricula also endorse a focus on purpose, audience and revisions; additionally, the Scottish principles and practice document (Education Scotland, 2012) highlights both the creation of a myriad of twenty-first-century texts and choice in writing. Choice is also foregrounded in the Welsh documentation (DfES, 2013). The Northern Ireland curriculum (DENI, 2011), rather more fully than the others, notes the importance of writing to express thoughts, feelings and opinions in imaginative and factual writing, and the need for children to learn to use various stylistic features to create mood and effect and to develop their own personal style.

PRINCIPLES

These curricula all recognise that writing involves both crafting and creating, although, in the last decade or so, it could be argued that teaching writing to 7–11-year-olds has tended to profile the crafting elements at the expense of creating, composing and completing whole texts (Frater, 2004; Cremin and Myhill, 2012). There is potentially a tension 'between the roles that writing has in identity construction, voice, performativity and dialogue on one hand, and academic achievement, perceived quality, convention and form on the other' (Jesson *et al.*, 2013: 218).

Creative teachers recognise this challenge and seek to achieve a balance between the technical aspects of writing and the compositional and content elements, as well as between writing as a finished product and writing as a process. Learning to write does not simply involve combining different skills, it involves the slow and complex consolidation of experiences and the gradual development of a more informed understanding about written communication. Such knowledge, experience and understanding will constantly be reshaped across life, as writers make choices and encounter different and more demanding text types, in new communicative contexts. Such knowledge will also be influenced by writers' dispositions towards writing and their identities as writers.

Furthermore, in this new media age, the nature of writing continues to change, and writing is recognised as an act of creative design, in which meaning is created, not just in words, but also through the visual layout (Sharples, 1999; Myhill, 2009). In their writing, children reflect their rich and diverse experience of reading multimodal texts, texts that make use of sound, image, colour and a variety of visuals, as well as words. In schooling, however, despite work in England to suggest alternative ways forward (QAA/UKLA, 2004, 2005), current forms of assessment do not acknowledge the multimodal nature of writing. In recognising the diverse voices and multimodal forms on which children draw, their own 'funds of knowledge' (Moll, 1992), teachers can help young writers connect the literacies of home and school and make more use of their text experiences and inner affective existences, as Fecho (2011) also argues. This increases the relevance of writing and motivates their involvement in the extended compositional process. In addition, research suggests that, when children are allowed to use their own resources and combine print, visual and digital modes, they demonstrate considerable imagination and creativity in the process (Pahl, 2007; Walsh, 2007). See Chapter 11 for an exploration of teaching visual and digital texts creatively.

Whatever the chosen modes and media, writers and designers need to be able to make choices about:

- the purpose and readership of the text;
- the most appropriate form of the text;
- the level of formality demanded;
- the amount of explicit detail needed;
- the form and organisation of the material;
- the technical features of syntax, vocabulary and punctuation suited to the particular text.

(Bearne, 2007: 88)

This list makes clear that, although skills and techniques matter and must be taught, they are only part of a complex picture; they benefit from being contextualised in meaningful literacy experiences that motivate and engage young people and enable them to use their knowledge of texts from outside school. In extended learning journeys, reading and response, as well as conversation and dramatic improvisation, contribute to interim drafts and final pieces of writing. This extended process of teaching literacy, developed initially in the UKLA/PNS Project *Raising Boys' Achievements in Writing* (Bearne *et al.*, 2004), has been widely used in England. Figure 7.1 shows this process, which enables children to become immersed in a text type, familiarise themselves with the genre and work creatively to generate, capture and explore ideas. They can then select from among these, developed, for example, through discussion and drama, and, supported by teacher demonstration, can commit to paper or screen as they work towards the creation of a final assessed outcome. This may be a multimodal outcome or may be presented just in words.

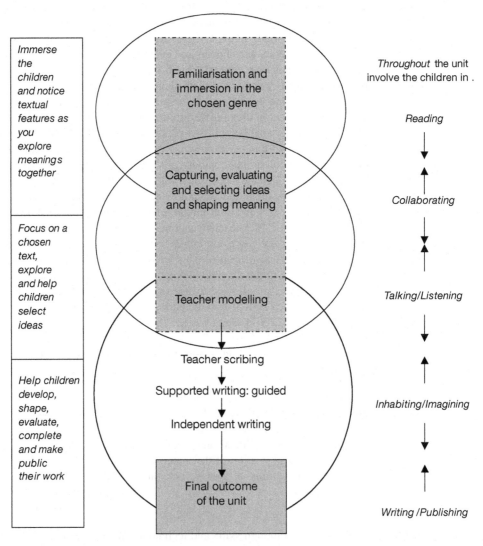

■ **Figure 7.1** The extended process of teaching literacy

Examples of extended learning journeys are shared in Chapters 8–11, and planning such work is discussed in Chapter 12.

READING, WRITING AND LEARNING

Writing involves exploring, generating, capturing and organising ideas in order to offer information to others through explanations, descriptions, persuasive and discursive arguments, as well as through more poetic and aesthetic forms. Narrative and poetry, in particular, are valuable tools for preserving the past, reflecting on ideas and experience and opening up conversations with others.

In terms of the process of writing, researchers in the field of composition studies suggest it encompasses *planning*, in which the imagination plays a central role, and ideas are captured and selected, *translating*, in which the chosen ideas are shaped into actual text, and *drafting and evaluating*, which involve revising and changing the piece (Flower and Hayes, 1980). Through the compositional process, writers develop, reshape and realise their ideas and meanings (Calkins, 1991; Graves, 1994). This model of writers as problem solvers, constantly juggling constraints, has parallels with conceptions of the creative thinking process (Guildford, 1973; Sternberg, 1999). Both involve dynamic stages, identifying or clarifying a challenge, generating possible responses and moving between divergent and convergent thinking in search of a solution. Although the act of composing is essentially a cognitive one, becoming literate depends on both social conventions and the relationship between meaning, form, social context and culture. Thus, written composition and, indeed, becoming literate depend on both social conventions and individual problem solving.

The transcriptional process involves paying attention to the spelling, grammar and punctuation of a piece of writing, as well as the presentation. Although both composition and transcription are important, children, parents and teachers may view the transcriptional elements of the process as more important than the compositional components. However, the value of transcription varies according to the purpose and audience of the writing; for example, writing to invite governors to a play requires more care and editorial attention than making a personal list of desired Christmas presents. In all writing contexts, having something to say, understanding the demands of the form and being able to monitor, evaluate and revise what is being written are important elements. Awareness of the purpose and audience of the communication is also significant.

It is widely recognised that writers collect ideas from the texts of their lives and their experience of many different textual forms, and that they draw upon this repertoire in their writing. Through sharing personal tales, young authors can revisit their lives and choose to resculpt their experiences as authors, voicing their observations on living through creating fiction (Armstrong, 2006). Additionally, books and films, as well as television and computer programs, can make a real contribution to children's involvement, response and eventual writing (Marsh and Millard, 2005; Cremin and Myhill, 2012). Research indicates that the three kinds of literary text that make the most impact upon 7–11-year-old writers are: emotionally powerful texts, traditional tales and stories containing 'poeticised speech' (Barrs and Cork, 2001). Reading and studying such texts in extended units of work, enabling children to connect to and engage with them, as well as appreciate the writer's craft, can enable them to lean on and learn from literature. Indeed, reflective reading and focused investigation of all types of text are integral to the development of young writers. Creative teachers identify different texts for different classes each year, although they may return to 'failsafe' favourites that they know evoke a rich and creative response. These might include, for example, the challenging story of *Coraline* by Neil Gaiman, Anthony Browne's *Voices in the Park*, Michael Rosen's *The Sad Book*, Elizabeth Laird's *Secret Friends*, Nicola Davies's *The Promise* or Gary Crew's *The Mystery of Eilean Mor*. All offer rich potential as engaging texts to support young writers.

TALK AND PLAYFUL ENGAGEMENT

The relationship between talk and writing has been demonstrated repeatedly, showing that both underachievers and high achievers benefit from opportunities to talk before, during and after writing (Andrews, 2008; Fisher *et al.*, 2010). Through talk at the initial stages of the writing process, children generate and share ideas, playfully experiment with options and capture, shape and consider what it is they might want to say. This offers them a rich resource when they come to commit their ideas to paper or screen. Furthermore, through developing confidence in playful and creative oral contexts, children learn to take risks with ideas, words and images, and this supports their fluency with ideas and enables them to make more divergent connections. Improvisation and playful engagement play a largely unrecognised role in the compositional process, and yet they are at the heart of developing creativity in writing.

For example, Holly, aged 10, had been involved in oral storytelling sessions in her class for a whole term, listening to and re-telling tales and extracts to others. At the close of the term, in an activity focused upon evoking rich written descriptions, she chose to evoke a moment from one of the tales she had heard her teacher tell, entitled the Weaving of a Dream (see Figure 7. 2). Her images and ideas are all new additions to the tale, in which a simple pearl is used for light in a fairy palace. In Holly's imagination, much more depth and detail are offered.

Talk and playful engagement are not only generative of ideas, but can be used during the compositional process. Through talking, children can reflect upon and refine their thinking, developing a metalanguage to talk about writing (Bereiter and Scardamalia, 1987). Working together as readers of each other's writing, they can explore ways of using language to clarify ideas and offer secretarial support. When discussing their writing, it is important, however, that children retain ownership and control, talking about their intentions as authors and what they are trying to achieve. This focus on the evolving text, its emerging meaning and the reader's needs and responses is crucial to break through to the 'what next' stage of writing (Sharples, 1999). Working with response partners, children can talk through their intentions, celebrate their successes, reinforce what they have learned and identify aspects that need attention. Such conversations benefit from teacher modelling and support (see Figure 7.8).

Once a piece of writing has been completed, the opportunity to make it public and share it, orally or through written publications, becomes important: children need to hear their voices and experience feedback and responses from their intended audience. Far too much writing in school remains unpublished and, as Frater (2001) asserts, is undertaken merely for the circular purpose of learning to write, rather than for communication and to develop the voice of the child. However, when children engage creatively in a community of writers and connect affectively with the subject matter, as well as publish their work, their voices ring off the page with conviction and commitment.

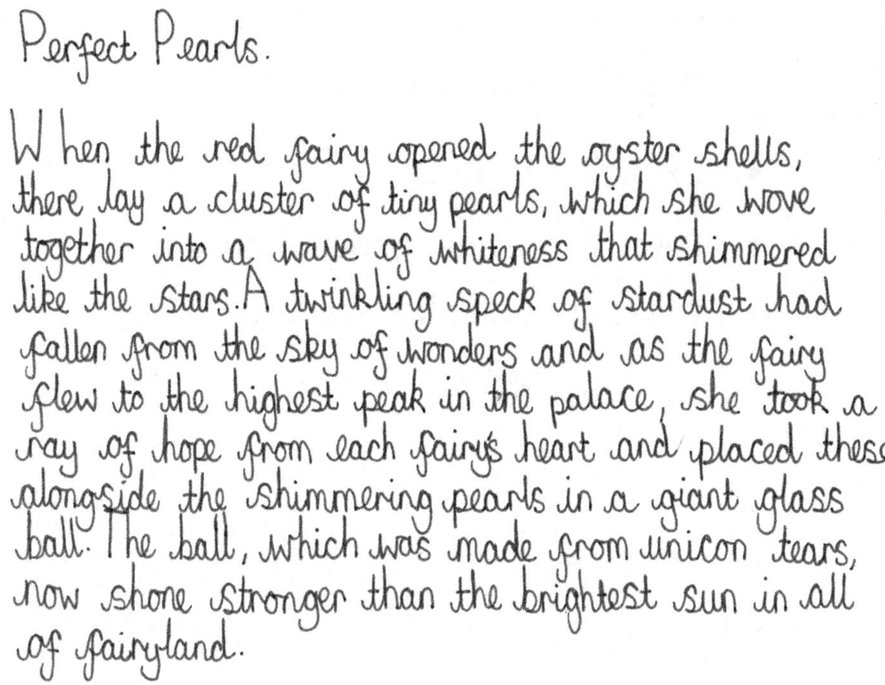

Perfect Pearls.

When the red fairy opened the oyster shells, there lay a cluster of tiny pearls, which she wove together into a wave of whiteness that shimmered like the stars. A twinkling speck of stardust had fallen from the sky of wonders and as the fairy flew to the highest peak in the palace, she took a ray of hope from each fairy's heart and placed these alongside the shimmering pearls in a giant glass ball. The ball, which was made from unicorn tears, now shone stronger than the brightest sun in all of fairyland.

Figure 7.2 The Perfect Pearls

In addition to talking before, during and after writing, children can write collaboratively; writing with a partner makes more explicit the social nature of writing. As some 8-year-olds commented, 'I love it when we write together because Sally's really good at ideas and I am good at punctuation and "wow" words – together we make a good team', and 'I much prefer writing with a friend – it's SO much easier and my writing SO much better'. Working together in this way can ease the challenge of writing, as well as create new demands, and can heighten the motivation to polish and craft work. Collaborative writing is particularly conducive to developing children's creativity in writing, as Vass (2007) has shown.

TEACHING GRAMMAR CREATIVELY AND IN CONTEXT

In England, the NC (DfE, 2014) includes challenging new requirements to teach grammatical knowledge to 7–11-year-olds. For example, these include, for 7-year-olds, preposition, prefix, clause and subordinate clause, and, for 10- and 11-year-olds, modal verbs, ambiguity, reflexive pronoun, active and passive voice and semi-colon. Focusing on such language features of texts and noticing and naming them are likely to be tedious and ineffective if children are not actively engaged in exploring issues related to the text's meaning. In Chapter 6, the REDM teaching grammatical sequence was introduced (Reedy and Bearne, 2013). This offers an evidence-based teaching sequence that pays attention to a text's constructedness in the context of establishing pupil engagement and developing their ability to make meaning through explicit attention to language in use (see Figure 7.3).

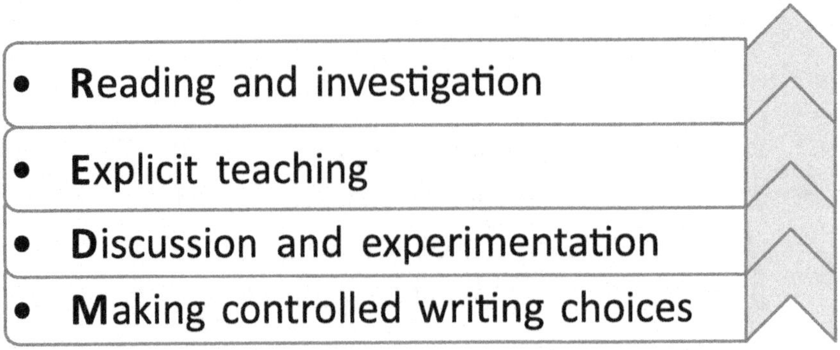

- **R**eading and investigation
- **E**xplicit teaching
- **D**iscussion and experimentation
- **M**aking controlled writing choices

Figure 7.3 Teaching grammar in context: the REDM process
(Reedy and Bearne, 2013: 7)

The sequence starts with reading and investigation of the specific language features, followed by explicit teaching and explanations. There is then a shift to discussion and creative experimentation, which will enable young learners to make more informed writing choices. Providing the context is meaningful and engaging, the children will become more aware of their options and connect these to their purpose and the effects they are seeking to achieve.

An example related to teaching the function of paragraphs will help to bring this process to life. As part of a unit about traditional tales, a teacher chose the book *Fairytale News* by Colin and Jacqui Hawkins, as it contains a fold-out newspaper that reports on the actions of various traditional characters. There are headlines such as 'Goldi-shocks' and 'Frog Fright at Piddle Puddle Pond', and clear models of well-constructed paragraphs are offered. The children were going to construct their own newspaper reports, based on other traditional tales they had been reading, being playful and creative with the narrative if they wished.

After reading the book to the class and seeing how the newspaper reports reflected (or not) the actions in the preceding stories, the teacher drew the children's attention again to the structure of the newspaper stories and pointed out their division into paragraphs. She explained that these usually have more than one sentence, and that the first, 'lead' sentence tells the reader what the paragraph is about, and the following sentence(s) reveals more about the topic. The children worked in pairs on one of the newspaper articles, finding the lead sentence in each paragraph and discussing what this told them the paragraph would be about. They then checked how the rest of the paragraph added more detail. As a class, they then agreed a set of criteria that would lead to a successfully constructed paragraph. Finally, the children wrote their own newspaper reports based on recently read traditional tales, using the success criteria to check their paragraphs. Later, their reports were made into a class version of the *Fairytale News*.

In another class, the teacher working with 10- and 11-year-olds wanted to extend the variety of punctuation that they used. She had already spent some time talking with the class about how punctuation captures the cadences of speech in dialogue and selected a unit of work on play-scripts in order to consolidate and develop this. As she modelled ellipsis, she explained it was a particularly good way to hook the reader in and keep them involved in the narrative as it unfolded. The class used their iPads to look for examples of ellipsis in a variety of texts and then shared what they had found. The discussion centred on the purpose of ellipsis and linked to how they could use it in their play-scripts. The teacher emphasised using it for maximum impact and avoiding overuse.

As the class had been reading different versions of the story of Theseus, the task was to take a part of the story and produce a play-script. The children then spent time improvising and enacting scenes from the story, in order to capture authentic dialogue and a sense of voice. All this preparation and support paid off; see, for example, Rugile's work: he used three examples of ellipsis in a lengthy play-script, each for a different effect. In Figure 7.4, the ellipsis indicates Aegeus's hesitation while he thinks about whether to agree to Theseus going to Crete. In Figure 7.5, it emphasises the tension and, in Figure 7.6, it creates a dramatic pause before a sound effect. In this way, through employing the REDM process, the class learned that they could use this punctuation device for a range of effects within a meaningful context.

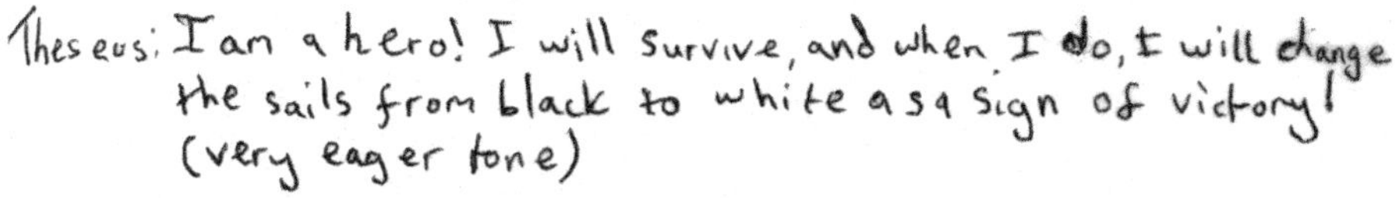

Theseus: I am a hero! I will survive, and when I do, I will change the sails from black to white as a sign of victory! (very eager tone)

Figure 7.4 Ellipsis indicating hesitation

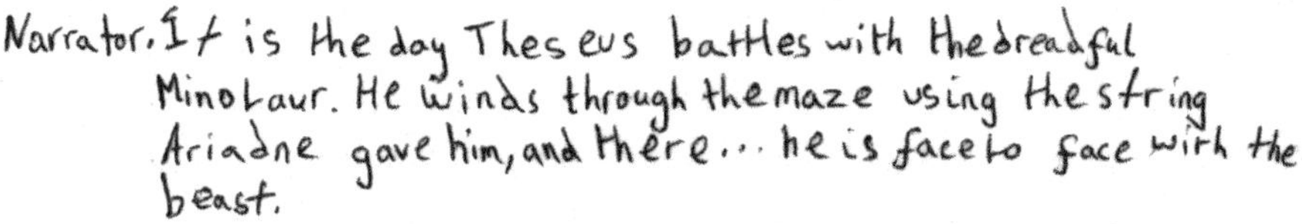

Narrator. It is the day Theseus battles with the dreadful Minotaur. He winds through the maze using the string Ariadne gave him, and there... he is face to face with the beast.

Figure 7.5 Ellipsis emphasising tension

Using drama to generate dialogue can also be useful to teach children how to punctuate speech and use speech verbs. If an improvised dialogue is scribed by the teacher in shared writing, then the class can revoice this in role to support the selection, placement and punctuation of speech verbs and adverbs. For example, in one class of 9–10-year-olds, during an exploration of the characters in *Clive and the Missing Finger* by Sarah Garland, the class improvised an ensuing row in role, in pairs, small groups, half and half and as 32:1, with their TIR as dad. Their teacher had previously looked with them at Garland's use of speech marks in a section of the text and explored through enactment the value of adding adverbs to describe the way in which the character spoke. The class was involved in experimenting with and discussing different adverbs and their impact on character creation. In the final assessed piece of work in the unit, they were invited to effectively convey the tension of the argument, using language appropriate to the characters, correctly punctuated, with speech verbs (in all four placements) and adverbs. See Figure 7.7 for an example. In this work too, reading, explicit teaching, discussion, drama and the children's creative engagement motivated and contextualised their learning about punctuation and enabled them to consider the impact of their language choices on the reader.

Narrator: As Ariadne leaves to get food Theseus sails away to abandon Athens, abandoning Ariadne.

Aegeus: Oh no! The sails they are black, Theseus must be dead ohhh... (SPLASH!)

■ **Figure 7.6** Ellipsis for dramatic effect

"If your'e 17, then act 17" dad snapped.
"But all the other parents let their children wear make-up" wailed Dorrie.
"Well, I'm not everyone else's parents I'm your father" dad replied angrily "and while your in my house, you'll do what I say".

Dorrie shouted at him furiously her face, as red as her lipstick, "you're out of order, I don't see why I should take it off!" "I'm not having you looking like that - everyone will laugh at you, you look ridiculous" dad exclaimed.

"I do not!"

"Go look in the mirror"
Dorrie stomped upstairs, her feet thumping on every step.

■ **Figure 7.7** A conversation in role

Examples such as those above show how creative and effective teachers of English can approach grammatical features and associated linguistic terminology in meaningful and effective ways. Through contextualising the teaching of grammar and punctuation, they can enable young writers to become more aware of the effect of their choices and the importance of making informed and appropriate choices (Myhill, 2011; Myhill *et al.*, 2011).

TEACHERS AS WRITERS

In order to teach writing creatively, teachers arguably need to model the writing process and share the pleasures and challenges of composing. Research suggests that some professionals, concerned about their ability to model specific literary features spontaneously and in public, prepare writing at home prior to sharing it, apparently spontaneously, in school (Luce-Kapler *et al.*, 2001; Grainger *et al.*, 2005) and express a lack of self-confidence as writers (Morgan, 2010; Dix and Cawkwell, 2011). However, children deserve to be apprenticed to real writers, who demonstrate that writing is a problem-solving activity, a process of thinking and evaluating involving an internal dialogue. Modelling writing authentically involves teachers showing children what strategies they use as writers when confronted with a difficult spelling or the need to write quickly, for example. It also involves talking about their blank spots, false starts and uncertainties, playing with language choices and demonstrating how meaning evolves and understanding develops, as authors exercise choices and write their way forward.

As Chapter 6 suggested, children benefit when their teachers are involved as writers, modelling writing for real and writing alongside them in the classroom. Such 'insider engagement' can foster new understandings about the process of writing; for example, in reflecting upon producing her short story, one teacher from Newham noted that she had learned:

> You can't do it overnight. You need a lot of thinking time and this is what has made me think with my children, that now when we have the start of a writing lesson and we know that this is the day when we are going to start writing it up – we've had an awful lot more time of thinking time or activity to support developing ideas and perhaps turning to our partners and talking about what we are going to write about. An awful lot of talking before we commit to paper and re-reading when we write.
>
> (Cremin, 2010)

Being involved as writers challenges teachers to create a pedagogy that recognises the importance of having a purpose in writing, making personal choices as the author and the value of re-reading at the point of composition. Teachers can model this, demonstrating that re-reading writing, listening to one's voice, is a critical, ongoing skill, not one to be left to the end of the composition (Grainger, 2005). Modelling re-reading and reviewing one's writing should be introduced gradually and reinforced throughout the primary years. In the process, writers can usefully consider the following prompts:

- ■ What am I trying to say?
- ■ How does it sound so far?
- ■ Why did I choose . . .? How else could I say this?
- ■ What do I want to say/do next?

■   How could I express . . .?
■   What will my reader be thinking/feeling as they read this?

Through engaging as writers and using writing to explore and evaluate possibilities, teachers can come to appreciate the complex, challenging and creative process of generating, shaping and evaluating ideas. When writing alongside children, teachers may begin to appreciate more fully the persistence needed, the role of talk and the significant influence of life experience and other texts. Though this role positioning can be challenging, (Cremin and Baker, 2010), teachers who write for real in classrooms often comment on how quickly children settle, how they value their teacher's efforts and come to recognise the difficulties they encounter when writing about subjects in which they have little personal investment or choice. The opportunities for co-authorship with children and for 'insider instruction' and the positive influences upon the children's attitudes to writing that can result from writing alongside them, suggest that being a writing teacher – a teacher who writes and a writer who teaches – is a potentially creative instructional tool in a professional's repertoire.

RESPONDING TO WRITING

During the writing process, formative assessment will be accompanied by response, spoken or written, involving teachers and children identifying the value in the young author's writing. Teachers' evaluative responses have tended, in recent years, to be related to specific teaching and learning objectives or individual children's writing targets. However, although tailored feedback is important at times, responding only to a child's use of similes or connectives, for example, or their ability to use complex sentences or 'wow' words limits teachers' responses to the skill-set required or techniques taught. This is unlikely to help young writers appreciate how their choices influence the reader's response and may not connect to the purpose of the endeavour: the actual communicative intent of the writing.

To develop children's ability to influence and shape readers' reactions to their texts, teachers need to foreground meaning in their responses, to read as readers first and as teachers second. This can be modelled through introducing children to responding to writing with EASE (see Figure 7.8). This involves readers/response partners:

■   revisiting the author's intention – asking what they were trying to achieve;
■   letting the author read it aloud or reading it to them;
■   responding – orally or in writing with EASE.

This response framework, developed from the work of D'Arcy (1999), can be used by teachers in responding to children's work and by children in responding to their teachers' writing. It can also be used to support children as response partners and to help them comment on and appreciate the work of professional writers. EASE operates as a potentially writer-oriented, meaning-focused evaluation framework; it profiles the engagement of the reader and seeks to recognise and identify the author's skills that created this engagement. Additionally, the reader is invited to suggest possible strategies for developing and extending the writing. Using EASE, teachers avoid making a one-sided commentary or critique of children's writing, seeking rather to prompt a genuine dialogue between reader

Engagement: internalising the message

What thoughts, feelings, visual impressions come into your mind as you read?

Appreciation: considering the writers' achievements

How did the writer make you engage in this way?

Suggestion: considering specific ways to develop the writing

What can you suggest to improve the writing as present?

Extension: considering possible strategies and ideas to extend the writing

What can you suggest to extend the writing, what more is needed or would enrich?

(Goouch *et al.*, 2009)

Figure 7.8 Responding to writing with EASE

and writer. As children learn to reflect independently and critically on their own writing, their ability to develop critical distance from their work and judiciously evaluate, edit and improve it is extremely important.

Another critical element of reflection, introduced in Chapter 6, is re-reading at the point of composition. Re-reading children's unfolding writing aloud to them and encouraging them to read it to themselves enable young authors to listen to their own voices, get a feel for their writing and develop a more self-evaluative and critical ear. In reviewing their emergent writing at the point of composition, writers become readers and then writers again; this can help them edit, reshape and reflect upon the sounds, tunes and visuals of their words and meanings.

Teachers seeking to foster children's creativity will want to select, present and publish, not only children's final writing/design products, but also their unfolding work, as well as the mediation and development of this. This may involve displaying annotations and children's EASE commentaries upon the work at different stages; these can help children reflect upon their own compositional journeys and enrich learning through reflection. Another strategy to help writers consider their writing journeys is to create compositional collages. Using materials from magazines and their own notes, children show the journey of a piece of writing and consider the myriad of influences upon this composition – the ideas, texts and memories, for example, that may have influenced it and the people, EASE comments and redrafting with which the author engaged in order to improve it.

FOSTERING CHILDREN'S AUTONOMY AS WRITERS

Although children deserve to be introduced to different written genres, they also deserve to assert their own agency as writers and authors. Do they see writing as merely performing the school game called writing? Fostering children's autonomy can increase young writers' personal involvement and investment in the process and can enrich their creativity, for, when adults exert less control during writing events, children express more interest and initiate more verbal interaction, producing less-conventional texts than when adults use a highly controlling style (Fang *et al.*, 2004).

Establishing writing journals, in which children can choose what to write about and in what form, can support their growing independence and help them develop a sense of their own voice as writers. In such journals, children tend to write for themselves and each other in ways that satisfy them and connect to their personal passions and interests. The time and resources given to these sessions enable children to draw on the media that best suit their intentions and to use 'the texts of their lives' (Fecho, 2011). Typically, teachers do not read children's writing journals unless invited to do so, although they are likely to encourage writers to discuss subject choices, write collaboratively and share their writing with each other. For more detail on establishing writing journals, see Graham and Johnson (2003).

In writing workshops, children can also select their purpose, form and audience, perhaps supported by an A–Z of forms and an ongoing list of writing ideas. In such contexts, children often chose to mix elements of their cultural capital with the cultural capital of the school, exploring their interplay and their sense of identity in the process. For example, Abbi, aged 9, had the following list of possible journal writing ideas; she chose several of these to develop, dropped others and added new ideas over time. See Figure 7.9 for her entry on hair styles; this has clearly been influenced by the magazines she reads and was followed in the journal by pages of accessories, such as shoes, handbags and jewellery, similarly treated. Abbi's early list of possible options that she might choose to write about included:

▓ review of Plain White T's latest album;
▓ my brother's madness about rugby;
▓ birthday present list;
▓ who I want to be with on the school trip;
▓ my birthday sleepover;
▓ top hair styles;
▓ my grandma;
▓ script for *America's Top Model*;
▓ my beautiful cat.

Setting time aside regularly to add possibilities to such a list is important, as is encouraging children to lean on their lives, on contemporary culture, on their views and concerns, and on drama and literature. In this way, a desire to write is evoked, and their young voices are activated through playful engagement with ideas and possibilities. In this way too, teachers 'create opportunities for students to use writing to explore who they are becoming and how they relate to the larger culture around them' (Fecho, 2011: 4–5).After taking part in open-ended activities (see below for suggestions), children can be invited to record provisional titles or ideas in their journal/workshop lists. Their selections, connections and decisions will make a significant difference to the degree of commitment, interest and perseverance that they demonstrate. In sharing their personal choice writing with one another, children reveal a sense of their emerging identities. Such 'inside–out

■ **Figure 7.9** An entry in a writing journal on hair styles

'writing' encourages reflection upon the expressive and social nature of writing and fosters a growing sense of control and authorial agency. This can contribute significantly to the creativity expressed in their writing, their voice and verve.

Activities to support choice

■ *Share personal stories*: Commencing with a teacher anecdote and using story titles, the class engages in swapping and sharing life stories in a story buzz. Each child will be able to share their tale many times and listen to others.

■ *Focus on story worlds*: Children draw and create new narrative worlds and populate these with creatures. See Figure 7.10 for 8-year-old Joe's drawing of a Navomark creature evolving; he imagined this species to exist in the stratosphere and protect the world from invasion.

■ *Create mood/emotions graphs*: The horizontal axis represents a period of time; the vertical axis represents the emotions (low to high). Children plot significant memories on the graph and label/write about a chosen event.

■ *Create timelines of life*: Children complete these at home, prompting stories to be told. After orally retelling one or two in school, a choice for writing can be made.

■ *Focus on families*: Prompted by literature, visitors or discussion, children share anecdotes, descriptions and insights about significant family members. Letters, character descriptions, poems or short stories may follow.

■ *Views and concerns*: Children share their views, concerns, complaints and perspectives on issues of interest to them. The class noticeboard, with newspaper/ magazine clippings, can help highlight issues, as can literature read. Persuasive, discursive or journalistic writing may follow.

■ *DVD shorts*: Children bring in favourite DVDs, and extracts are viewed, prompting explanations and discussions. Children may then create play-scripts, sequels, adverts or reviews.

■ **Figure 7.10** A Navomark creature evolving

■ *Focus on personal passions*: Children bring in material related to personal interests –pop groups, hobby, sport and so forth. Pamphlets, poems, fact files, diagrams, letters or stories may follow.

FOSTERING IMAGINATIVE ENGAGEMENT: WRITING IN ROLE

Writing in role offers children fictional purposes and audiences for writing. The lived experience of drama becomes a natural writing frame, charged with the emotions and experiences of the imagined world, promoting voice, choice, stance and passion in writing. Drama in literacy time is a valuable precursor to writing, supporting the generation and selection of ideas; in drama, children compose multimodally and shape their ideas in action, prior to committing these to paper or screen. In using drama as a bridge to writing, teachers align drama conventions to forms of writing, so that the drama offers opportunities for oral rehearsal of the text type. This is motivating and enables the imagined experience to operate as an effective prompt, contextualising the act of composing. See Chapter 3 for examples of this significant bridging function.

Exploring texts through process drama in extended units of literacy work can also contribute to children's writing, as both qualitative (Crumpler and Schneider, 2002; Cremin, Goouch *et al.*, 2006) and quantitative (Fleming *et al.*, 2004) studies demonstrate. Classroom/process drama proceeds without a script, employs elements of both spontaneous play and theatre, and involves the teacher in weaving together an artistic experience and building a work in the process. In such drama, both teachers and children engage in active make-believe, adopting roles and interacting together to create fictional worlds of their own making (Cremin and McDonald, 2012).

Research suggests that creative teachers remain open to 'seize the moment/s' to write during process drama, allowing themselves to follow the learners' interests, rather than working towards a particular written genre (Cremin, Goouch *et al.*, 2006). They offer the learners considerable choice of the form and content of their writing, which often become a vital and connected part of the imagined experience. In contrast to using drama in a 'genre-specific' way, to prepare for a particular form of writing, 'seize the moment' drama and writing is less explicitly framed: teachers respond spontaneously, and writing arises naturally in response to the dramatic situations encountered. Three threads appear to connect process drama and writing and foster creative and effective compositions; these are: the presence of tension, emotional engagement and incubation, and a strong sense of stance and purpose, gained in part through role adoption (Cremin, Goouch *et al.*, 2006). Through adopting different viewpoints and examining new and more powerful positions in both drama and writing, young learners experience alternative ways of being and knowing. As a consequence, and in response to their engagement in the tense dramatic experience, when the moment to write is seized, the work produced frequently demonstrates a higher than usual degree of empathy, a stronger and more sustained authorial stance and an emotively engaged voice. Such writing very effectively captures and maintains the readers' interest.

Using process drama on extended learning journeys across the curriculum can also promote high-quality writing in role and writing alongside role. For example, in an exploration of issues about the rainforest, writing in role might include letters or diaries of aid workers, European news reports or personal writing as the Huaroni. Writing alongside role, after the drama, might include a TV documentary script or a magazine article discussing the situation. Choice is again critical, as the imposition of a single written task does not sit comfortably with the various viewpoints developed in extended classroom drama.

CONCLUSION

Writing takes time. Children's journeys towards writing in extended units of work involve considerable reading, talking, playful exploration and close examination of texts prior to writing. Teachers offer explicit instruction and model and demonstrate the genre to support children in imitating, innovating and drafting their compositions. The process also involves children in re-reading and responding to their own and each other's writing, in guided writing and response partnership contexts, and editing, evaluating and publishing their work. In separate, independent writing contexts, young writers exert their authorial agency and, leaning on their lives, the world of popular culture and the multimodal texts they encounter, choose their content, form, purpose and audience in writing-journal/writing-workshop time. This combination of teaching and learning, instruction and support, experience and opportunity, as well as the exploration of freedom and form, has the potential to foster creativity in children's writing.

FURTHER READING

Bearne, E. and Reedy, D. (2013) *Teaching Grammaar Effectively in the Primary School*. Leicester, UK: UKLA.

Cremin, T. and Myhill, D. (2012) *Writing Voices: Creating communities of writers*. London: Routledge.

Fecho, B. (2011) *Writing in the Dialogical Classroom: Students and teachers responding to the texts of their lives*. Urbana, IL: National Council of Teachers of English.

Myhill, D. (2005) 'Writing creatively', in A. Wilson (ed.), *Creativity in Primary Education*. Exeter, UK: Learning Matters, pp. 58–69.

Walsh, C. (2007) 'Creativity as capital in the literacy classroom', *Literacy*, 41(2): 74–80.

CHILDREN'S BOOKS

Browne, A. (1998) *Voices in the Park*. London: Walker.

Crew, G. and Geddes, J. (2005) *The Mystery of Eilean Mor*. Melbourne, Australia: Lothian.

Davies, N. (2013) *The Promise*. London: Walker.

Garland, S. (1994) *Clive and the Missing Finger*. London: A & C Black.

Gaiman, N. (2003) *Coraline*. London: Bloomsbury.

Hawkins, C. and Hawkins, J. (2005) *Fairytale News*. London: Walker.

Laird, E. (1997) *Secret Friends*. London: Hodder.

Rosen, M. (2004) *The Sad Book*. London: Walker.

CHAPTER 8

IMAGINATIVELY EXPLORING FICTION

Teresa Cremin

INTRODUCTION

Children's literature, and fiction in particular, is at the heart of the English curriculum. It has the potential to play a powerful role in children's creative development. Literature can inspire, inform and expand the horizons of young people, challenging their thinking and provoking creative, multimodal responses in art, drama and dance, as well as on paper and on screen. As all national curricula documentation across the UK recognises, literature plays a key role in children's development culturally, emotionally, intellectually, socially and spiritually. This chapter explores how to teach fiction texts creatively in literacy and shows how, if the eight key features of creative practice are employed, children can make rich connections, interpretations and representations of meaning. At the primary phase, teachers use literature to teach literacy, teach through literature in cross-curricular contexts, teach learners about literature and encourage independent reading for pleasure.

FICTION TEXTS

It is widely accepted that literature enables readers to develop an understanding about the human condition, and that the power of narrative underpins this. As Hardy (1977: 12) famously argued, 'narrative is not to be regarded as an aesthetic invention used by artists to control, manipulate, and order experience, but as a primary act of mind transferred to art from life'. As a way of making meaning, narrative pervades human learning and, therefore, deserves a high profile in the curriculum.

Fiction can enable children to safely experience a range of emotions; it illuminates human behaviour in different cultures and societies and facilitates reflection upon universal themes of existence, such as love, hate, envy, greed, prejudice, sacrifice, loss and compassion. Fiction affords the chance for children to journey through other worlds, to take on other roles and to learn, breaking down barriers in the process (Ee Loh, 2009); it cannot, though, do this alone (Hope, 2008). The pedagogy of teachers is crucial: the nurturing effect of literature and its potential to educate the feelings can only be tapped in school if fiction and poetry are valued as more than mere resources for teaching literacy (Cremin, 2007).

Many young people find narrative fiction very appealing: it offers a strong motivation for reading and viewing and, in the past, has been the preferred reading choice of both boys and girls (Whitehead, 1977; Hall and Coles, 1999). Today, it remains popular and is among the top reading choices for primary-aged children outside school, who, in England, report a preference for adventure, comedy, horror, crime, war/spy, animal, science-fiction, sports and romance stories, in that order (Clark, 2013). Story writing is also frequently cited as a popular written genre (Myhill, 2001; Grainger *et al.*, 2002), perhaps because, in this form, children are able to take control of their own world-making play and express their creativity more freely. When reflecting upon why they love stories, two avid 10-year-old readers replied: 'You can lose yourself in another world and just kind of live there' and 'I like being in a hot tub in my imagination'. Such a hot tub enriches children's creative capacity, offering ideas and possibilities and the opportunity to ponder, hypothesise and problem solve their way forward.

Narrative fiction appears in a wealth of formats and can be found in magazines, in short-story collections, in comics, graphic novels, picture fiction, novels, television and films. Characters from popular culture such as Danger Mouse, Bagpuss, Clarice Bean, Dora the Explorer, Sponge Bob Square Pants and the Simpsons also belong to the world of fiction that children encounter and on which they draw in their writing. As well as narratives from TV, films and computer games, series fiction in book form – whether as hard copy or in ebook format – is often extremely popular with the young, prompting many children to get hooked and persevere as readers. Quality examples that are also highly popular include: the *Horrid Henry* tales by Francesca Simon, F.S. Said's *Varjak Paw*, Michele Paver's *Wolf Brother*, Jeff Kinney's D*iary of a Wimpy Kid* (a novel in cartoons), Helen Dunmore's *Ingo*, Toni DiTerlizzi's *The Spiderwick Chronicles* and Paul Stewart and Chris Riddell's *The Edge Chronicles*.

The lessons children learn about reading are shaped by the actual texts they encounter (Meek, 1988), as well as classroom interaction around texts offered by their teachers. It is clear that, if they learn to read in the company of talented authors and illustrators, this positively influences their motivation, persistence and success. Likewise, in the stories children compose, the influence of the books they have read, heard and studied is visible (Cremin and Myhill, 2012). This is evident in 6-year-old Alex's ant story, in which the 'Where is Spot?' principle of many young children's narratives is evident (Figure 8.1). In this tale, the poor ant nearly meets his demise when an anteater pops up out of the bushes. Fortunately, however, Alex's ant is saved when a lion chases the anteater away.

TEACHERS' KNOWLEDGE OF CHILDREN'S LITERATURE

In addition to offering supported choice, it is a professional responsibility to introduce young people to new and classic fiction, as well as picture fiction. Yet research suggests that teachers are not always sufficiently well acquainted with authors and picture-fiction creators to enable them to plan richly integrated and holistic literature-based teaching or foster reader development (Cremin, Bearne *et al.*, 2008; Cremin, Mottram *et al.*, 2008). In the UKLA survey (Cremin, Bearne *et al.*, 2008; Cremin, Mottram *et al.*, 2008), 1,200 primary teachers from eleven local authorities in England were asked to list six 'good' children's writers. In their responses, 48 per cent of the practitioners named six, and 10 per cent named two, one or no authors at all. Roald Dahl gained the highest number

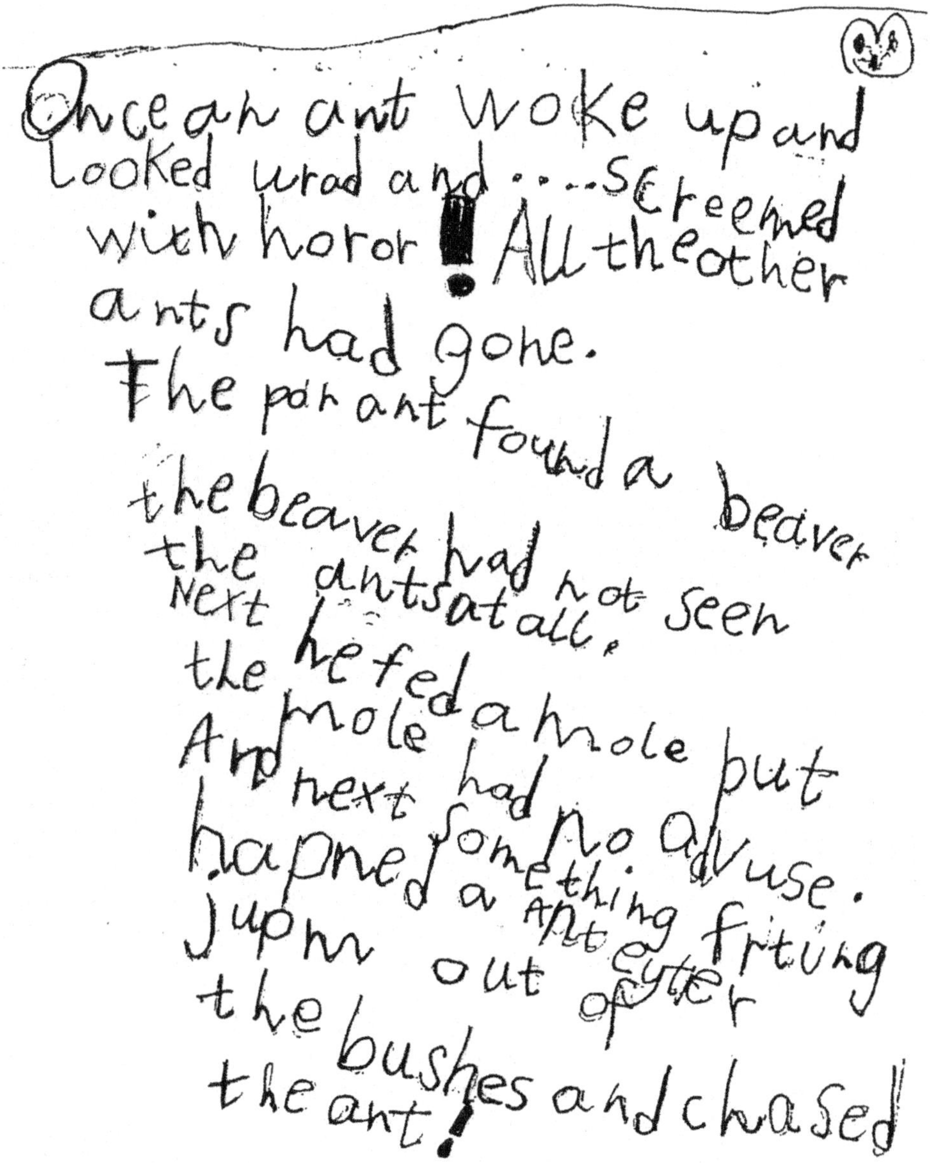

Once an ant woke up and
Looked wrad and ....screemed
with horor! All the other
ants had gone.
The por ant found a beaver
the beaver had not seen
the ants at all.
Next he fed
the mole a mole
And next had no advuse. but
hapned something frtuing
a ant eyter
jupm out of
the bushes and chased
the ant!

Figure 8.1 The opening of 'The Ant's Adventure'

of mentions (744). The next, in order of number of mentions, were: Michael Morpurgo (343), Jacqueline Wilson (323), J.K. Rowling (300) and Anne Fine (252). The only other authors who received more than 100 mentions were: Dick King Smith (172), Janet and Allan Ahlberg (169), Enid Blyton (161), Shirley Hughes (128), C.S. Lewis (122), Philip Pullman (117), Mick Inkpen (106) and Martin Waddell (100). There was reliance upon a limited number of arguably celebrity writers. In terms of range and diversity, relatively few writers of novels for older readers were included, and there was little mention of writers from other cultures, or even writers writing about other cultures, and yet, as Appleyard (1990) reveals, there is a distinct kind of pleasure in finding oneself in texts, and all children deserve to experience this regularly.

The teachers' knowledge of picture fiction was also limited, with only 10 per cent of the teachers naming six picture-fiction creators, and 24 per cent naming none at all (Cremin, Mottram *et al.*, 2008). There were very few mentions of named picture-book makers who offer complex visual texts for older readers. Arguably, the teachers, 85 per cent of whom reported relying upon their own repertoires to select books for school, were not sufficiently knowledgeable to introduce children to contemporary literature and, the survey responses suggest, were using fiction and poetry mainly as a resource for instructional purposes. However, it is reassuring to note that these teachers read in their own lives: nearly three-quarters reported reading a book within the last three months (Cremin, Bearne *et al.*, 2008). Popular fiction topped the list of their favourite reading (40 per cent), followed by autobiographies and biographies and other post-1980s novels (both 14 per cent). A small percentage (6.5 per cent) had recently read children's fiction, including crossover novels such as *Harry Potter* (J.K. Rowling) and *The Curious Incident of the Dog in the Night-Time* (Mark Haddon).

The lack of professional knowledge of and assurance with children's fiction that this research reveals, the over-dependence on a small canon of writers and the minimal knowledge of global literature have potentially serious consequences for all learners, particularly those from linguistic and cultural-minority groups. Without a diverse knowledge of children's fiction and an awareness of key authors and illustrators whose work is potent enough to foster the creative engagement of teachers and younger learners, classroom literacy practice at the primary phase will necessarily be limited.

Teachers who read themselves and read children's literature widely are arguably better placed to make judgements about quality and appropriateness in selecting books and in matching books to individual readers. Such professionals have been called Reading Teachers – 'teachers who read and readers who teach' (Commeyras *et al.*, 2003) – and build strong personal relationships with children (Cremin *et al.*, 2014). This is a key characteristic of all creative teaching professionals, who, Craft (2005) argues, tend to adopt a humanitarian stance with regard to education. For more details on Reading Teachers, see Chapter 5.

Teachers who read widely and keep up to date with children's literature are more likely to see it as a rich source of possibility, a place for imaginative involvement and reflection, and may be less likely to treat it merely as a model for writing or a resource for cross-curricular work.

TEACHING FICTION CREATIVELY

The teaching of fiction arguably suffers as a consequence of the twin pressures of prescription and accountability and the overuse of text extracts to teach specific linguistic features. Professional authors, concerned at what they perceived to be an extract-focused 'analysis paralysis' approach to fiction, have argued that what was at stake was 'nothing less than the integrity of the novel, the story, the poem . . . valued for its own sake and on its own terms' (Powling, 2003: 3; Powling *et al.*, 2005). This group, which included Chris Powling, Bernard Ashley, Philip Pullman, Anne Fine and Jamila Gavin, were not alone in expressing their dissatisfaction; others have also voiced their concerns about the ways in which children's literature has been positioned and can be used in the classroom (Cremin, Mottram *et al.*, 2008; Lockwood, 2008).

Nonetheless, many primary professionals realise that what they choose to read aloud, recommend, share and study and how they explore literature in the classroom are crucial to fostering learner creativity. So, they seek to develop pedagogic practices that are open ended and give space to the children's views, harnessing their curiosity through playful engagement with powerful fictions that have the potential to interest, involve and challenge them. Bringing a literary text to life, through layered, multisensory, collaborative engagement, can include drama, artwork, writing, discussion, digital work, dancing and singing, for example, and will prompt the generation and evaluation of new meanings and interpretations. It is also likely to inspire children to read independently, provoking curiosity about characters, narratives or poetic content (O'Sullivan and McGonigle, 2010; Landay and Wootton, 2012). Literature is often used creatively across the curriculum, for example in mathematics (Pound and Lee, 2015), geography (Lintner, 2010) and history (Cooper, 2013).

There is strong evidence that picture fiction can make a rich contribution to children's creativity (Arizpe and Styles, 2003). Meek argued long ago that quality picture-fiction books 'make reading for all a distinctive kind of imaginative looking' (1991: 119) and highlighted their potential for creatively engaging all readers. More recently, Arizpe *et al.* (2014) have shown the myriad benefits, personal and cultural, as well as social and in relation to literacy learning, of immigrant children reading pertinent and powerful wordless picture books, such as Shaun Tan's *The Arrival*. Authors such as Tan, Neil Gaiman, Emily Gravett, Anthony Browne and Gary Crew, for example, often experiment with the interplay between words and pictures and set up gaps between the literal and metaphorical interpretations of their narratives. As a consequence, their demanding texts provoke multiple interpretations, as well as discussion about the issues, themes and values expressed by the author/illustrator, and the language, characters and narrative structure used.

Complex novels can also prompt involvement, enabling children to sustain their engagement with longer texts and develop persistence. The talented work of Berlie Doherty, Philip Reeve, Marcus Sedgwick, David Almond, Malorie Blackman and Geraldine McCaughrean, for example, often produces considerable discussion and debate. In addition, flash fiction and picture-strip and cartoon-style stories by authors such as Bob Graham or Marcia Williams, as well as graphic-novel partnerships (e.g. between Mariko and Jillian Tamaki), offer a rich expression of the potential of the imagination. Powerful fiction texts, whatever their format, leave space for the creativity of the reader to be brought into play. Creative teachers exploit these reverberating spaces and join learners in a range of problem-finding/problem-solving activities that seek to advance their understanding, their comprehension and their creativity.

READING AND RESPONDING ACTIVELY TO FICTION TEXTS

Although the act of reading fiction is likely to be seen as a private affair, and children need to be able to make sense of texts for themselves, comprehension develops in large part through conversation and interaction. Meaning emerges and is shaped and revised as readers engage with and respond to what they read, often in the company of others. Each reader brings him/herself to the text, their life experience, prior knowledge and understanding of the issues encountered, as well as cultural perspectives and insights. Meaning is thus created in the interaction between the author, the text and the reader. Benton and Fox (1985) argued long ago that teachers should focus more on the creative act of reading and, in particular, on the expression of personal responses. Their position remains of value; this is where young children's deep delight in literature resides. Through discussing their responses, children can make connections, interrogate their views about the world and learn about themselves in the process. In order to achieve this, teachers need to investigate the layers of meaning in a text and help children draw upon their prior knowledge. So, although teachers' own responses are important, batteries of comprehension questions should be avoided, and the children's questions, puzzlements and interpretations should lead the conversations.

Reading journals can also support a focus on active interrogation and reflection upon texts. Creative professionals develop their own ways of operationalising journals with each class. Some may offer a bank of possible prompts at the back of the journal and invite children to record their responses following discussion; others may encourage children to

Predicting/ hypothesising	I think what might happen is . . . although it might not because . . . . What if the character . . . ? I wonder what the character is thinking at this moment?
Picturing	When I read that I vividly saw a picture of . . . in my head – did anyone else see any moment/character very clearly?
Connecting/comparing	This reminds me of . . . (other stories/films/TV or life experience) so it makes me feel . . .
Questioning	I wonder . . . why . . . what . . . .whether . . . if . . . .?
Engaging emotionally/ empathising	I'm not sure what I feel about this character, I used to think . . . but now I wonder if . . . .
Responding to issues	I wonder what the author/illustrator is trying to examine? I used to think he/she was exploring . . . but now I am less sure . . .
Evaluating	I like . . . but I'm less keen on . . . Exploring likes, dislikes, puzzles and patterns (Chambers, 1995)
Noticing language/ style/presentation	I noticed . . . were there words or phrases that anyone else noticed – what do you think made them leap out at you? I wonder why the author chose to present character X in this . . . way? The writing reminds me of . . . style – is anyone else reminded of another writer's work?

▪ **Figure 8.2** Strategies for active reading

annotate the text during reading, using post-it notes to highlight key phrases/passages, puzzles or patterns. Reading journals can effectively integrate reading and writing and can support both literature circles and private reading. If a bank of prompts is offered, those noted in Figure 8.2 could be adapted, and children can be encouraged to record their initial impressions and questions/predictions, for example. In addition, teachers may suggest children draw responses to the narrative, encouraging visualisation of particular characters or scenes at significant moments in the tale.

There are a number of other classroom practices that prompt exploration and engagement and multimodal responses to texts, examined in Chapters 4 and 5. Drama, for example, can enable children to inhabit the narrative, experience its tension and examine character motivation and perspective. Art, photography, music and dance can also encourage representations of the themes and the meanings identified, helping to develop children's intercultural awareness and layered understandings (McAdam and Arizpe, 2011). Multiple suggestions for active exploration are also noted later in the chapter, as part of work encompassing written responses.

READING IN GROUPS

In small, guided groups, literature circles and independent, choice-led reading groups, children take part as interested conversationalists, talking their way forward creatively and establishing new insights and understandings, as well as developing a shared language for talking about texts reflectively and evaluatively. In group discussion, the reading-comprehension strategies used by both children and teachers are important. These can be modelled and will often be framed as tentative statements or open questions to prompt extended conversations. They reflect the kinds of strategies effective readers employ to make sense of the text (see Figure 8.2) and link to Philosophy for Children work that itself prompts focused enquiry around a key question identified by the group (see Buckley, 2012, for details of the process). As Fisher (2013: 41) acknowledges, 'creative dialogue cannot be left to chance, it must be valued, encouraged and expected'.

Literature circles involve children reading a text in common, mostly outside the session, and meeting regularly to discuss it, often with the support of an adult and/or reading journal (King and Briggs, 2005). They seek to foster increased autonomy within a community of readers, and time is usually set aside to develop a sense of anticipation prior to reading. In addition, children will be involved in mulling over ideas together, identifying questions and confusions and seeking clarification, as they share their interpretations with one another. Literature circles can help children internalise the process of engaging in such exploratory talk, and so, again, teachers are likely to scaffold children's learning by modelling the use of reading strategies (Figure 8.2) to help them anticipate and reflect upon the text.

Establishing independent, child-choice-led reading groups can also enrich opportunities for children to exercise their agency as readers. Many schemes exist that involve children in voting for a favourite text or shadowing a book award. The CILIP Carnegie Kate Greenaway Shadowing Scheme was the UK's first, and arguably remains the premiere award for children's literature in Britain. It draws on the expertise of experienced and knowledgeable librarians (Butler *et al.*, 2011) who annually award the Carnegie Medal, to the writer of an outstanding book for children, and the Kate Greenaway Medal, for distinguished illustration in a book for children. Working in shadowing groups, which are predominantly extracurricular, young people read, discuss and carry out activities on the books short-listed for one or both awards, and they can then compare their views with those of the judges. The shadowing scheme has a dedicated website, with author interviews and videos, children's reviews of the shortlisted texts and a Greenaway gallery, where teachers can upload children's related artwork. It represents a potentially rich educational opportunity that affords scope for developing interest, discussion and perseverance and for introducing readers to new fiction.

Young people interviewed as part of recent research into the scheme indicated that reading fiction is sometimes difficult to fit into their weekly routine, but that the scheme provides a focus and a reason to prioritise reading:

> I read a lot more now, I'm attempting to read for at least an hour a day. This is because I'm on this mission to finish them all [the shortlisted books]!

> I really enjoy talking about the books, as well as reading them, this gives me something to aim for.
>
> (Cremin and Swann, 2012)

Group members who met with teachers or librarians in book clubs, in the lunch hour or after school, viewed the scheme enthusiastically, in part because there was scope to 'say what you want about books' and take the 'time to stop and think about books'. Those young people who were involved in shadowing as a curricular initiative were rather less positive, but they also valued the chance 'to talk about books', to 'choose which books we wanted to read' and to 'read such great books' (Cremin and Swann, 2015). Talk in shadowing contexts was often observed to be a fairly unrestricted exchange of ideas and was unconstrained by assessment, as in the following interview comments from a group of young readers:

A: It is quite informal so umm, you are like, Greg was saying we don't have to read a certain book by a certain time, we can just read what we want to and write a review and things like that and just talk about it freely.

I: That's interesting, what do you mean by talk about it freely?

A: Like you don't have to write a review or anything, we don't have to say certain things about it, we can say what we actually think.

I: OK

B: We are free to have our own opinions.

C: People can understand and then debate with you whether it is a good book or not, so it is supposed to have like other people's opinions, listen to other people's ideas because it shows that people have different tastes in reading.

Disagreement was common in shadowing discussion, whether this was focused, for example, on *Solomon Crocodile* by Catharine Rayner in a class of young readers, or the novel *Trash* by Andy Mulligan in an extracurricular group of 10–11-year-olds. The scheme encouraged and validated diverse views (Cremin and Swann, 2012). It is clear that establishing reading groups, such as literature circles or shadowing groups, can, if choice is afforded, and quality literature is offered, provide opportunities for mutual respect between readers to develop, for difference and diversity to be foregrounded and for readers to develop both perseverance and commitment.

WRITING FICTION TEXTS: EXPERIMENTING WITH FORM AND FREEDOM

It is widely recognised that reading enriches writing, and that literature offers a repertoire of possibilities for writers. Through open-ended explorations and focused discussions, children learn more about how texts are constructed, and such deconstruction can lead to reconstruction in their own writing. At times this will be imitative, but, at others, literature will be engaged with as a source of inspiration and ideas. As part of the extended process of composition, creative teachers map in opportunities to inhabit and explore texts through drama, discussion, storytelling, art, dance, music and performance. Such explorations encompass oral, kinaesthetic and visual approaches and provoke children's intellectual and emotional engagement in the narrative, generating new ideas for writing. For example, through improvising with puppet characters from a story, children can collectively co-author new fictions, or, through listening to oral stories and re-telling personal and traditional tales, they can learn a great deal about narrative structure and language features (Cremin and Myhill, 2012). Children's involvement with computer games has also been shown to influence their story writing (Bearne and Wolstencroft, 2007), as has their involvement in film (Bhojwani *et al.*, 2009). Both can be supported through a multimodal approach to writing that recognises that the fiction (and other) texts children enjoy at home combine the modes of print and image, sound and gesture, as well as movement. Leaning on literature, life and a range of popular cultural resources supports young writers, although teachers will wish to help them make their implicit knowledge about the multiple languages of narrative more explicit and make judicious choices, according to context.

In creatively encountering a text, children's attention can be drawn to its construct-edness, so that their growing awareness of a writer's skill develops alongside their pleasure in the meanings conveyed. Young authors can develop the craft of writing, in part through conscious use of the fictional models around them. The Teaching Reading and Writing Links project demonstrated that critical reading and investigation of texts are integral parts of the writing process, and children's metacognitive development and awareness of the reader can be enhanced through thoughtful teaching about the literary language of fictional texts (Corden, 2001, 2003). The teaching on this project, however, was not at the expense of the meaning or purpose of the fiction, and children were provided with opportunities to work on extended pieces of writing in which they could make use of their new knowledge and skills in context.

Specific response to text activities that allow children to interpret and reconstruct stories, as well as to increase their awareness of the author's craft, can pay dividends. Children can develop their knowledge about language through a range of affectively involving text activities that focus upon the key elements of fiction: character, language, setting, story structure and the theme. To enhance their understanding of these elements, teachers can use activities that foster children's serious but playful engagement in narrative (see Figure 8.3).

Such activities need to be employed in the context of a text. For example, one teacher, recognising the popularity of Lauren Child's two series, focused on Clarice Bean, (e.g. *Utterly Me, Clarice Bean, My Uncle Is a Hunkle Says Clarice Bean*) and Charlie and Lola (e.g *Charlie and Lola: We completely must go to London, Charlie and Lola: I will not ever never eat a tomato*), and planned an extended unit of work around them. She chose to focus on the author's amusing characters and the ways in which Child brings them to

Awareness of character

Role-play   Character pockets
Speech/thought bubbles   Character ladder
Interior monologue   Emotions graph
Emotions map   Hot-seat

Awareness of structure

Story journeys   Bookzip
Stepping stones   Mural
Freeze-frames   Timelines
Story maps   Retelling

Awareness of language

No quote without comment   Puzzle possibility game
Reading journals   Dog's tail
Phrase/clause wall   Telling down
Forum theatre   Like, dislike, puzzle, pattern

Awareness of theme

Backbone summary   Share the essence
Thematic bracelets   Hint hunt
Contents focus   Sentence game
Sculpture and paragraph   Poster of the film

▤ **Figure 8.3** Activities that can help explore narrative elements

life through drawings, language, behaviour and other characters' attitudes towards them. In one activity, the teacher, having focused in a recent reading on Marcie (Clarice's older, teenage sister), brought in a pair of her own daughter's jeans and proceeded to empty 'Marcie's pockets', inviting the 7–8-year-olds to predict the contents. They did so and explained their reasons for suggesting, among other items: 'bright pink lipstick', 'receipts from Boots', 'cigarettes', 'love heart sweets', 'her mobile' and 'a purse with a photo of her boyfriend'. The teacher then invited the class to choose their own character from one of the series and imagine what might be in their pockets. After some discussion, these were drawn. The children then invented stories in which some of the pocket objects played a part. Saabir, who chose Charlie (see Figure 8.4), developed a tale that involved Charlie lending his younger sister Lola some gum. This ended up stuck behind her ear and got caught in her hair, and so his brush came into play. . . . Later, Lola insisted on borrowing his headphones too, so her new bald patch would not be seen!

Another practitioner, exploring Jez Alborough's book *Where's My Teddy?*, chose to focus on the characters Eddie and the great Big Bear. Both have lost their teddies and find each other's in the wood. The class of 5- and 6-year-olds created freeze-frames of significant moments in the tale and engaged in interior monologues, speaking out loud the thoughts

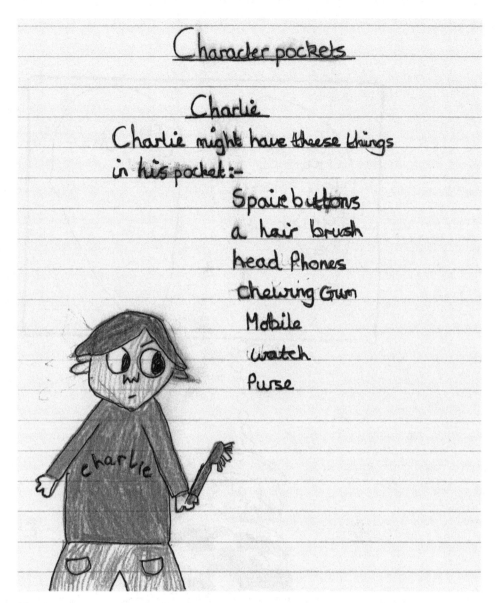

Figure 8.4 Character pockets

of Eddie and the Big Bear at the moments they had depicted. Once safely home, with their TIR as Eddie's mum and the children in role as Eddie, they retold their stories about meeting the Bear and his giant-sized teddy and finding their own beloved teddy. The teacher then re-read the book and focused on the end, when both the Bear and Eddie are in their own beds, 'huddling and cuddling their own little teds'. Through role-play in pairs, the children improvised their chosen character's conversation with their teddy and rapidly recorded these conversations. For an example, see Figure 8.5. Jenny's conversation between Eddie and his teddy suggests that the little teddy had rather enjoyed his adventure with the Big

Jenny

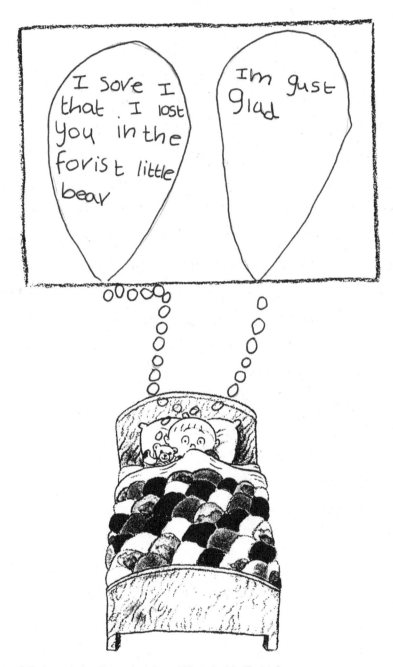

Figure 8.5 Jenny's bedtime chat from *Where's My Teddy?*

Source: Copyright ©1992 Jez Alborough, from *Where's My Teddy?*, by Jez Alborough. Reproduced by permission of Walker Books Ltd, London SE11 5HJ

Bear, hinting at another story within Alborough's story. In fact, Jenny had a lengthy tale to tell about a cave in the mountains and the other animals the tiny teddy had seen while travelling with the Big Bear. Her story was shared and celebrated as a novel interpretation, and, later that week, children were observed in the forest role-play area, acting out the tiny teddy's adventures.

Yet another practitioner, working with 9–10-year-olds, chose to focus on the theme of the text *The Ice Bear* by Jackie Morris. She used a visualiser to enlarge the pages and explored the tale of how raven steals a white cub from his ice bear mother, later turning the cub into a human child who is brought up by a hunter. For seven years, the hunter and his wife, who have longed for a child, hold him close and sing him songs, but he seldom speaks, and 'always the raven watched over him'. One day, the raven tricks the boy out on to the ice, and, as darkness falls, the pack of ice bears comes for him. He is reunited with his mother bear (whose skin is scarred by her tears of loss), but his human father swears to kill the bear that has taken his child. . . . The story ends in a traditional truce, with the boy spending winter with the bears and summer with his human family, and yet one is left pondering the consequences of this arrangement and the role of the trickster raven.

The teacher read sections of the tale at a time, stopping to explore issues through talk and drama. For example, the class explored the bear mother's emotions through interior monologues, hot-seated the raven, seeking to understand his motives, and later, in role as ice bears or humans, sought to persuade the boy to stay with them through a decision alley. Once the teacher had completed the reading of the book, she invited the class to gather in groups and create a group sculpture to represent one of the key themes of the text as they saw it. Much discussion ensued, and titles were added to the visuals physically created with their bodies; some groups also noted what their sculpture was made from, adding to the metaphor offered. Their titles included:

- One bad turn does not deserve another.
- Love and loss travel together.
- Life scars you.
- Who am I?

There is evidence here of the children exploring divergent ideas, supported by their imaginative exploration of the words and images in this potent text; the group sculpture activity prompted them to think in new ways and exercise their collaborative creativity.

PROFILING FICTION IN EXTENDED LEARNING JOURNEYS

When fiction is being profiled across several weeks in the primary classroom, there are a number of available options. Teachers might choose to focus on a particular form of fiction, such as myths or legends, for example, and explore how storytellers convey their narratives orally or in written form. Or they might lean on a theme such as friendship or bullying and draw together a number of texts to read and explore, considering how different authors, illustrators and poets examine the issue. Alternatively, teachers might choose to focus on one or two significant children's authors and read across a range of their works, reflecting upon their craft and style as writers. In each of these and other possible units of work, creative teachers are likely to draw upon narratives presented in a number of media, including, perhaps: printed and graphic novels, oral tales, short stories in anthologies, and narratives on radio, television and film.

If the focus is on a children's author, then, during the period of immersion and exploration of their fictional texts, children can be invited to search relevant websites (the author's own, publishers' and other book sites) for additional information. It is also possible that radio or filmed interviews will be available to watch, and supplementary materials might be found to help make connections between the writers and their work. Many authors respond to seriously written letters of enquiry and also visit schools to work alongside children. In the Carnegie Kate Greenaway research, it was noted that many authors were prepared to Skype shadowing groups to talk about their books, and this represents another option.

If the focus is on themes or is linked to cross-curricular work, then diversity will again be key, and making use of the Literacy Shed (www.literacyshed.com) may support focused yet playful examinations. This website offers multiple resources and advice, as well as children's examples from teachers who have used the materials. There are foci such as fantasy, ghosts, contrasts and many more to help teachers, and multiple video clips and animated picture-fiction texts such as Martin Waddell's *Owl Babies* and David Weisner's *Tuesday*. As with any resource, however, the key issue is not the use of stand-alone activities, but a planned unit of work that progresses over time, places literature at the heart of the work and makes use of the eight characteristics of creative teaching to foster creative learning. See Chapter 12 for a discussion of such planning.

If a creative learning journey based on the autobiographical tales and short stories of some contemporary children's writers is planned, for example, the route actually travelled will be shaped by the children's emerging needs and interests and their response to the tales and their themes. Letting the children lead during the journey will ensure that they take a degree of ownership and control of their learning, fostering their possibility thinking and creative engagement (Cremin, Burnard *et al.*, 2006). The learning intention/long-term outcome of such a unit could be for each child to write and publish a short story, connected in some way to their own lives.

Initially, the teacher could work with the class to create a short-story collection, perhaps borrowing from local libraries, inviting children to lend any from home, and seeking out such tales in children's magazines and on websites. The focus could be on traditional tales, such as those found in Crossley Holland's *Short* collections, or on personal tales, as in Morpurgo's *Singing for Mrs Pettigrew* and Naidoo's *Out of Bounds*, both of which draw upon their childhood experiences to recreate and re-envision narratives. Still others, such as Ahlberg's *The Boyhood of Burglar Bill* and *The Bucket*, are explicitly autobiographical.

Creative teachers will want to find tales within these collections that engage and excite them as adult readers, but might valuably start with Ahlberg's opening tale in *The Boyhood of Burglar Bill*, entitled 'One-armed man, three-legged dog'. This deliciously evokes his childhood, in which his love of football and a 'madman teacher' play a significant role. Commencing with this is likely to trigger personal connections and tale telling, which could be supported by drawing timelines of life and talking to parents and carers about significant events. In school, pairs could swap stories in a story buzz and identify possible titles for their own and each other's tales. An emphasis on ambiguity, brevity, intrigue and/or subtlety may be foregrounded, and another story buzz with their titles might enable the children to revisit and reshape their chosen life stories by sharing them with different partners. In a story buzz, as the children move around the class, pairing up, listening to and telling each other their tales, their narratives will not only be rehearsed and reshaped, but will be expanded on. In one class of 10–11-year-olds engaged on a similar auto-biographical journey, the teacher found several of the children chose to write, not about family members, but about friends, and significant memories surfaced. See, for example, Jo's recollection of his friend's death in Figure 8.6.

A later focus on this journey could involve studying tales from *Singing for Mrs Pettigrew* and sharing Morpurgo's fascinating commentaries on each. In these, he explains

A Senceless death

I entered the classroom.
Everyone was sitting down.
There was Just one empty seat.
Where was my friend
I felt sick and my heart felt heavy with grief.
Black ice on the road.
His dads car skidding out of control.
His life brought to an end.
The Whole day was in silence.
Nobody wanted to play.
Nobody wanted to work.
Even his enemies were sad.

■ **Figure 8.6** A senseless death

his connections to the place, people and predicaments examined and recreated in the tale. By now, the children will have chosen the stories they wish to retell/develop and may have begun to map these out on page or screen. They might also create their own commentaries, like Morpurgo, or as compositional collages, using cut-outs from magazines and the Internet and adding drawings and photographs to indicate the many influences on their narratives. Shared and guided work through the unit will highlight particular objectives, and the teaching, both planned and responsive, will allow children to pursue their interests and self- chosen narratives, with support and tailored instruction being offered on the journey.

Finally, it will be important to celebrate the children's completed stories, ensuring that copies of the class anthology are available, in print or on the school website, and readings of the tales in class and assembly are undertaken. Reviews can be sought from parents, peers and children in other classes/schools. Making children's work public is important: it enables young writers to receive feedback from their readers and recognise themselves as authors, alongside the authors whose work they have read and studied. It might also be that the final collection could be offered to local community centres, doctor's surgeries and libraries, to extend the reach of the class's publication.

CONCLUSION

Creative teachers seek out fiction texts that require children to actively participate in making meaning – texts that trigger multiple questions and deep engagement and that build bridges of understanding. In exploring such texts, creative teachers employ a wide range of open-ended strategies that foster children's curiosity and develop their personal and creative responses, enriching their understanding of narrative and prompting related talk, reading and writing, inspired by the powerful literature chosen for study. At the same time, creative teachers read aloud a wide range of other potent, affectively engaging texts.

FURTHER READING

Arizpe, E. and Styles, M. (2003) *Children Reading Pictures: Interpreting Visual Texts*. London: RoutledgeFalmer.

Cremin, T. (2007) 'Revisiting reading for pleasure: Diversity, delight and desire', in K. Goouch and A. Lambirth (eds), *Understanding Phonics and the Teaching of Reading*. Berkshire, UK: McGraw-Hill, pp. 166–90.

Evans, J. (2009) 'Reading the visual: Creative and aesthetic responses to picturebooks and fine art', in J. Evans (ed.), *Talking Beyond the Page: Reading and responding to picturebooks*. London: Routledge, pp. 99–117.

CHILDREN'S BOOKS

Ahlberg, A. (2006) *The Boyhood of Burglar Bill*. London: Puffin.

Alborough, J. (1995) *Where's My Teddy?* London: Walker.

Child, L. (2000) *My Uncle is a Hunkle Says Clarice Bean*. London: Orchard.

Child, L. (2002) *Utterly Me, Clarice Bean*. London: Orchard.

Child, L. (2007) *Charlie and Lola: I Will Not Ever Never Eat A Tomato*. London: Orchard.

Child, L. (2012) *Charlie and Lola: We completely must go to London*. London: Orchard.

Crossley Holland, K. (2011) *Short Too! A second book of very short stories*. Oxford, UK: Oxford University Press.

Morpurgo, M. (2006) *Singing for Mrs Pettigrew*. London: Walker.
Morris, J. (2010) *The Ice Bear*. London: Frances Lincoln.
Mulligan, A. (2011) *Trash*. London: David Fickling.
Naidoo, B. (2003) *Out of Bounds*. London: Puffin.
Rayner, C. (2011) *Solomon Crocodile*. London: Macmillan.
Tan, S. (2007) *The Arrival*. London: Hodder.
Weisner, D. (1991) *Tuesday*. New York: Houghton Mifflin.

PLAYFULLY EXPLORING POETRY

Teresa Cremin

INTRODUCTION

Poetry, a highly crafted kind of written language, offers a rich resource for teaching literacy creatively: its particular structures and forms generate interest, and its multimodal nature incites physical movement from the lips to the fingertips. Poetry deserves to be read and responded to actively and imaginatively, prompting a desire to read more and discuss, perform, represent and write it. All of these activities, supported by teachers reading aloud and providing opportunities to engage with both contemporary and classic poetry, are endorsed by national curricula across the UK. As well as contributing to creativity and literacy, poetry can increase children's awareness of, and pleasure in, language. This chapter focuses on teaching poetry creatively, employing the eight strands of creative literacy practice.

POETIC TEXTS

Outside the classroom, children's lives are packed with poetry: they engage in a world of rich language play and experiment with and imbibe playground rhymes, songs, football chants, jingles, jokes and lyrics, often without recognising their essentially poetic nature. Their first experiences of poetry are often oral, for, as Michael Rosen (1989) argued long ago, poetry and fiction have their roots in everyday speech, and, from their earliest years, children meet poetry in word play, nursery rhyme, rhythm and song, taking particular pleasure in the playful and often subversive nature of poetic language. Recent research on playground games (Marsh and Bishop, 2014) affirms that children still find intense pleasure in verbal play, and that the repertoire of rhymes that accompany clapping games or regulate counting activities, for example, is expanding, influenced in part by their knowledge of the media.

There are multiple definitions of poetry, ranging from 'memorable speech' (Auden and Garrett, 1935) to 'the right words in the right order' (Hughes, 1967), but, as Zephaniah (2001) observes, although experts make it their business to tell readers what kinds of poem they should like, individuals of all ages make their own decisions and develop their own preferences. Teachers need to introduce children to a wide range of forms and styles, through reading aloud, shared and guided reading and closer examinations of free verse and many forms. These might include: shape poetry, list poetry, narrative poetry, rap, rhyming forms such as nursery rhymes and playground games, and short, patterned poetry such as haiku, kennings and cinquains. Children can be encouraged to draw upon these and other forms, as well as free verse, in their writing. They can also be encouraged to be poetry detectives – on the lookout for poetry in picture fiction (e.g. Jeanne Willis's *Grill Pan Eddy*), in assembly, on the TV and elsewhere. In addition, children's texts about poetry, such as Gary Crew's *Troy Thompson's Excellent Poetry Book* and Sharon Creech's *Love that Dog* and *Hate that Cat*, are invaluable.

Poetry employs a range of features, including: sound effects – repetition, alliteration, onomatopoeia, rhythm and rhyme; visual effects; well-chosen and often powerful vocabulary; surprising word combinations; and repeated patterns for effect. Noticing, discussing and using such features in various poetic forms are part of teaching and learning about poetry, but are not the *raison d'être*, for such features are harnessed to create meaning and achieve effects. Pleasure and engagement precede full understanding, and so priority must be given to the meaning and message of poetic text through creative approaches that foster the development of positive attitudes and dispositions towards this rich and varied art form.

The experience of poetry is important. Through developing an open and creative ethos in the classroom, teachers encourage experimentation with poetry in all its forms, building upon the early sounds and savours found in nursery and playground rhymes and linking to the lyrics of popular music, as well as other forms. Playground rhymes, songs and chants have much in common: they often encompass repetition and rhythm, are easy to recall, are highly adaptable, social and physical and are affectively engaging. Children of all ages can brainstorm these, perhaps after a session in the playground, and can read and share such rhymes, also examining examples from elsewhere, such as John Agard and Grace Nichols' *Caribbean Dozen*. Identifying patterns and features of such rhymes and classifying them into collections of two-ball, skipping, clapping and counting rhymes will both build on and expand the class's repertoire and foster experimentation and performance. The children may well know rhymes in other languages, and if so these will be important to share. Through such playful engagement, reading and response are nurtured, and later compositions may follow, as in the case of the poem composed by Liam, aged 8, which has the patterning of playground chants, while being influenced by other poetry also (see Figure 9.1).

TEACHERS' KNOWLEDGE OF POETIC TEXTS

It has been argued that teachers' confidence in knowing and using children's literature, and particularly poetry, may be limited (Arts Council England, 2003; Cremin, Mottram *et al.*, 2008). In a UKLA survey of 1,200 primary teachers, when asked to name six children's poets, 58 per cent of the teachers named only two, one or no poets, 22 per cent named no poets at all, and only 10 per cent named six poets. The highest number of mentions by far was for Michael Rosen (452), with five others gaining over a hundred mentions, namely: Allan Ahlberg, Roger McGough, Roald Dahl, Spike Milligan and Benjamin Zephaniah. After these, only three poets were mentioned more than fifty times: Edward Lear, Ted Hughes and A.A. Milne. Few women poets were mentioned, and, with the notable exception of Benjamin Zephaniah, black poets received very few mentions. The teachers, drawn from eleven different local authorities, tended to note poets whose poetry might be seen as light hearted or humorous (e.g. Rosen, Dahl, Ahlberg or Milligan), or writers whose

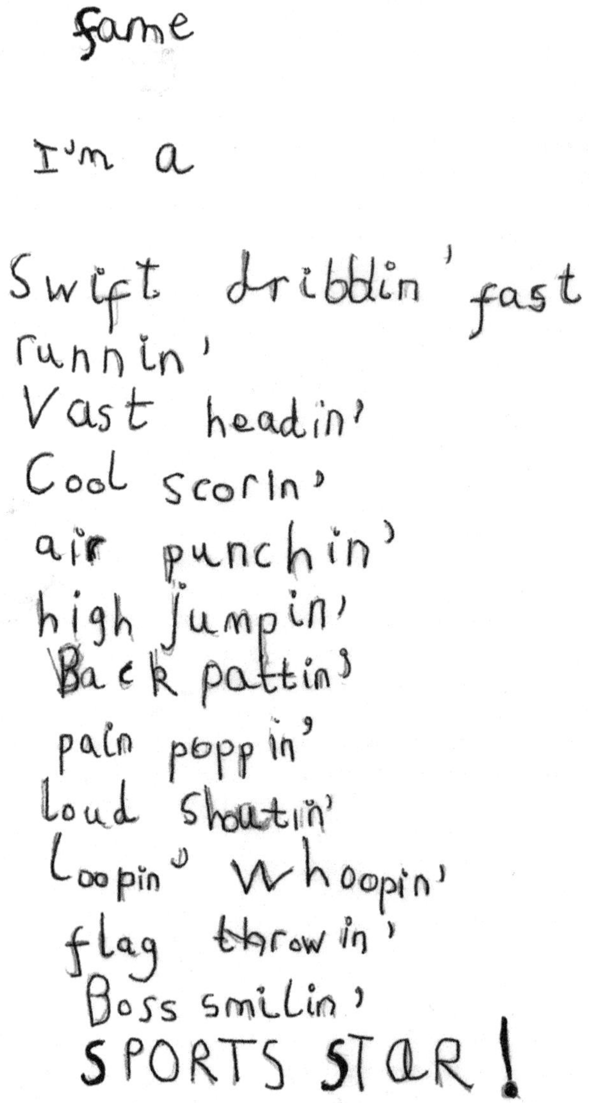

fame

I'm a

Swift dribblin' fast
runnin'
Vast headin'
Cool scorin'
air punchin'
high jumpin'
Back pattin'
pain poppin'
loud shoutin'
Loopin' Whoopin'
flag throwin'
Boss smilin'
SPORTS STAR!

■ **Figure 9.1** Fame by Liam

work might be categorised as classic (e.g. Rossetti, Browning, Blake, Wordsworth, Stevenson, Hughes, Milne). Most of the poems named by title in the survey were classics that teachers had probably studied in their own schooldays (e.g. Carroll's 'Jabberwocky', Stephenson's 'From a Railway Carriage' and Davies's 'Leisure'). This may suggest that teachers are focused more on poems than poets, may be reliant upon poems recalled from childhood, and may be using poetry to teach linguistic features, at the expense of reading, responding to, and enjoying poetry for its own sake.

In addition to this weak subject knowledge, research indicates that teachers, even subject leaders, lack confidence both in teaching poetry and in selecting appropriate verse, and, as a consequence, poetry tends to be confined to particular units of work (Lambirth *et al.*, 2012). Poetic practice may thus be somewhat tethered to publishers' resources, probably reducing the likelihood that poetry is taught creatively. Additionally, this lack of knowledge may be restricting children's access to poetic voices in all their energetic and reflective diversity, and preventing teachers from recommending, reading or sharing the work of women poets, or poets from different cultures.

In order to teach poetry creatively, teachers need to become acquainted with the widest possible range of writers, encompassing both older and newer voices, such as Edward Lear, Spike Milligan, John Agard, Benjamin Zephaniah, James Berry, Gareth Owen, as well as Jackie Kay, Grace Nichols, Andrew Fusek Peters, Tony Mitton and Claire Bevan. The work of writers from further afield (e.g. Sheree Fitch, Shel Silverstein and the Caribbean poets, whose work is celebrated in the new anthology *Give the Ball to the Poet*, edited by Horrell, Spencer and Styles) and the poetry of popular novelists (e.g. Berlie Doherty and Kevin Crossley Holland) are also worth getting to know. Any list, however, is invidious and incomplete. The professional challenge is to keep up to date and to get to know those whose work has immediate appeal and those whose writing is more layered and demanding.

Leaning on Michael Rosen's A–Z of poets, the class might make their own anthology over the year, widening their repertoire alongside the teacher's. In creating their own class anthology, children will be involved in reading, composing and performing poems, as well as discussing selection and presentation issues. They could also create friezes and displays of favourite poems, explore poets' websites and survey their parents'/grandparents' favourite poems, songs and rhymes. One group of 9–10-year-olds, finding that all their parents remembered 'Jabberwocky', chose to create their own version, which playfully embroiled teachers at their school and was performed in assembly (see Figure 9.2) for an extract of this.

READING AND RESPONDING TO POETRY

Creative teachers seek to ensure poetry is read aloud, with voice and verve appropriate to the text, so that children can hear the patterns and language and find pleasure in the text. Listening to the poet's own voice too can be enriching and is feasible through the online Poetry Archive (both the adults' and children's sections are worth exploring), poet's own websites and through CDs (e.g Jackie Kay's *Red Cherry Red*). Poetry also needs to be voiced by the learners themselves: it is not enough for them to hear poetry read to them; they need to bring it to life by tasting the word textures, feeling the rhythms and discerning the colour, movement and drama in the text. Copies of poems and poetry books need to be in the children's hands, and opportunities need to be made available for them to release the words from the page and read, chant, move and sing verse into existence. Pedagogic practice that helps both children and teachers find pleasure in the sounds and rhythms, music and meaning of poetry is essential. Too much assiduous attention to poetic analysis can constrain children's playful engagement. As always, developing a balanced approach is key, though recognising poetry's multimodal and aesthetic qualities remains important.

In class, the meditative nature of one poem can be contrasted with the effervescence of another, not only through a teacher's exposition, but also by the children themselves making meaning together in small groups. They can be supported in such endeavours by using Chambers's (1993) reflective structure, 'like–dislike–puzzle–pattern', to prompt conversations about the texts. In one class of 7–8-year-olds, the teacher read aloud John

Jabbercane

'Twas twilling and the tardy thwocks,
Did humph and flub upon the burple,
All frapsy were the wee dumpocks,
And the babe wooths did wurple,

Beware the jabbercane my son,
The purple legs and squat green body,
Beware the Webb Webb bird and push,
the jumptious Nettisnatch,

And so he took his lethal spear,
Longtime he sought the jabbercane,
And stood in tougt by the fell of wier,
But still he searched, he searched in vain,

■ **Figure 9.2** Jabbercane

Agard's 'My telly' several times. It starts with the memorable lines, 'My telly eats people especially on the news', and goes on to explore the kind of 'little people' that the TV devours (e.g. 'little people with no shoes, little people with no food, little people crying, little people dying'). It closes with the line, 'if you don't believe me look inside the belly of my telly'. The children chatted in pairs about their likes and dislikes about the poem, before sharing these and noting them on a copy of the verse. They then played the puzzle possibility game, in which several children voiced their puzzles, and others sought to offer possible responses to these. Many felt the poem was 'too simple' and 'boring', 'because it keeps on saying my telly this and my telly that'. Few grasped the meaning of the verse, and most were puzzled by the telly eating people; some read this literally.

As individual children's puzzles and questions about the poem were voiced and responded to, the issues of famine, death and the depressing nature of much news coverage was gradually foregrounded through the discussion. The anthology was seized, and other books by John Agard were found, prompting further discussion about the presence of such a potent poem in a '*rather young looking*' book of rhymes. Some weeks later, in a class assembly, one group chose to read this poem repeatedly while a PowerPoint series of images of people facing famine, downloaded from the Internet, was displayed. Stephen then read his poem 'Ethiopia', while a single visual image remained on the screen. The silence in the room was palpable.

> Ethiopia
> The face of the dying,
> Feeling helpless,
> Feeling weak,
> His mother can do nothing
> To help her struggling child,
> The tattered cloth of the people's sorrow,
> The horror of watching people fade away,
> Humans begging for just one grain of wheat,
> Flies on the sores of a dead child.
> Stephen

Stephen's poem reflects his developing understanding of the issues, enriched by previous experience. Thus, if meaning and purpose are foregrounded, and opportunities for collaboration and engagement are offered, alongside focused discussion of the poem's language features and form, children's comprehension will be enhanced. This avoids poems being subjected to analysis for the sake of naming literary techniques and reduces the tendency of teachers to ask endless rhetorical questions that result in predictable, convergent answers. Instead, the children's own questions and thoughts need to take centre stage, and their problems and confusions need to be voiced, discussed and responded to, through active examination and reflection.

PERFORMING POETRY

Classroom approaches need to connect to and build on children's early oral experiences of poetry and their social, physical and emotional nature. Creative teachers plan opportunities for children to perform poems in diverse ways, as this can nurture their affinity with rhythm, rhyme and beat and capitalise upon their pleasurable engagement with language. The marriage of poetry and music is centuries old, and so percussion and song, and even something as simple as the ostinato of a line of the verse can help demarcate the rhythm and point up the meaning and the tune. The physical embodiment of verse is also important and can trigger alternative ways of responding to poetry. Children's performance readings and explorations may additionally include dance and drama and mime and movement, which can energise their engagement and provoke multiple interpretations of the sense and savour of the words. Such verbal and visual performances can be enriching to both listeners and performers.

A focus on pop songs and lyrics can also pay dividends, as can developing an *X Factor*-style poetry competition and performing poems from contemporary edited collections (e.g. Julia Donaldson's and Roger Stevens').

The popularity of the national competition Poetry by Heart, run by the Poetry Archive, affirms the pleasure found in voicing poetry, inhabiting its words, tunes and textual patterns.

As Andrew Motion (2014), the ex-Poet Laureate observes, poetry is, 'emotional noise. That is why it's often able to move us before we completely understand it. Its sounds allow us to receive it in our hearts, as well as in our heads.'

Children can use poetry as a form of play-script, with groups re-voicing verses, perhaps leaning on the conversational poetry of Kit Wright and Michael Rosen, for example. Richard Brown's collections are helpfully marked for many voices and prompt collaborative play-script-like readings of his verse. Using poetry as play-scripts can facilitate spontaneous readings, as well as more thoughtfully prepared group or class presentations. Collaborating with others to bring the dead words on the page to life is a powerful way of reading and performing poetry. In seeking to understand poetry in this way, children will be experimenting with language, interpretation and meaning in their small-group discussions and shared readings and performances, as well as through experiencing the multimodal representations of others. Supported by their teacher's creative engagement and their own felt experience of the verse, new insights about particular poems' meaning, rhythm and structure can emerge. Performance can also encompass making use of digital media to augment and re-present the group's chosen poem with images, still or moving, and/or with sound and music. Capitalising on children's own digital expertise, Hughes (2013) describes how 11-year-olds created their own digital poems, connected to social-justice issues. In another class, of 9–10-year-olds, small groups selected poems to perform, and one group of girls chose 'Mary and Sarah' by Richard Edwards. During their exploration of it and in preparation for a performance of this play-script-like poem, the group decided to write their own poem, 'Boys and Girls', based loosely on Edwards' poem, and performed that instead (see Figure 9.3).

Given time to share poetry performances and reflect upon them, learners can come to understand more of the theme, structure, style and meanings of their chosen poems. In this instance, the girls' journey of understanding, appreciation and, later, composition had been largely led by their interests and engagement, supported by their teacher and the initial choice of texts. As this book argues, autonomy and ownership are key features of creative practice and contribute markedly to the children's creativity, expressed in words, both written and spoken, and in their performances.

WRITING POETRY: EXPERIMENTING WITH FORM AND FREEDOM

Poetry repays playful engagement and experimentation, both in reading and writing. A greater awareness of the power of pattern, repetition, literary language and creative energy inherent in poetry can be developed through open-ended group exploration and can then be employed in writing. Additionally, poetry can be creatively danced or sung into existence. Children may borrow a rhythm from a poem they have performed, write new lyrics to the tune of a well-known song or choose to use the form of a particular poem, imitating and leaning upon it and their experience of it gained through performance. Such imitation will not necessarily lead to close replication and may, if children are offered opportunities to playfully engage with a variety of forms, lead to invention and innovation. The deeply creative nature of poetry is highlighted by the poet James Berry when he observes:

> Poetry is a form of music that stirs connections. It's the human experience in discovery. It opens up ideas that you didn't know existed until you tried to put them

into words. Writing poetry is a way of striving to see as deeply as possible, as widely as possibly, as accurately as possible.

(Berry, 2011: 14)

In order for children to put new ideas into words, leaning on known forms can help, but first they need the opportunity to fully engage with the forms. Otherwise, their writing

Boys like messy things,
Things that Smell:
Mud fighting, football and being cheeky, it's hell.

Girls like slugy things,
Things that glow:
Make-up, sweets and marshmallows

Boys like rude things,
Things all cheeky:
Woopee cushions, fake bugs, things all freaky.

Girls like polite things,
Things all gentle:
Teddy bears, cudly toys, they go mental.

Give me, Say boys,
A football to play,
A motorbike to ride
To Zoom away

Give me, Say girls,
A pink frilly dress,
Maybe Some sparkly shoes,
To go with the rest.

Boys Say - football
Girls Say - netball
Boys Say - bike
Girls Say - Skip

Girls say - pink
Boys Say - blue
Girls Say - Sun
Boys Say - rain

Boys and girls -
They'll never agree
Till later in life
They may, maybe...

■ **Figure 9.3** A group poem, 'Boys and Girls'

may well be limited to 'knowledge telling', a limited re-description of an experience trapped by a chosen form, rather than 'knowledge transformation', transforming the experience through experimenting with the form or content to convey new meanings (Bereiter and Scardamalia, 1987). However, if children are offered the chance to experience the form, feel a particular poem's rhythms and connect to its content, this can support them in composing and shaping their thoughts. For example, two 6-year-olds, Paul and Halcyon, had been reading and miming actions to 'My Cat Jack' by Patricia Casey with the rest of the class and later wrote poems about their hamsters (see Figure 9.4).

Finding a balance between form and freedom is part of the challenge of creative literacy teaching. Although children deserve to be introduced to forms so that they can craft their own versions, they also deserve to be recognised as authors and artists and given the space and time to compose and shape their own work, finding their voices in the process. One 10-year-old, Anne Marie, leaning on Jack Ousbey's poem 'Gran Can You Rap?', cleverly borrowed the form and played with the content to create a poem about her teacher, which was both apt and amusing (see Figure 9.5). This was self-initiated, in that her teacher had shared different poems about families and invited groups of children to select one to re-read and discuss. After a period of supported exploration, during which the class found other related poems, a class poem was composed and performed. Finally, each child was invited to write their own poem about a member of their family. Anne Marie, asserting her authorial agency, however, composed this engaging verse about her teacher instead and performed it with friends in assembly.

■ **Figure 9.4** Two poems about hamsters

Mrs Q Can You Rap?

Mrs Q, was in her chair, marking all the books,
When I tapped her on the shoulder and she gave me
funny looks,
Mrs Q can you rap? Can you rap Mrs Q??
She said "Yeh I've got the knack too, who told you?
For I'm the best rapping teacher this schools ever
seen,
I'm a book reading, book marking, rap rap queen."

Mrs Q jumped on her desk in the corner of the room,
She started to dance and sing with a zoom,
She started grooving and her feet were tapping.
"The children jumped up and started clapping,
"I'm the best rapping teacher this schod's ever seen,
I'm a pencil sharpening, ruler snapping, rap rap queen."

Mrs Q whirled and twirled straight out of the door,
Gliding and sliding across the hall floor,
She danced with the caretaker, the cook and the nurse,
"As she pranced out the lobby she picked up her purse,
"She's the best rapping teacher this schod's ever seen,
She's a table teaching, word spelling rap rap queen."

By Annemarie Foster. 2010

■ **Figure 9.5** 'Mrs Q Can You Rap?'

Underpinned by a deep commitment to making and communicating meaning creatively, creative teachers seek to increase children's poetic repertoires and respond critically and evaluatively to their compositions. It is important, as Barrs and Styles (2013) observe, to avoiding eliding teachers' response to children's poetry with assessment of their writing. Rushing to assess their poetry and judge it using levels or assessment criteria is not only highly problematic, but also sidelines the significance of sensitive dialogic responses and interventions that can move learners forward. Such formative assessment is needed to enhance young writers' ability to communicate in this genre. To view poetry as a form of self-expression, as research suggests many teachers do (Collins and Kelly, 2013; Lambirth *et al.*, 2013), and thus protected from any evaluative commentary, is to fail to recognise that creativity involves both the generation and the informed evaluation of ideas. Teachers need to offer support for both. Working as co-authors and also as response partners can also help young writers and prompt them to examine the effect of their writing on an audience (see Chapter 7 for ideas about responding to writing).

Children write most effectively about aspects of life that matter to them, that have emotional relevance and connection (Fecho, 2011). They can be supported in choosing their subject matter by discussing life experiences and valuing these as a source of writing material. Starting points might include the following, though poetry may not always be the child's choice for later writing:

■ *Timelines of life*: Children complete these at home and use them in school to retell stories and revisit memories orally. After sharing some tales of lived experience in pairs and small groups, they can make a choice for writing.
■ *Treasured possessions*: Children bring in objects that remind them of someone/an event, and words that describe the object can be brainstormed. Through discussion and reflection, ideas for writing are pooled, and choices are made.
■ *Conversations or monologues*: Children think of someone and list all the things that person (mum/my teacher/brother/gran) often says. They then create poems out of these sayings, supported by Rosen's/Wright's/Ahlbergs's conversational/monologic poetry.
■ *Favourite places*: Children identify some of their favourite places and seek to revisit, remember and reflect upon them. They write about them, perhaps using their senses.
■ *Passions and persuasions*: Children share their personal perspectives on a range of issues, their hobbies, likes and dislikes, irritations and fascinations. They select a subject to examine and, perhaps, a particular poetic form.

In addition, fictional and imaginary prompts can support poetic writing, although, again, offering elements of choice will enable young writers to compose poems that connect to their thoughts and feelings and are not just limited to mirroring the form or demonstrating their knowledge of similes or metaphors, for example. Starting points might include:

■ *Magic shoes*: Decorate a pair of old shoes with glitter, wings, buttons, beads etc. Then use them as a starter; for example, 'In my magic shoes I can fly to . . ./walk over . . ./dance with . . ./see as far as . . ./travel to . . ./become. . .'.
■ *Borrow from the book blanket*: Spread the class library over the tables; children peruse in pairs, collecting titles for possible poetry writing. Pairs choose, discuss and write collaboratively, borrowing or adapting a title and generating ideas based on this.
■ *Secrets*: Children write in role as a character in a tale and share imagined/real secrets. They could start with the line, 'It's a secret but I'm really . . .' or 'It's a secret, but although Mrs Cremin thinks I'm climbing the wall bars/sharpening my pencil/reading quietly, really I'm . . .'.
■ *Desires and wishes*: These can be shaped as whole verses or one-liners. Initially, children might focus on literal desires for the world or themselves, but, with work, these can be expanded to more evocative ideas and imaginary poetic possibilities (see Figure 9.6 for some wishes composed by 9–10-year-olds).

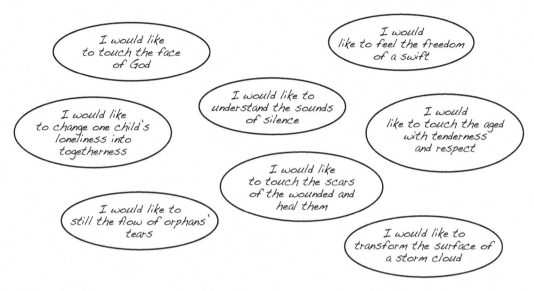

Figure 9.6 Children's poetic wishes

PROFILING POETRY IN EXTENDED LEARNING JOURNEYS

Through playful exploration and thoughtful contemplation on focused learning journeys, children can widen their knowledge and enhance their understanding and pleasure in poetry, as well as shape their own poetic voices. Creative professionals plan open-ended learning journeys involving periods of immersion in poetry and active exploration, re-presentation and discussion, as well as time for composition and reflection. They also become fully involved as artists in the classroom, participating in such explorations with the children, experimenting with language, ideas and meanings and modelling their own responses, as well as composing poetry themselves. In the process, they model being open to others' ideas and thoughts, as well as critically evaluative of their own emerging interpretations and personal poetic writing. As Hyland (2003: 10) observes, expressive approaches to poetry teaching, are 'likely to be most successful in the hands of teachers who themselves write creatively', as reflecting upon their own creative processes can help teachers teach writing from the inside out and bring their skills to class as vehicles for authentic learning (Spiro, 2007). When teachers write alongside children, as well as share their work, this can offer significant support to young writers and helps adults appreciate the challenge and pleasure in poetic writing (see also Chapters 6 and 7).

Working towards a school arts festival, for example, children might be invited to read, write, research and select a themed collection of poetry, experimenting over time with their group's representations, using music, movement, images, drama or whatever they choose, and sharing these with a visiting poet or dancer as they build towards and shape their final performance and compose pieces for publication on the school's website. The sense of ownership offered by such open, but purposeful, endeavour is likely to prompt a creative response, as it allows time for detours, aesthetic connections, the examination of alternatives and critical evaluation, as well as formative assessment and tailored teaching.

Additionally, linking poetry to work across the curriculum can be fruitful, perhaps using Gaby Morgan's World War I anthology or Grace Nichols's book inspired by art at the Tate Gallery. In one class, having interviewed various visitors as part of Black History month, the 8–9-year-olds were given free choice to write related poetry. Ahmari, leaning on Richard Brown's 'Spirit of Place' (a poetic horror story), which his teacher had read to the class several times, became unusually engaged and wrote 'The Spirit of the Boy' (see Figure 9.7). This focuses upon someone who had had a similar experience to his great-great-grandfather, who was a passenger on board the *Windrush* in 1948, when it travelled from the Caribbean to Tilbury docks. Though they had never met, Ahmari's personal connection and interest in the unit of work enabled him to produce this highly emotive and empathic poem, a testament to his creative imagination.

In extended units of work of this nature, reflection, review, feedback and celebration can be given due space and time, and children can revise their work as they prepare for a full public sharing of it. Publication and review of children's work is a significant part of the process of exploring poetry and may take many forms, including:

- *a class/school poetry anthology*, with contributions from teachers, TAs and other school staff;
- *class, group or individual poetry posters*, with some of their own poems and some chosen verse;
- *a poetry CD*, sold to parents, with musical interludes or backing music;
- *a poetry assembly*, with the words read while a looped PowerPoint display runs with images and children's designs;
- *a school poetry festival*, with groups/classes sharing their work;
- *poems in the school newsletter*;
- *poetry displayed around the school*, like the Poems on the Underground project; poetry can be enlarged and printed and prominently displayed, with accompanying children's artwork;
- *laminated poetry cards* of the children's poetic writing for guided reading;
- *a cabaret evening of poetry*, with staff and children performing poems in various ways to the parents;
- *poetry on the school website*, both printed text and filmed performances.

CONCLUSION

Poetry must be experienced before it can be analysed and deserves to be engaged with playfully, actively and creatively, as a multimodal art form. If teachers offer rich reading and response opportunities, introduce children to a wide range of poets and encourage them to suggest poems to be read and performed, then a positive climate around the art form will be established. This will be enriched by ensuring there is time to investigate and explore chosen poems in detail, and to use multiple modes and media to appropriately highlight the special nature of this intriguing game with words. Writing poetry will be an integral part of such extended explorations, not a separate activity, and one that draws upon the children's life experiences, interests and passions, as well as their experience of the work of published poets, including each other.

The Spirit of the boy

There was a boat
a crowded boat
a hopeful, crowded boat

on that boat there was a boy,
a poor boy
a poor, brave boy

And in that boy was a heart
a dripping heart
a broken dripping heart,

But within that heart there was hope
Strong hope
Strong hope and Spirit

a Spirit that kept him going
and got him a Job
a very good Job in England

The Spirit of the boy
The Spirit of boat
The Spirit of Jamacia

Figure 9.7 The Spirit of the Boy by Ahmari

FURTHER READING

Bryan, B. and Styles, M. (20113) *Teaching Caribbean Poetry*. Sheffield, UK: NATE.

Cremin, T. (2013) 'Exploring teachers' positions and practices', in S. Dymoke, A. Lambirth and A. Wilson, *Making Poetry Matters: International research on poetry pedagogy*. London: Bloomsbury, pp. 9–19.

Lambirth, A., Smith, S. and Steele, S. (2013) 'Responding to children's poetry', in S. Dymoke, A. Lambirth and A. Wilson, *Making Poetry Matters: International research on poetry pedagogy*. London: Bloomsbury, pp. 71–83.

Spiro, J. (2007) 'Teaching poetry: Writing poetry – teaching as a writer', *English in Education*, 41(3): 78–93.

CHILDREN'S BOOKS

Agard, J. and Nichols, G. (2011) *A Caribbean Dozen: Poems from 13 Caribbean poets*. London: Puffin.

Berry, J. (2011) *A Story I Am: Selected poems*. Tarset, UK: Bloodaxe.

Brown, R. (1995) *The Midnight Party*. Cambridge, UK: Cambridge University Press.

Creech, S. (2001) *Love that Dog*. London: Bloomsbury.

Crew, G. (2001) *Troy Thompson's Excellent Poetry Book*. Melbourne, Australia: Lothian.

Donaldson, J. (2014) *Poems to Perform: A classic collection chosen by the Children's Laureate*. London: MacMillan.

Horell, G., Spencer, A. and Styles, M. (2014) *Give the Ball to the Poet: A new anthology of Caribbean poetry*. London: Commonwealth Education Trust.

Kay, J. (2007) *Red Cherry Red*. London: Bloomsbury.

Morgan, G. (2014) *Poems from the First World War: Published in association with Imperial War Museums*. London: MacMillan.

Nichols, G. (2004) *Paint Me a Poem: New poems inspired by art in the Tate*. London: A & C Black.

Rosen, M. (2009) *Michael Rosen's A–Z: The best children's poetry from Agard to Zephaniah*. London: Puffin.

Stevens, R. (2013) *Off By Heart: Poems for Children to Learn and Remember*. London: A & C Black.

Willis, J. (2011) *Grill Pan Eddy*. London: Walker.

CHAPTER 10

EXPLORING NON-FICTION IMAGINATIVELY

David Reedy

INTRODUCTION

Creative teachers support their pupils in exploring a wide range of non-fiction texts, in print and multimedia forms, during literacy sessions and across the curriculum. They recognise the imaginative possibilities offered when children become interested in information they are listening to, reading and watching, and know that writing and presenting in role are powerful ways of helping children understand the content and forms of non-fiction texts. This chapter explores how to teach non-fiction texts creatively, providing opportunities for speaking, hearing, watching, drawing, reading and writing these texts for real purposes and real audiences. Creative teachers recognise the importance of engagement, motivation and playful interactions in children's encounters with information text, so that affective aspects of these texts are explored, as well as factual elements. In addition, such teachers do not see textual genres as fixed and unalterable, and so they recognise and encourage boundary crossing between genres when appropriate.

TEACHERS' KNOWLEDGE OF NON-FICTION TEXTS

'Non-fiction' is something of a portmanteau term – lots can be crammed into it. It covers a vast range of materials and continues to expand, as advances in technology offer access to new ways of creating and accessing non-fiction texts. At home and in school, a large proportion of the texts children encounter, see, hear, read and create are non-fiction. Many will be used to get things done in their everyday lives, such as replies to party invitations, text messages to communicate information, forms to fill in, lists to remember what to take to school, emails to friends, and information books and ICT-based texts to find out some specific information. Adults and children watch, read and write non-fiction for pleasure and to enhance or share knowledge of something interesting, and they engage with hobby magazines, biographies, blogs, Wikipedia, information books, reference books, docu-mentaries, 'faction' series on television, video and DVDs and so on. Non-fiction texts are also used to persuade people, perhaps to buy things, believe a case, visit places, donate to charity or put their names to a campaign. Visuals, text and sound can be used separately or combined, and a wide variety of designs and forms are experienced in books, newspapers, comics and magazines, as well as in leaflets, manuals, maps and diagrams, for example. Texts are increasingly multimodal and ICT based, as well as paper based. Children starting school in the twenty-first century are likely to be familiar with television, DVDs, computers, Internet, email, mobile phones, talking books and so on. As Bearne and Wolstencroft (2007: 78) speculate, 'It may be that there will soon be different ways of describing the mass of non-fiction encountered every day'. In the meantime, creative teachers exploit this rich variety held within the term 'non-fiction' and do not confine themselves to a limited or fixed range of texts, forms and modalities.

However, the development of creative engagement with information/non-fiction texts has been, to say the least, mixed. The introduction of the National Literacy Strategy in England in 1988 (DfEE, 1998) had a significant impact by ensuring that non-fiction texts had a central place in the English curriculum, both in reading and writing. Prior to this, teachers rarely used non-fiction texts in their teaching of reading and writing (Wray and Lewis, 1997). However, it could be argued that the approach employed in many classrooms led to teachers looking at information texts purely as a way of demonstrating fixed structural criteria by which a small set of text types could be identified and using these to write highly controlled and limited examples. Although using non-fiction text types in cross-curricular contexts was later recommended (DfES, 2006), in order to enhance their authenticity, concerns remained.

These focused on the way the range of non-fiction text types (or genres) could be seen as fixed and rigid, leading, however unintentionally, to an inflexible view of the range of text types 'permitted'. The underlying theories (Rothery, 1985; Kress and Knapp, 1992; Wray and Lewis, 1997) argue that textual genres are created by the speakers'/authors' communicative purpose in creating a text, and thus textual genres can be infinitely varied, as there are infinite reasons for creating texts. However, this was not always fully understood by busy teachers, who were guided solely by prescribed objectives that focused on the features of different text types, including those that are discursive, explanatory, persuasive, instructional or comprise non-chronological reports and recounts. Mixed non-fiction texts, such as a tourist leaflet that contains elements of persuasion, report and instructions, were also seen as problematic in some classrooms where a narrow range of non-fiction text types was taught. Teaching in these classrooms was guided by a focus on technical details of the textual structures and language features of text types, rather than on *why* they were created, *who* would read/listen to them, and *how* this impacts on form and language features.

There needs to be a focus on purpose, audience and thus construction, and a less rigid interpretation of genre, enabling children to select and use appropriate text types, remains important. However, the overwhelming emphasis in the programmes of study for English in England (DfE, 2013) is on technical features, and there is scant attention paid to why children might wish to read and write non-fiction texts. Children are expected to read, retrieve and record information from such texts, to distinguish between statements of fact and opinion and write non-narratives, using simple organisational and presentational devices (e.g. headings and subheadings, bullet points, underlining).

Creative teachers know they have to move well beyond the basic requirements of the above. They need to take into account children's interests, address audience and purpose in reading and writing, and appreciate that, in the real world, non-fiction texts do not sit in clearly marked text-type boundaries. Hybrid and playful texts, such as well-researched historical fiction, parody texts (fictional versions of non-fiction texts) such as the many different non-text parodies inserted into *The Jolly Postman* by Allan and Janet Ahlberg, or narrative non-fiction that mixes factual information with imagined actions, thoughts and feelings of a real protagonist, do not fit into neat fiction/non-fiction categories. Creative teachers will explore boundary-shifting texts with their pupils, which are often highly motivating and imaginatively conceived. Examples include *Archie's War* and *My War Diary* by Marcia Williams, Michael Morpurgo's *Only Remembered*, *Auntie Dot's Atlas* by Eljay Yildirin and Colin and Jacqui Hawkins' *Fairytale News*. Creative teachers seek to explore the affective and aesthetic aspects of non-fiction texts, as well as their efferent impact.

TEACHING NON-FICTION TEXTS CREATIVELY

The pedagogical principles outlined in the chapters on developing creatively engaged readers and writers apply just as much to non-fiction texts as they do to fiction texts. Creative teaching involves building a supportive, creative ethos, where talk and reflection around non-fiction texts, active and interactive approaches to using and creating such texts, collaboration, cooperation and risk taking are encouraged. It involves many of the same text-based activities that teachers might employ to encourage children to enjoy and be knowledgeable about fiction texts. These include, for example, reading aloud from engaging non-fiction texts, sharing enthusiasms and views on non-fiction texts, encouraging children to discuss non-fiction books and comment on them in their reading journals, pointing out series, such as the excellent National Geographic collection, and allowing children opportunities to choose their own non-fiction reading materials. As Mallett argues (2005: 229), teachers need to:

> start from the young learners – their questions, comments, wondering and curiosity about the topic in hand. The desire to know is a powerful motivator and work organized round this is likely to arouse a high level of interest and commitment.

Creative teachers of non-fiction understand that engagement and motivation are critical to learning. These dispositions shape the breadth and depth of a learning experience. When children or adults are interested and committed to something, or can see its relevance, they are more likely to explore it deeply and persist with it, even if it becomes challenging, and some non-fiction texts can be challenging if worthwhile information is to be both found and understood. The best non-fiction texts touch something within the reader. Potent, affectively involving non-fiction texts can bring a child into an experience and provide the starting point for engaged reading and creation of their own texts.

Selecting meaningful non-fiction experiences and materials that reflect authentic purposes, make links to life and offer opportunities to adopt affective as well as efferent stances towards the experience supports the creative teaching of non-fiction. Teachers should select information texts with the same care they reserve for fiction texts and should look out for a wide variety of attractive and appealing texts and ICT-based texts that invite children to become involved. This can be done in many ways – for example, through the fascination of detailed drawings, amazing photographs, three-dimensional (3D) cross-sections and diagrams, through information presented in a variety of ways – newspaper formats, fact files, realia documents, a quality written text – through a strong authorial/ personal voice and through the use of multimodal forms. Teachers should also look for content likely to engage children's interests, reflect their lives and hobbies, broaden their horizons, link to topics being studied across the curriculum and give interesting, quirky or humorous insights into well-worn subjects. These should include non-fiction texts from popular culture, such as card collections, sticker books, football programmes, catalogues and so on.

READING AND RESPONDING TO NON-FICTION TEXTS

Reading non-fiction texts can present particular challenges for the young reader. There may be technical or topic-specific vocabulary, many complex sentences, the use of the passive voice and more formal registers than those used in narrative texts. Teachers can scaffold children's reading of such texts by:

■ helping children see a genuine purpose for engaging with the text;
■ helping them activate any prior knowledge they have on or around the topic;
■ preparing them for the kind of vocabulary they might meet;
■ giving them experience in hearing and using formal registers;
■ modelling active reading of the text and the strategies they use;
■ supporting children in understanding the text;
■ ensuring that any response to the text involves the reader in remodelling the information.

One powerful way of ensuring that children make a text or texts their own and read with a real purpose is to ensure they come to them with questions and curiosity. In a class of 6–7-year-olds, a sequence of work focused on healthy living was coming towards its conclusion. The teacher encouraged the children to reflect on what they now knew and understood, and to note down anything they thought was important new knowledge to them. They were then asked if there was more that they wanted to find out and to formulate questions as the basis for further research. The teacher modelled how questions could be composed using a variety of question structures and the words 'why', 'when', 'what'. One trio of boys, Hassan, David and Bradley, decided that a really interesting thing they now knew was that getting plenty of fresh air was important, and they came up with three questions that intrigued them:

■ Can you feel air?
■ Does air help us breathe?
■ Do trees give us air?

With these questions in mind, which did not lean upon the given structure, they searched for information in the school library and online. Working in their small group, they collected books that looked relevant and used chapter headings to find sections that might be helpful. They shared information and discussed whether it answered any of their research enquiries. Occasionally they got frustrated, and adult help was needed to navigate some of the most complex texts, but they persevered. They decided to make a simple board book, either for their own class library or for a younger class. Each page would be devoted to one of their three questions. The children took their implicit knowledge of how information is displayed in expository texts in school and designed pages that contained writing text, illustration and diagrams. In Figure 10.1, one of the pages is illustrated, along with the front cover of their information book.

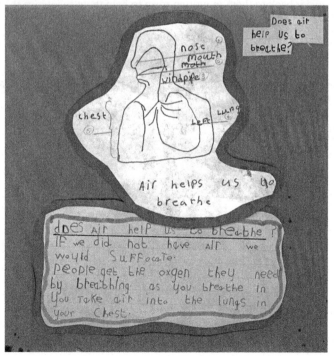

■ **Figure 10.1** Extracts from an information book on air

The paragraph in Figure 10.1 reads: 'Does air help us to breathe? If we did not have air we would suffocate. People get the oxygen they need by breathing as you breathe in you take air into the lungs in your chest.' The diagram shows how air can get from your nose and mouth into the lungs in your chest. Throughout this process, the children themselves were making the key decisions: what was of interest to them, where to go to find and read the information needed, what information they thought was relevant, the vocabulary and register they would use for the text to communicate what they had found, and the design of their final text. They were at the centre of their own work and worked creatively and with agency to pursue their own interest, supported by their teacher.

Many teachers use grids to help children to read non-fiction texts purposefully and critically and avoid them merely recalling or parroting large chunks of continuous prose. This is always alongside offering real reasons for reading. These grids and frames, or other ways of interacting with the text, such as text marking or text sequencing, help children actively engage with the text and deepen understanding. For example, one class of 6–7-year-olds were set the task of deciding which plants to purchase from a garden centre in order to plant hanging baskets for the school. They knew that only certain plants would be suitable and had to find out which plants would be best. Their teacher supported them in several ways. First, she led a discussion on what they knew already and summarised the emergent criteria – for example, the plants couldn't be too tall/wide, they should be colourful and eye catching, they should smell nice, they could have interesting leaves as well as flowers. From this scribed list, the class jointly created a research grid (see Figure 10.2). In creating this, the teacher used the children's criteria to introduce the technical vocabulary they would encounter when they came to look in gardening reference books and gave it back to them in written form to help them recognise the words later. Involving the children in making the grid, rather than simply giving them one prepared earlier, created a real sense of ownership. The teacher then modelled how to use information books to

Name of flower	Height	Spread	Flowers	Colour	Leaves	Perfume

Figure 10.2 The children's research grid

complete a row on the grid. As she modelled using an index, locating the page and scanning the text, she talked about what she was doing and why, in order to make this accessible. The children then undertook research in pairs. Throughout their research, the grid reminded them of what they needed to know; it acted as a scaffold, helping them move from joint action with an experienced teacher towards independent action.

During their research, the class used a variety of skills because they needed to use them. This purposeful, contextualised teaching, using information-gathering skills, helped keep them motivated even when the task was difficult. Persistence and resilience in the face of difficulty are key to creativity (Claxton, 2002) and were actively fostered in this work. Most of the children were willing to try several different techniques, if their first attempt to find an answer failed. The subsequent activities – sharing of suggestions, class discussion and selection, visit to the garden centre to buy the plants, planting up of the baskets and returning to information books for advice on aftercare – gave the young learners powerful reasons to read and write non-fiction texts. They experienced pleasure and pride in their hanging baskets and could see, smell and touch the results of their successful non-fiction reading.

CONNECTING NON-FICTION AND FICTION

Reading non-fiction can also be creatively enhanced by linking it to reading fiction. This can help children understand that facts are not neutral and can heighten the children's emotional engagement in, and understanding of, both the fiction and non-fiction texts being studied (Soalt, 2005), thus opening up new creative possibilities. See Chapter 3 for an example exploring pollution and the environment. A wealth of historical novels and texts linked to other learning areas exists; seeking these out and exploiting useful synergies between fiction and non-fiction representations of issues can be extremely valuable. Picture books such as *Encounter* by Jane Yolen (an alternative perspective on Columbus), *Memorial* by Gary Crew and Shaun Tan (examining society's debt to those killed in war), *I Am the Mummy Heb-Nefert* by Eve Bunting (focused on ancient Egypt), and many more, offer creative teachers considerable scope for extended explorations.

Using picture books such as the above can be a way of approaching controversial subjects for further investigation. For example, a class of 5–6-year-olds were thinking about a visit to the zoo. They generated what they knew about zoos and were invited to record this in any way they chose. Their teacher then read *Zoo* by Anthony Browne to them – a powerful picture book telling the story of a family visit to a zoo that, by careful juxtaposition of images and words, raises questions about the ethics of zoos. This led to a lively discussion about why the animals look so unhappy; the tiger, for instance, paces continuously up and down the cage, and the children's mother comments, 'poor thing'. Different perspectives began to be revealed, and the discussion led to a series of questions that children wanted to find out more about, scribed by the teacher. These included:

- What do animals do in zoos?
- What do zookeepers do?
- How are zoos good for animals?
- How are zoos bad for animals?
- Why aren't animals free?

Non-fiction books were gathered to investigate these questions, which now intrigued the class, and an authentic purpose for reading non-fiction was created. However, the children's books found were of little use, as none addressed these ethical issues. The teacher had to find more-adult texts and read them to the children, while they listened carefully to see if they answered their questions, satisfying their curiosity and concerns. Eventually, using a writing frame, they wrote about their findings. Two children wrote:

> We think zoos are good. Our first reason is because they get fed. Each animals has different food prepared for it. Our second reason is they get looked after by the vet. Our last reason is the zookeeper cares for animals. Although some people think that zoos are bad because the animals get taken away from their homes we think we have shown our point.

In this instance, it was the use of a picture book, rather than the limited information texts available to the children, that stimulated their interest and, ultimately, developed new knowledge and understanding.

In another example, a group of gifted and talented 10–11-year-olds were reading Michael Morpurgo's *Private Peaceful*, which tells the life story of a village boy and his family leading up to World War I, and his experiences there. They were also exploring the non-fiction ICT text *Fields of Glory*, the true story of Britain's first black, non-commissioned officer, from his early life as a Barnardo's boy to his later work as a professional footballer and his war service, as well as his death in action. This is told through a variety of non-fiction genres – letters, diary entries, newspaper articles, film clips and so forth. The teacher linked these two texts to an authentic non-fiction text in the children's own lives – one that many of them passed every day, often barely noticing it and rarely reading it: she took them to visit the village war memorial, with its list of names from both world wars. Reading the names, the children were struck for the first time by the realisation that some of the experiences, factual and fictional, that they were reading about and watching in class probably happened to families who lived in the village. This had a powerful emotional impact on the group. It increased the children's level of engagement and motivation, and they undertook further research into the histories behind the names on the memorial. Later, they gave a talk about this research in assembly, leading up to the sale of Remembrance Day poppies.

Throughout this cross-curricular work, the young learners used a range of research skills, interrogated primary sources, including interviewing older people in the village, and made notes and wrote brief biographies based on what they discovered. They also used drama and role-play to explore different scenes in Morpurgo's novel. This was enhanced and deepened by their exploration of the non-fiction texts, which in turn fed into their understanding of the real experiences that must have taken place in homes in their village. For example, they discussed why Charlie and Tommo's letters home make little mention of the horrors of the war, and they re-enacted the scene from the novel when Charlie explains to Tommo why, when he was home on leave, he avoided mentioning the horrors of the trenches to his wife and mother. Afterwards, children wrote their reflections on 'Why we stayed silent'. These were both factual and empathetic, as Simon's example demonstrates:

> Soldiers in the trenches often didn't let their families know how bad it was. They didn't want their families to worry. They also felt

that men should not complain. The public was protected from knowing too much. There was very little film or photographs for them to see at the time. Letters were censored so the soldier knew they had to be careful what they wrote. It must have been very hard not saying anything when you were back with your family on leave. Many soldiers took years to recover from the war. They still did not talk about it. Mrs Edwards said her father never talked about the war. He often jumped at loud noises and sometimes he cried but he tried to hide it.

In the examples outlined, the final response to non-fiction reading was action: letters were written, questions were formulated to ask on the visit to the zoo, hanging baskets were planted, and children did an assembly presentation and sold Remembrance Day poppies.

However, responses to non-fiction texts can take many forms. They can be visual, 3D, oral, drama/role-play, musical, written, or any combination of these. Some of the many possibilities that creative teachers have developed include the following:

■ After receiving a letter from the headteacher asking for ways to spend £500 on playground equipment, each class researched playground games and equipment, decided on their 'bid' and prepared an oral–visual presentation to give to the school council (which made the final decision).

■ After gathering information about the Earth in space, a class created a music-movement presentation showing the movement of the planets. They designed costumes to reflect the nature of each planet.

■ After reading about the location of towns, examining maps and visiting local bridges, children made a 3D topographical model showing their town's position on the crossing point of a river and the roads that converged at that point.

■ At the end of a unit of work on pirates, a class of children had a pirate day, when they dressed up, spoke in pirate language, made hard tack biscuits and role-played various aspects of pirate life. Some children acted as roving reporters, taking photographs, videoing and interviewing 'pirates'. They shared this at parents' evening.

■ After watching the opening sequence of the BBC series *The Blue Planet*, children generated questions about blue whales, their habitat and lifestyles and then researched in books and online to gather information to answer their enquiries. This was then communicated in a variety of forms: information leaflets, blogs, posters and a display in the school hall.

WRITING NON-FICTION TEXTS: EXPERIMENTING WITH FORM AND FREEDOM

Non-fiction writing is a complex business, involving both compositional and transcriptional skills. As the compositional aspects may be particularly challenging for children, it is tempting for them, when faced with apparently authoritative texts and maybe several sources of information, to copy or cut and paste chunks of the original(s). In order to help them

overcome this, teachers need to ensure that children engage in an extended process of teaching and learning (see Chapter 7 for a diagram of this) and during this:

■ have plenty of experience of the kinds of text they are producing;
■ engage creatively in order to examine the information;
■ find ways to gather together what they want to say;
■ make this information their own, perhaps in collaboration with others, so they can 'speak' on the topic with confidence;
■ be supported in exploring the best way to communicate the information;
■ use their own knowledge of the presentation of print and online texts;
■ shape, revise and publish their own work.

Decisions about what information to include and how to present it should depend on the purpose and audience of the communication. Thinking about this helps children see what textual and visual features can help them get their message across in the most effective way. For example, in advertising her ice-cream machine, 10-year-old Lara was prompted to make multiple decisions about presentation, colour and impact (see Figure 10.3). Another class voted on the success of the children's adverts, prompting a fuller discussion of the significance, quality and placement of both visual features and words.

SCAFFOLDS FOR NON-FICTION WRITING, PLANNING AND INFORMATION GATHERING

A range of graphic and planning frames can be helpful in supporting children to gather information and to organise how to present it. Although children should be encouraged to regard these as flexible and changeable, they can help children capture information and initial thoughts and select ones appropriate to the final outcome. So, an 'argument for/argument against' grid or an 'argument/counter-argument' grid would be helpful when preparing to write a discussion, take part in a debate or write a persuasive letter, and a 'compare and contrast grid' would be helpful if children were, for example, comparing change over time, or the characteristics of several items.

In one class, children were introduced to the idea that some parents choose to educate their children at home themselves, rather than sending them to school. This surprised them, and they were keen to think through and discuss the issue. They generated reasons why they thought children should go to school, with no one taking the opposite position. The teacher then went into role as a Mr Smith, and the children formulated questions to ask him about why he had decided to educate his child, Curtis, at home. After discussing Mr Smith's responses, they made notes on a grid (see Figure 10.4) about the pros and cons of educating children at home. This helped the children juxtapose the two viewpoints and structured their thinking in a concrete manner. They then wrote letters to Mr Smith, using a writing frame, to convince him that his son would be better off at school, explaining, for example, that he would have friends at school, would learn to cope with different people and might feel less left out (Riley and Reedy, 2005).

Creative teachers also encourage children to write mixed-genre texts, use genres from modern life and parody genres, and sometimes challenge expectations by using an unusual genre to get a message across. These forms of writing encourage risk taking and a playful approach, which help develop creativity. Genre exchange and parody texts, in particular, can help children focus on form in a playful manner. Such experiences often make children reconsider the information they have gathered in the light of this new context. In genre exchange, children gather information and then present it in a form unlikely to have been current at the time (e.g. a Roman newspaper), or in a form not usually used for presenting the kind of information given (e.g. work on class rules and respect for individuals undertaken in PSHE could be written up as 'A Recipe for a Happy and Harmonious Classroom', rather than the more usual 'Our Class Rules'). Parody texts involve placing unlikely or fictional content within a well-recognised non-fiction form, such as an instruction manual or a field guide, and foster alternative creations and playful exploration of both forms.

For example, a class of 8–9-year-olds read *How Dogs Really Work* by Alan Snow. This parody text looks like a technical manual and is a combination of non-chronological report and explanation text. The children enjoyed the humour and the detailed 'technical' illustrations and discussed the form of the book and what made it work, noting the formal register and apparently technical language and illustrations. They then went on to create, in groups, their own versions – *How X Really Works* or *A True Guide to X*. The challenge was to make the books look as convincing as non-fiction texts. Groups decided on the pages to include and allocated a page to each child, roughing out their ideas and holding editorial meetings to share and critique these. Finally, they added non-fiction elements, such as contents, index and blurb. The books became immensely popular reading resources

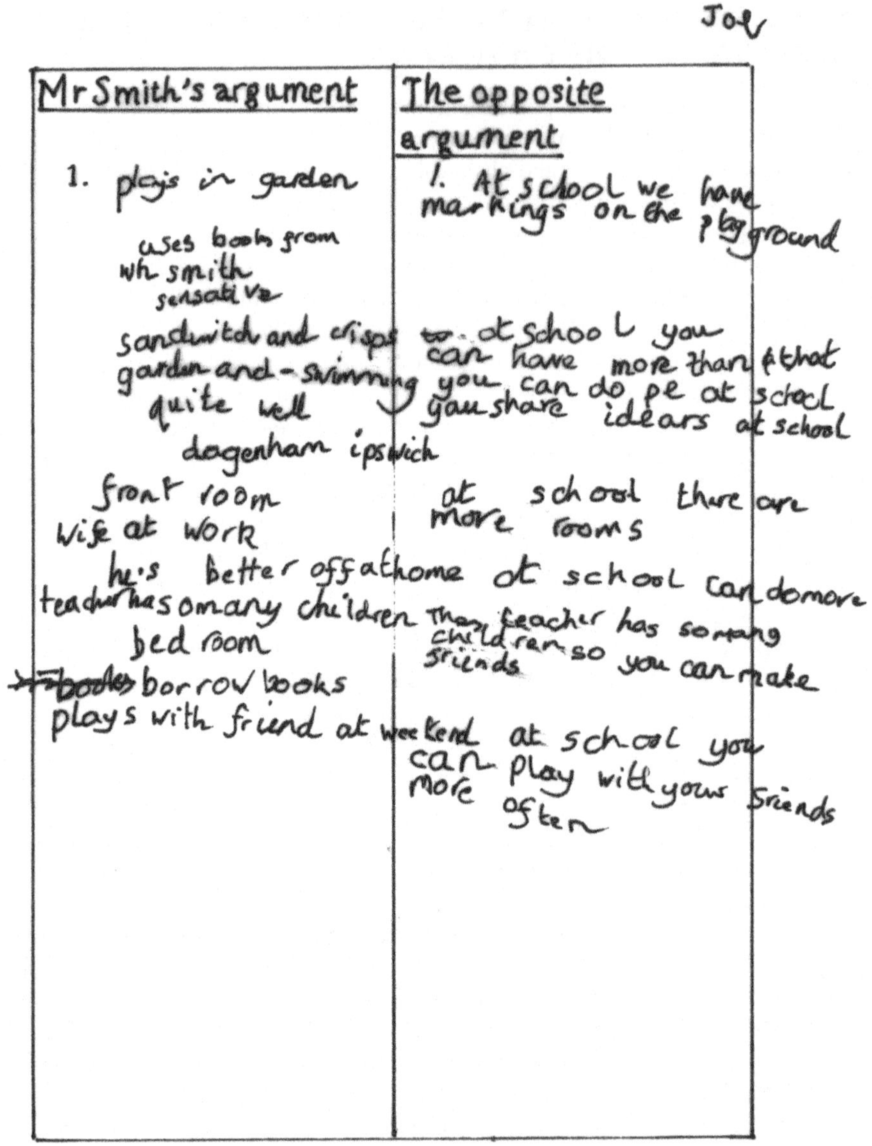

Joe

Mr Smith's argument	The opposite argument
1. plays in garden	1. At school we have markings on the playground
uses books from wh smith sensative	
sandwich and crisps garden and - swimming quite well	so at school you can have more than that you can do pe at school you share ideas at school
dagenham ipswich	
front room wife at work	at school there are more rooms
he's better off at home teacher has o many children bed room borrow books	at school can domore The teacher has so many children so you can make friends
plays with friend at weekend	at school you can play with your friends more often

▪ **Figure 10.4** Arguments for-and-against grid

in the classroom. In addition, each group prepared a talk on its specialist subject and role-played talking as an 'expert'. Through this, the children learned a considerable amount about the structures and language features of non-chronological reports and explanations. (See Figure 10.5 for an extract from one group's *The True Guide to Teachers*.)

Another example involved a class of 9–10-year-olds, who listened to and discussed *War With Troy*, an oral retelling of Homer's Iliad, by Hugh Lupton and Daniel Morden, on CD. Although the main emphasis was upon speaking and listening activities, a wide range of creative responses to the story was enabled, including writing activities (for example,

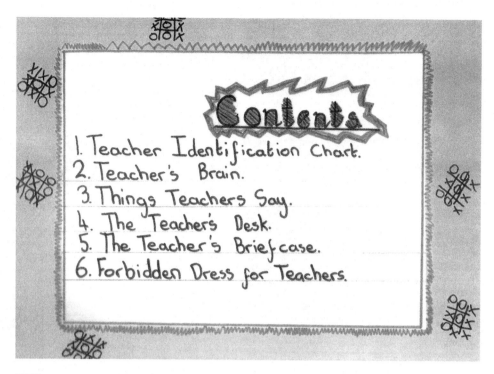

■ **Figure 10.5** The Contents to *The True Guide to Teachers*

character descriptions over time) and art activities, such as designing an *Iliad* book cover and painting a Greek vase. The major outcome was a dance performance. Towards the end of this unit of work around the story, the pupils were given free choice of creative activity, in response to the story as a whole or a favourite scene. Many children chose to make 3D models of their favourite scene (see Reedy and Lister, 2007, for examples), whereas others made newspapers to illustrate episodes in the narrative (Figure 10.6).

The extensive newspaper parody included a range of perspectives relating to the story, including: news reports of the outcome of the battle, opinion pieces exploring the reasons leading to this event, interviews with participants, human-interest stories with the family of Hector, quizzes, sports and fashion pages, and predictions/prophecies in the style of astrologers. Deep knowledge and experience of the newspaper genre were used to compose and design this very amusing text, read with enthusiasm by adults and children alike across the year group. This example demonstrates the importance of the children being given the opportunity to decide themselves what their creative response could be and thus owning both the purpose (to entertain, amuse and describe from multiple viewpoints) and the audience (the rest of the year group and the teachers). This ensured there was a genuine focus for the writing, as well as shaping the inventive final product.

Creative teachers of writing look out for real reasons for children to write and create non-fiction multimodal texts. These might include:

■ setting up genuine enterprise initiatives, so that children make posters, sales information sheets, letters to sponsors, launch information and so on;

THE WINGED MESSENGER

BRINGING NEWS TO TROJANS EVERYWHERE   3RD MARCH 1250BC

The Brutal Death of a Trojan Prince

A nation mourns

BY LOUISE LEE
EPIC REPORTER

Yesterday saw the death of the Trojan hero and prince, Hector.

He was forced into battle against the Greeks because his younger brother Paris, had kidnapped Helen, Queen of Sparta and wife of Menelaus, after Aphrodite had promised him the most beautiful woman in the world, following the golden apple incident. Hector killed Patroclus, the best friend of mighty Achilles, so Achilles wanted revenge in the shape and form of DEATH! Hector's death followed a mighty battle, between the two heroes. Hector was taken by surprise, when he first saw Achilles, as he thought he had killed him the day before, but it was really Patroclus dressed in his best

GLORIOUS HECTOR, TRAGICALLY KILLED YESTERDAY

Continued on Page 3

Achilles Exclusive 2 Paris or Helen ; Who is to blame? 4 Priam, Hecuba and Andromache mourn 5 Golden Apple Quiz 7 Fashion 8 Cassandra Predicts 9 Sport 10

---

3 ||| A Hero's Death   3:3:1250 BC

WE WERE CHEATED BY THE GODS

Continued from page 1.
recognisable armour. The death of his best friend, made Achilles return to battle, after he sulkily refused to fight, following his argument with Agamemnon. The battle was raging on the plains of Troy, when spoilt Achilles and glorious Hector met for the last time. Pretty Prince Paris and his brother brave Hector, had just watched swift-footed Achilles spear to death their youngest brother godlike Polydorus. Glorious Hector stood no chance against selfish Achilles, as he had new armour from Hephaestus, the God's blacksmith. Whilst heroic Hector and

ZEUS' SCALES ARE HECTOR'S DOWNFALL

the plains of Troy, up on Mount Olympus the Gods and Goddess' fought over who would be mourned over the next day. Golden Apollo, our great protector and stunning Aphrodite, Helen's protector argued against wise Athene, who looked after Achilles and ox-eyed Hera protector of the Greeks. As Hector watched Polydorus fall, he ran to Achilles, who seeing the magnificent frame of glorious Hector was clearly scared, but his anger at brave Patroclus' death made him fight. As stroppy Achilles charged, Golden Apollo created a mist, which confused the sulky Greek, and allowed our Trojan Prince the chance to escape, but

The moment of Hector's death; watched by the Gods

brave Hector. Later that day, Achilles found our hero, and called him a murderer. Glorious Hector tried to run, but sly Athene pretended to be Deiphobos, Hector's favourite brother, and this let selfish Achilles get close to glorious Hector. At this moment, father of the Gods, Zeus, who could not decide who should win, was putting death powder into his golden scales. On one side the powder was for brave Hector, on the other it was for stroppy Achilles. As he held out the scales they fell on one side, just at that moment Achilles' spear pierced the side

THE REALLY BIG SPEAR

SALE STARTS TODAY THE TROJAN SPEAR CO.

---

5 ||| A HERO'S DEATH   FAMILY'S DESPAIR

A FAMILY MOURNS

EXCLUSIVE; HOW WILL WE GO ON

King Priam, Queen Hecuba and Andromache came outside their picturesque palace to speak about their splendid son and heroic husband. Priam commented first "You must understand that we have all been affected by Hector's death, I've starved myself silly, Hecuba has had no sleep and Andromache is crying herself to sleep, but this war will go on. If Achilles has read our published copy of The Winged Messenger he will know that I will beg and beg and beg if I can have my son's precious body back. I know Achilles is grieving himself recently so he must know what I'm

HECUBA ON LEARNING OF THE DEATH OF HECTOR

Priam fought back the tears as he tried to speak some more when an old, wrinkly pale Hecuba speaks of her misery, "My son, my boy, I remember when he was eight or nine I could see a thirst to fight, oh not like Achilles though, who would pick a fight with anyone, no my child had a thirst to fight for his country and die for it. I have been through what no parent should go through, your own flesh and blood die before you, it breaks my heart to see my eldest son dying helpless on the dusty plains, trying to protect Troy and it did him no good, he had the perfect life, a pretty yet wife and a bouncing baby boy, and what did he chose to do? The easy life or the wicked, disastrous hard one, he chose the life-eating hard one. I can't bear this stupid war, I have lost three wonderful sons in this battle. I could not image what I would do if Deiphobus and Paris were killed!"

A tear-stained Andromache cried. "My son will never know who his father is, alas I will keep the memory alive. He confided in me that he didn't agree with Paris bringing Helen here, but he cared too deeply about what Paris thought so he kept it a secret. As far as that scumbag Achilles is concerned, how dare he treat my beloved husband's body like it was some sort of wild boar, it is unbelievable. Did he think of my son and how he would never grow up to know his dad when he savagely murdered Hector? Did he think of Priam and Hecuba when he killed their child? When he brutally disrespected Hector, did he think of me watching my husband die, as he gleefully mistreated Hector? No he did not. I hope he rots in Hades Hall!"

A TEARFUL ANDROMACHE

PRIAM SPEAKS OF HIS HEARTACHE

going through. I will give him anything to get my son's body back, even if that means he invades my palace or kills me first, I'll get Hector's body back, I promised him that, Hecuba can confirm this, but he is the first thing I think about in the morning and the last thing I think about at night!"

---

9 ||| THE WINGED MESSENGER   PREDICTIONS

CASSANDRA PREDICTS
WHAT DO THE GODS HAVE IN STORE FOR YOU?

Born under the sign of ZEUS;
The Gods have a surprise for you, not necessarily a good one, that doesn't mean that Zeus has given up on you.

Born under the sign of HERA;
You will gain from someone else's losses and will think greater of yourself, but it may get you into deep water.

Born under the sign of APOLLO;
You are reliable and people will consider you a God, alas don't believe this yourself or something bad will happen!

Born under the sign of APHRODITE;
You will search for family secrets, but will have to put a friend's trust on the line to discover it.

Born under the sign of POSEIDON;
You will suddenly want to entertain people at a feast; you will become a great success. Hip, hip Hooray

Born under the sign of ARTEMIS;
You will give up your bow and arrows for some leisure, Good for you!

Born under the sign of ATHENE;
You will climb up the career ladder like there's no tomorrow, from promotion to promotion, but remember to spend some time with your families.

Born under the sign of HERMES;
You get kinder by the second, and you never know why you have masses of friend!

Born under the sign of DEMETER;
You are always searching for something; you may soon find it. Don't let a loved one eat pomegranate seeds.

Born under the sign of DIONYSUS;
You have a busy social life, you will party day in and day out. So get the wine out!

Born under the sign of HEPHAESTUS;
You have to work hard for a living, but you will marry a beautiful woman.

Born under the sign of ARES;
Troubled times are near, but you are willing to fight. Be brave your country needs you.

WANT A MORE PERSONAL PREDICTION?

VISIT CASSANDRA AT THE PALACE

■ **Figure 10.6** Extracts from the Trojan newspaper

■ writing a letter to the class that demands research and a response; for example, from the local Wildlife Trust, asking them to advise on where to site bird boxes in the school grounds;

■ creating documentaries on a topic being studied in another curriculum area, writing the voice-over and performing it;

■ creating non-fiction book-making opportunities – from books for younger children to fanzines and hobby magazines;

■ engaging the class in setting up a mini-museum in school and opening this to the community;

■ undertaking an extended drama in which a tourist shop for a place is established;

■ making safety films, posters and information leaflets to inform other children in the school, as part of science topics, such as electricity;

■ preparing a non-fiction text on paper/screen about an out-of-school activity they are passionate about;

■ getting involved in genuine community-based campaigns/or national initiatives, such as recycling or responding to national calls to look after rare butterflies;

■ creating advertising leaflets for a local venue or a place visited on a school trip;

■ contributing to the school handbook or making their own child's prospectus.

PROFILING NON-FICTION TEXTS IN EXTENDED LEARNING JOURNEYS

Creative teaching around non-fiction texts takes place in both literacy sessions and across the curriculum. The two contexts are often combined to provide an extended creative journey, where children learn from first-hand experiences, use non-fiction skills in context and read and write for real purposes. Teachers can model creative involvement and guide the experience by taking an active role on such extended journeys.

For example, working with a class of 8–9-year-olds, a teacher planned an extended thematic unit on World War II. In both history and literacy sessions, the children undertook research on evacuation, using information books and newsreel film cuttings and interviewing local people. To make the experience more real, the teacher also planned an extended role-play. The children had made cardboard suitcases in design and technology and brought clothes from home and a toy to pack. The class was taken to the school hall, labelled and made to sit in rows. In role – and in costume – their teacher played a WRVS volunteer and was thus able to organise the evacuees. The children all walked in a crocodile to an actual local station and took a train journey. Some mothers waved them off and 'cried'. Unbeknown to them, the children were taken to a rather drab community hall, and a group of adults (parents from another class, role-playing host families) came in to select the child/children they wanted. Many of the adults had dressed in period costume. The atmosphere changed as children were taken away, friends were separated, and just a few remained. Some 'late' host families turned up. Soon, only two children were left, unallocated and unwanted.

Afterwards, the children discussed their experiences and feelings. They reflected on what they had learned, and how it added to the research and reading they had already undertaken on evacuation. They wrote 'faction' accounts of evacuation, drawing on their journey and their research, and read these to writing partners, who commented on factual accuracy and atmosphere. Throughout the unit, the teacher continued to weave role-play and factual investigation together. For example, ration cards were issued one day, and a special wartime school lunch was served. A bomb shelter was created in the classroom, sirens sounded, and bomb-raid sound effects were played as the children sheltered in it. The teacher led community singing to keep their spirits up. Note taking and research skills were taught in the context of guided-reading sessions, using books about the war, and children selected their own areas for further research. They recorded some of these as wartime radio broadcasts, using the call sound 'London calling, London calling'. This example shows how creative teachers undertake extended explorations and weave seamlessly together learning about a period and learning about non-fiction texts, through involving the children in playful and imaginatively engaging experiences that foster their curiosity and provide 'real' purposes for reading, research and text production.

CONCLUSION

Young people and adults continue to need to read and write non-fiction texts, as these help us organise our life and work. For many readers and writers, they offer pleasure and satisfaction too. Increasingly, non-fiction texts are multimodal and ICT based. The need for teachers to support children as they read and write non-fiction texts on paper and on screen is now well accepted in primary schools. However, the recognition that purpose and audience shape their encounters with non-fiction texts, and that the necessary skills are best taught in the context of needing to use them, is perhaps less well established. Creative teachers of non-fiction lead the way in promoting this recognition and ensuring that children's experiences with non-fiction texts in school become as rich and engaging as their encounters with narrative and poetic texts.

FURTHER READING

Mallett, M. (2007) *Active Encounters: Inspiring young readers and writers of non-fiction 4–11*. Leicester, UK: United Kingdom Literacy Association.

Mallett, M. (2011) *The Primary English Encyclopaedia* (4th edn). London: David Fulton.

Reedy, D. and Lister, B. (2007) '"Busting with blood and gore and full of passion": The impact of an oral retelling of the *Iliad* in the primary classroom', *Literacy*, 41(1): 3–9.

Wilson, A. and Scanlon, J. (2011) *Language Knowledge for Primary Teachers* (4th edn). Oxford, UK: Routledge.

CHILDREN'S BOOKS

Ahlberg, A. (1995) *The Jolly Pocket Postman*. London: Penguin.

Browne, A. (1994) *Zoo*. London: Red Fox.

Cambridge Schools Classics Project (2005) *War With Troy*. Cambridge, UK: Cambridge University Press.

Crew, G. and Tan, S. (1999) *Memorial*. Sydney, Australia: Lothian.

Dowswell, P. (2014) *The Story of the First World War*. London: Usborne.

Hawkins, C. and Hawkins, J. (2004) *Fairytale News*. London: Walker.

Morpurgo, M. (2004) *Private Peaceful*. London: HarperCollins.

Morpurgo, M. (2014) *Only Remembered*. London: Jonathan Cape.

National Geographic (2010) *Wild Animal Atlas: Earth's astonishing animals and where they live*. National Geographic.

National Geographic (2014) *Infopedia*. National Geographic.
Powell, J. (2005) *Fields of Glory: The diary of Walter Tull*. London: Longman Digitexts.
Snow, A. (1995) *How Dogs really Work*. London: Collins.
Williams, M. (2007) *Archie's War*. London: Walker.
Williams, M. (2008) *My War Diary*. London: Walker.
Yolen, J. and Shannon, P. (1992) *Encounter*. New York: Harcourt Brace Jovanovich.
Yilirim, E. (1997) *Auntie Dot's Atlas*. London: Collins.

CREATIVELY EXPLORING VISUAL AND DIGITAL TEXTS

Eve Bearne

INTRODUCTION

Visual texts make an important contribution to our lives. Images, on paper and on screen, inform, direct, amuse, entertain and help us relax or pass the time. In terms of paper-based texts, words are now almost always accompanied by photographs, diagrams or drawings, and print is often enhanced by a variety of font sizes and shapes. For children, particularly, there is a wealth of complex and challenging picture books, as well as detailed information books where the images carry as much meaning as the words. These developments have been made possible by the use of digital technology, which has enhanced production and colour processes. Equally, however, digital technology has had an immense impact on screen texts: computer games, the Internet, television and film. A wide range of multimodal texts exist, in paper form, on screens and as dramatic performances; everyday texts include the visual – maps, icons, advertising, television, film – so that visual literacy is an essential element of contemporary literacy. This chapter describes some of the creative ways that teachers have used visual texts in the classroom and how they have harnessed the children's home experience and expertise in digital and popular cultural texts.

Although the NC in England (DfE, 2014) does not specify the use of visual texts, there is scope for including them in the wider repertoire. Picture books, graphic novels and comics, for example, will form part of the range from the early years to the end of primary education. In the reading comprehension section, there is emphasis on children experiencing a wide range of poems, stories and non-fiction, and books that are structured in different ways. In writing composition, children are expected to write narratives based on personal experiences and, later, consider how authors have developed characters and settings in what they have read, listened to or seen performed. In relation to spoken language, there is ample scope both for drawing on visual and dramatic sources and making and performing multimodal texts. In Wales and Scotland, there is more overt recognition of visual literacy, and teachers are expected, for example, to ensure that children themselves can understand how something can be represented in different ways – for example, in moving image, multimodally and in print.

VISUAL AND DIGITAL TEXTS

The increase in use of images and the screen means that many everyday texts are now multimodal, accompanying words with moving or still images, sound and colour. Teaching, too, is enhanced by the availability of different technologies that make discussions of the role of image, sound, colour and variations in typography much more possible through different media:

■ the computer – Internet information and PowerPoint presentations;
■ paper-based texts – picture books, graphic novels, comics, magazines, information books;
■ sound and visual media – radio, television, videos and DVDs.

Visual literacy, Moline (2012) argues, is fundamental to learning. He says that we are all bilingual – that our second language, which we do not speak but which we read and write every day, is visual. The everyday ubiquity of visual texts makes demands on teachers helping young learners become discerning and critical readers and writers. Teaching about these multimodal texts means more than concentrating on the words; it involves being explicit about the contributions to meaning made by different combinations of modes. These include:

■ gesture and/or movement;
■ images – moving and still, diagrammatic or representational;
■ sound: spoken words, sound effects and music;
■ writing or print, including typographical elements of font type, size and shape.

There is ample evidence of even very young children's experience of media and digital technologies (Marsh *et al.*, 2005; Bearne *et al.*, 2007; Vanderwater *et al.*, 2007; Wohlwend, 2009). In the street, home and school, they are surrounded by texts that merge pictures, words and sound. They expect to read images as well as print, become attuned to the design of texts (Kress and van Leeuwen, 2006), increasingly use computers in seeking information and composing their own texts, and are capable of handling the demands of the technology from the earliest years.

TEACHING VISUAL TEXTS AND DIGITAL CREATIVELY

As the range of available texts grows, and a more integrated approach to the curriculum becomes increasingly important, visual literacy is certainly an area that needs attention in school. The term has evolved from different theoretical sources, including aesthetics, art history, cultural studies, education, linguistics, media studies and semiotics, and has a complex theoretical history, but, in a very useful document, Bamford defines visual literacy as the ability to construct and interpret meaning from visual images. She suggests that it involves:

developing the set of skills needed to be able to interpret the content of visual images, examine the social impact of those images and discuss purpose, audience and ownership. It includes the ability to visualise internally, communicate visually and read and interpret visual images.

(Bamford, 2008)

This definition offers clear similarities to the development of print literacy. There are parallels between elements of different kinds of written text, with different organisational features and stylistic aspects, and visual texts. Both can be engaged with, enjoyed, critically appreciated and analysed. Like written texts, multimodal texts have structures that can be discussed, explained, modelled and taught. However, as children bring rich resources in terms of their experience of visual texts, it is as well to start there – with their knowledge and experience drawn from exposure to the visual from birth (Marsh, 2005).

Children's familiarity with visual texts gives them a good grounding for their appreciation and response to other kinds of text. Films and other screen texts are ideal vehicles for involving all pupils and for developing their collaborative creativity; not only do children have experience and expertise in reading visual texts, but everyone views them together, generating curiosity, problem solving and collaboration, as they make sense of what they see together. Screen texts offer teachers a perfect opportunity to adopt a more flexible and creative approach to language, interpretation and meaning. In this way, viewing and making visual texts can contribute to a classroom atmosphere of openness and the development of an environment that encourages children to offer their own views, ask their own questions and play with ideas and possibilities. Teachers can seize opportunities to pay more attention to screen texts in extended units of work. This may involve comparing the presentation of a narrative as a novel and as a film – for example, exploring the different ways in which meanings are conveyed in both Ted Hughes' book *The Iron Man* and the film *The Iron Giant*. Additionally, teachers can creatively explore a chosen film as a core text and enable the children to develop their literacy skills in the process. It is worth remembering, however, that films are texts in themselves that can be read, studied and enjoyed for their own worth, not only as vehicles for developing reading and writing (Bearne and Bazalgette, 2010).

TEACHERS' AND CHILDREN'S KNOWLEDGE OF VISUAL AND DIGITAL TEXTS

Although there is considerable evidence of children's affinity with multimodal texts, and the capacity of young people to respond flexibly to new technologies as they emerge has been well documented (Robinson and Mackey, 2006; Parry, 2014), there is much less evidence of teachers' experience of screen texts and confidence in using digital technology. There seems to be significant variation in the levels of confidence and expertise brought by pre-service and serving teachers to using digital technology in the classroom (Hague and Williamson, 2009). However, research indicates increasing levels of confidence and enthusiasm for using digital technology in schools, particularly in primary schools (Smith *et al.*, 2008; Graham, 2012). On the other hand, although teachers may feel more confident about using digital technology in their teaching, it seems that, for a variety of reasons, their experience and competence can be ignored in classrooms (Honan, 2008). In addition, research has shown a level of 'blindness' on the part of teachers to the levels of expertise and experience of digital texts, particularly popular cultural texts, that children bring to the classroom (Arrow and Finch, 2013; Cremin *et al.*, 2015). This means that many of the assets brought to the classroom by children – and teachers themselves – are being sidelined, with potentially serious consequences for creative engagement.

In seeking to teach creatively and develop children's creativity, teachers may need to reconsider their own views, experiences and attitudes towards visual and digital texts and also find ways to recognise and build upon the children's strengths. Where teachers have been prepared to bring together popular cultural texts and school literacy, the results have been promising, as shown in research in New Zealand schools: 'The more links we make to the children's real world, the more effective our teaching. For reluctant readers and writers, linking to topics that they find motivating can make a huge difference' (Dickie and Shuker, 2014: 35).

The teachers involved in this research project discovered the powerful effects of hooking into children's knowledge of characters such as Ben 10, a range of superheroes, Barbie, princesses, Harry Potter and sporting heroes. Some built on the children's knowledge of computer games, pop stars and favourite characters in animated television films and were impressed by the children's in-depth knowledge and engagement with their favourites. Not only did these teachers make important links between home- and school-based learning, they demonstrated that innovative teaching has benefits for teacher and learners.

READING AND RESPONDING TO VISUAL AND DIGITAL TEXTS

Working within the requirements of routine literacy sessions, Rowena Watts (2007) set out to use film creatively, to encourage close reading of the text and multiple responses. Drawing on Woods's (2001) definition of 'creative reading' and Craft's (2000) conception of possibility thinking, she developed a teaching unit where her class of 6–7-year-olds learned how to read film and designed storyboards for their own films. After the project was over, she interviewed the children about whether being taught about reading film had made any difference to their watching films at home. Rosie commented, 'Yeah, it has made you um actually understand more about how a character is feeling – and his actions and how it makes it look more exciting or magical' (Watts, 2007: 106). Rowena observed that the children had:

> learned to identify and use cues for character development; to use colour as silent signs to create mood or convey feeling. Ultimately they had learned the craft of the meaning maker and in doing so had improved their ability to understand through inference, deduce meanings, use context, interpret ideas and respond to them.
>
> (Ibid.: 108)

All of these elements contribute to children becoming creative readers, readers who ask questions of texts, use available evidence and each other to make multiple interpretations and personal connections, and imagine, appreciate and understand the texts they read on several levels.

As the UKLA *Reading on Screen* project discovered (Bearne *et al.*, 2007), many children not only use sophisticated screen reading processes, but can also explain how they go about reading screen texts. Listening to the voices of two 10-year-olds, Peter and Poppy, reveals how these experienced readers vary their strategies according to whether they are reading on paper or on screen:

> When asked where they started to read a book, comic or magazine, Poppy said: *With books you start at the first page, start reading at top and stop if it gets boring.* With magazines: *you flick through and look for a good picture and read about it.*

Peter said he starts reading comics at the same place as a book *but maybe flick to the end*. He uses a more strategic process with magazines: *flick through, look for football, game cheats, check for games I'm playing at the moment*.

With computer game reading, Peter *looks for important buttons on the keyboard* at the start of the game and Poppy looks for the *main symbols*. During a game Peter explained: *if it's a racing game, you keep your eyes on the car . . . if it's a fighting game, then keep your eyes on the other person*. Poppy concentrated *on the main character*.

(Bearne *et al.*, 2007: 15; italics in the original)

Although children's comments on their approaches to reading on screen are illuminating, there is still a need for teachers themselves to get to grips with reading moving image texts. After a British Film Institute project designed to develop leading teachers' confidence in using film in the classroom, the teachers involved were asked to reflect on the project:

I think it's opened our eyes really. A light went on in my head when I thought you could read a film like you read a book and get the inference and deduction out of there, so it's been a huge change for me.

(Marsh and Bearne, 2008: 18)

The leading teachers involved in this project found similarities between reading written narratives and reading multimodal narrative texts. To do either means being able to:

- understand the narrative, even if it involves flashbacks or fantasy episodes;
- notice how colour and motif (in sound or in images) are used to help the reader/viewer keep the thread of the story;
- comment on how sound, music, colour, viewpoint/camera angle and focus contribute to creating atmosphere or establishing setting;
- read facial expression, gesture and posture;
- discuss the use of perspective and camera angle or point of view in communicating with the reader/audience.

All of these features – story structure, setting, characterisation and author's intention or theme – are familiar from reading books with children. Any of them can become the focus for viewing a film as a whole class and for teaching film creatively.

WRITING VISUAL AND DIGITAL TEXTS: EXPERIMENTING WITH FORM AND FREEDOM

As the earlier explanation of multimodality might suggest, there is an inherent problem with using the word 'writing' for the multimodal texts that children compose. When children make visual texts, they are combining modes – whether in picture books, information texts, moving images or in PowerPoint presentations. Of course, these may well include writing at some stage, in preparation or production of the texts, but the power of the text will not rely on the written word alone. Presentational software allows for a range of composing activities – poetry, information and persuasive texts, and narrative.

Although there are parallels between writing and composing multimodal texts, elements of movement, sound, colour and design have to be taken into account. Composing multimodal texts includes:

■ *deciding on mode and content for specific purpose(s) and audience(s)*:
  – choosing which mode(s) will best communicate meaning for specific purposes (deciding on words rather than images or gesture/music rather than words);
  – using perspective, colour, sound and language to engage and hold a reader's/viewer's attention;
  – selecting appropriate content to express ideas and opinions;
■ *structuring texts*:
  – paying conscious attention to the design and layout of texts; organising texts using pages, sections, frames, paragraphs, screens, sound sequences;
  – structuring longer texts with visual, verbal and sound cohesive devices;
  – using background detail to create mood and setting;
■ *using technical features for effect*:
  – handling the technical aspects and conventions of different kinds of multimodal text, including line, colour, perspective, sound, camera angles, movement, gesture, facial expression and language;
  – choosing language, punctuation, font, typography and presentational techniques to create effects and clarify meaning.

Further to these text elements, there is the need to reflect on and evaluate both the process and the product:

■ explaining choices of modes(s) and expressive devices, including words;
■ improving the composition: reshaping, redesigning and redrafting for purpose and readers'/viewers' needs;
■ commenting on the success of a composition in fulfilling the original design aims.

MAKING MULTIMODAL TEXTS

The following example shows how a class of 6–7-year-olds created their own comic strips, after reading and analysing a range of comics.

In an inner-city primary school in Balsall Heath, Birmingham, most of the pupils have English as an additional language. Two teachers worked with a small group of 6–7-year-olds whose literacy ability was high, on a two-week teaching sequence designed to introduce children to how multimodality works in comic-strip formats. The teachers began by using a range of comics to familiarise the children with the features of comic-book texts, including speech bubbles, captions, font shape and size, and the shape and size of the frames. They then asked the children, in pairs, to come up with questions they could ask about a given comic strip:

Zubair and Muhammed: Why are some pictures dark or light?
Saynab: Light pictures show something happy; dark pictures show something sad.

Saynab and Ameena: Why are the boxes different sizes?
Miryam and Summayah: Something is happening slowly and something is happening fast.

The children talked about how these different features affected how the story was told, and the teachers noted these as a plan to help the children compose their own endings of the Daedalus and Icarus story, as told in the comic-book-format version of Greek myths retold by Marcia Williams (2006). The class worked in pairs to present freeze-frames of different events in the story, and these were photographed and printed off for the children to create the speech for each frame. The idea was to concentrate on characterisation (*What do we know about the characters? How do we know?*) and feelings. While they were doing this, one of the teachers noted what they were saying so that they could use their own words for later work on a comic strip. One pair for example said, 'Stop! Don't go, you're too close to the sun', and the other called, 'Help! Help! I'm melting from the sun!'

Finally, the children were asked to work out a different ending for the story and role-play their ending. They composed their own versions, planning first with sticky notes and then drawing their own comic strips (see Figure 11.1).

The children evaluated their planning in pairs, giving each other advice about improving their comic strips before the final version. They showed differences in understanding about multimodality: some were more word focused; others were more image focused. Una suggested that Saynab should do more captions and movement lines, whereas Saynab said that Una needed more writing. However, Una defended her choice of not including a caption for every picture, as, 'it's obvious from the picture what's happening', showing a good sense of how words and pictures interact to make meaning in a multimodal

■ **Figure 11.1** A comic strip

text. This project was the first time the two teachers had tackled reading and writing multimodal texts, and the children's engagement and achievement encouraged them to plan for more work on multimodality.

VISUAL APPROACHES TO WRITING

In a class of 5–6-year-olds, a teacher developed an extended unit of work on narrative designed to develop descriptive writing skills. Starting with the Disney film *Ponyo*, directed by Hayao Miyazaki, and a selection of non-fiction texts, she planned for a range of written outcomes over the course of an extended learning journey covering reading comprehension, writing composition and vocabulary, grammar and punctuation elements from the National Curriculum for English.

Reading comprehension

Children should be taught to:

- link what they read or hear read to their own experiences;
- discuss word meanings, linking new meanings to those already known;
- understand the book by:
  - drawing on what they already know or on background information and vocabulary provided by the teacher;
  - discussing the significance of illustrations and events;
  - making inferences on the basis of what is being said and done;
  - predicting what might happen on the basis of what has been read so far;
- participate in discussion about what is read to them, taking turns and listening to what others say;
- explain clearly their understanding of what is read to them.

Writing composition

- write sentences by:
  - saying out loud what they are going to write about;
  - composing a sentence orally before writing it;
  - sequencing sentences to form short narratives;
  - re-reading what they have written to check that it makes sense;
- discuss what they have written with the teacher or other pupils;
- read aloud their writing clearly enough to be heard by their peers and the teacher.

Writing – vocabulary, grammar and punctuation

Children should be taught to develop their understanding of concepts set out in English Appendix 2 (DfE, 2013) by:

- leaving spaces between words;
- joining words and joining clauses using 'and';

- beginning to punctuate sentences using a capital letter, full stop, question mark or exclamation mark;
- using a capital letter for names of people and the personal pronoun 'I';
- using elements of grammar from Year 2: nouns, noun phrases, adjectives.

The teacher planned session 1 to familiarise the children with the film. They began by watching the first five minutes or so and then stopped to discuss what the film might be about. Through open-ended questioning, they discussed clues in the introduction that might help them predict the story-line. In the following session, they watched the trailer of the film to refresh their memories, and the teacher uploaded images of the main events of the film on to the IWB, so that the children could discuss the sequence:

- Was this in the beginning of the film?
- Who is this character?
- Which part of the film is this?

As the discussion progressed, she wrote key words on the board, such as characters' names and 'tsunami', and then gave the children a set of four images from the film to sequence correctly, stick in their books and write captions for what was happening at each point of the story.

In sessions 3 and 4, the children were to research a sea creature to write their own sea-creature fact file. The teacher explained that a non-fiction text is based on real facts and information and showed the children clips of sea creatures on the IWB. She asked them to focus on what the creature looks like and any information about how it moves, what it eats and how big it is, and she noted their comments on the whiteboard. They then looked at a big non-fiction book together, discussing the main features. In groups, the children decided on their own sea creature to research, from a variety of non-fiction books. Each child was responsible for researching a particular aspect of the creature. On the visualiser, the teacher showed the children her own fact file, indicating the main features of non-fiction books: titles, captions, subheadings, images, labels and different fonts and typographic styles.

For session 5, the teacher wanted to focus on noun phrases and commas. She planned for the children to write list poems describing what it would be like to be a deep-sea diver. On the IWB, she showed children clips of deep-sea divers swimming in the ocean, asking:

- What do they see (creatures, shipwrecks etc.)?
- How big do the creatures look in comparison with the divers?
- What colours can you see?

In role, the children pretended to be deep-sea divers swimming around the classroom, while the teacher played background sounds of sea creatures, waves and deep-sea divers' breathing. As a class, they then wrote a list poem that the children could use as a model for writing their own poems describing what a deep-sea diver might see in the ocean: 'In the ocean I can see … noisy dolphins and furious sharks, darting and diving, glittery rainbow fish swimming slow, sharp and scary'.

As the culmination of the unit of work, the children were going to use their list poems as a basis for longer pieces of descriptive writing, drawing on their imaginations, knowledge of other stories and knowledge of sea creatures. They first watched a video of a deep-sea dive; their teacher had explained that they were going to imagine they were deep-sea divers and write their own description of a deep-sea dive experience, which was to be read to a younger class – so it had to be interesting, and this could be achieved by using suitable adjectives. The class worked with their talk partners to think up adjectives to describe what they saw in the video, and, as they fed back their ideas, the teacher modelled how to make writing more interesting by the effective use of adjectives in noun phrases. After a reminder about full stops and capital letters, the children wrote their descriptions. Oman's (aged 6) remarkable piece is shown in Figure 11.2.

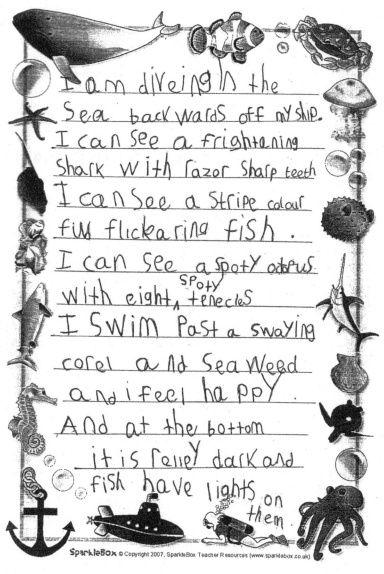

SparkleBox © Copyright 2007, SparkleBox Teacher Resources (www.sparklebox.co.uk)

■ **Figure 11.2** A description of a deep-sea dive

Oman shows his audience just what he can see, including details of how a diver enters the water, using language vibrantly to bring a picture to the minds of his readers.

Through the children making their fact files and writing their descriptions, the teacher built their knowledge of the underwater world, consolidating and confirming where children had understood ideas and where they needed more support. At every stage, she used visual texts: a feature animated film, images of sea creatures in books and on the IWB and a video of deep-sea diving. Throughout the sequence, she used visual prompts and role-play to support the children's learning. Each class began by reading and investigating texts, with explicit discussion of their features and the effects they created. Through drama and discussion, they experimented with ideas, before making choices about how they would write their own versions. The teacher's focus was on the children making their writing vivid through interesting noun phrases, choosing effective adjectives to create descriptions that would engage a younger class. This sequence of reading, explicit teaching of specific features, discussion and trying out ideas reflects the process of teaching grammar in context, outlined by Reedy and Bearne (2013) and noted in Chapter 7.

As shown by the examples in this chapter, creative approaches to teaching mean that reading visual texts can lead to insightful language study and the development of writing that has a strong individual voice.

PROFILING VISUAL TEXTS IN EXTENDED LEARNING JOURNEYS

This section outlines how an extended unit of work based on film can lead to individual, multimodal narrative composition. *The Wrong Trousers*, designed by Nick Park and the Aardman studio (1993), lasts for 30 minutes and is about friends stumbling over a plot to carry out a robbery, thwarting the villain and restoring the stolen goods – a recognisable narrative structure. The outline follows the teaching process, as described in Chapter 7, and the planning process, as described in Chapter 12. This learning journey extends to between three and four weeks and can be used with any age group. As with any outline plan, however, creative teachers will want to select and adapt the ideas to suit specific classes and are likely to change elements of the plan as the work unfolds, in response to the needs and interests of the learners. Initially, it will be important to identify an assessable outcome: this could be a multimodal mystery story presented as a PowerPoint display, as a digital film or even as a complex picture book. The teacher-selected, key narrative learning objectives for the age group need to fit with the genre of an adventure narrative.

The focus in the first half of the extended exploration will be on familiarising the children with the genre and capturing ideas. Thus, the focus of the session is likely to be on setting, perspective, sound, characterisation and editing, as the children build towards a storyboard that will be the basis of the multimodal outcome.

The class could view the film in sections, pausing at key moments to discuss what might happen next. At this stage, the idea is just to enjoy the film with the children, simply recording the stages of the narrative, identifying the key sections and noting them on the IWB or flipchart. These sections might include the following, although, with younger classes, this might need to be simplified:

▪ *establishing section*: a domestic setting with several characters/friends;
▪ *development*: a new character is introduced who causes trouble/disrupts the harmony;

■ *complication*: there is a mystery to be solved associated with the character;
■ *action*: the 'hero' discovers the plot and tracks down the villain;
■ *resolution*: there is a chase, where the friends deal with the villain;
■ *conclusion*: domestic peace is restored.

In order to generate and capture ideas, the class could be asked to freeze-frame an episode from each section; the teacher could usefully take digital images of these for later work and annotation or, alternatively, could take screen captures from the film's key incidents, for the same purpose. When the setting is analysed, notes could be added to the appropriate sections on the saved IWB/flipchart notes.

In preparing for the visual outcome, the class will need to re-view the film and discuss selected episodes that illustrate how atmosphere and narrative tension are created. Discussion might focus on a specific aspect of the film – for example, setting, character-isation, perspective or the creation of atmosphere. The children will be preparing to compose a new episode that might be inserted during the 'action' part of the story. The episode will be a short, storyboarded sequence where the hero follows the villain to a place not shown in the film. In preparation for the independent work, the teacher may need to model how to establish the setting for this episode. In order to ensure the children are encouraged to work independently, pairs could identify and draw a new setting for an additional episode, perhaps downloading pictures from the Internet as inspiration.

Work on perspective during this first half of the extended unit could involve analysing camera angles to identify the director's point of view. This is best done by taking one section of the film that has suitable variation in perspective and camera angles. One excellent sequence is the part where Gromit leaves the house at night, thinking that he has been replaced in Wallace's affections by the Penguin. Discussion on perspective can be guided by explaining that often, but not necessarily always:

■ a long shot establishes setting or tells the action of the film;
■ a mid shot is used to show relationships between characters, as well as action;
■ a close-up tells us about a character's thoughts or feelings;
■ perspective shot from below often indicates difficulty or threat for the main character;
■ perspective shot diagonally can mean confusion, fear or disorientation;
■ perspective shot from above can mean superiority of another character or can create narrative tension.

As part of their independent group work, children could continue working in pairs to create an 8-frame storyboard of the new episode, using different angles and perspectives for each frame. They might use the one discussed in class or think up their own to fit the setting they have designed.

Work on sound could involve the teacher in selecting a section of the film where the music/sound effects are particularly effective and, having covered the screen, inviting the children to note what they think is happening as they listen. As it is difficult to find language to describe atmosphere created by music, they might be given pre-prepared envelopes of words to choose from. With older pupils, these might include words such as, 'haunting, intriguing, melancholy, tense, mysterious'. They will need time to discuss these with their partners, before feeding back to the whole class. After noting their descriptions, they should then view the section of the film that they have just listened to and discuss the differences and similarities between their guesses and the film itself. The children could then, in their independent work, add notes to their storyboards about what sounds they want to use, to create atmosphere or tell us something about characters.

Work on characterisation might involve the teacher again selecting parts of the film for the children to concentrate on the characters and discuss how the film director makes the audience know that some characters are 'good' and some 'villains'. The emphasis should be on how facial expression, posture and gesture indicate characteristics and feelings – for example, raised eyebrows or hands on hips to show anger; drooped body posture to suggest unhappiness. After the independent work, notes for the three main characters – Wallace, Gromit and the Penguin – could be recorded on the IWB/flipchart for all the main characters, under the headings 'What the character says' and 'What the character does'. As a consolidation of reading character in film, a section of the film where the camera concentrates on the feelings of one of the characters can be selected, and the children can be asked to discuss how the character is feeling, and how they know this. They might also be asked to write a short diary/journal entry from the point of view of the character, describing her/his feelings. This writing could be enhanced by using drama conventions such as interior monologue, hot-seating or role on the wall to explore the characters more fully. See Chapter 3 for ways to bridge between drama and writing. Alternatively, screen captures of images of characters could be used for the children to attach speech or thought bubbles, prior to their adding dialogue in speech bubbles to their own storyboards.

Work on editing is important, as this process creates narrative drive in film. Sometimes it is slow and reflective, which gives some sense of how the characters are feeling; sometimes it is fast and creates narrative tension. The power of editing can be shown by selecting a section of the film where the editing either develops character or narrative tension and reviewing it several times, while the teacher models how choices about changes of shot help build up narrative tension or characterisation. Both the sequence in which the Penguin is stealing the diamond and the final chase sequence are ideal for this. Afterwards, the children can annotate their own storyboards to show length of shots.

At this point, after approximately two weeks, each pair should have an 8-frame storyboard, with a particular setting (annotated to explain details) of a new episode, showing angles and perspective. During the ongoing sessions, the children should have added notes about sound to create atmosphere or characterisation, given some indication of length of shots and attached speech bubbles. In the later sessions of this extended unit of work, the focus will be on shared composition of the multimodal text, to make a PowerPoint presentation, a digital film or complex picture book. If this has not been done before, it might be best for the teacher to model making a whole-class presentation, film or picture book, involving the children in groups for each aspect – for example, writing dialogue, designing and drawing settings, separate double-page spreads and so on. Alternatively, they could work in their pairs to create their own movies/PowerPoint presentations. Both presentations and films can have sound effects and dialogue added. The children might download images for settings and software designed for drawing, or draw their own screens based on the storyboards. Equally, they could act out the extra episodes, taking digital images of freeze-frames, or use small-world play figures or puppets.

Time will need to be spent on:

- designing, drawing/downloading settings and characters and making them larger or smaller according to the perspectives chosen in the storyboards;
- drafting, trying out, editing and finalising dialogue;
- deciding on sound for each screen/shot and recording/making it;
- timing length of shots or transitions between screens;
- planning what will be on each double-page spread;
- putting it all together;
- designing advertising for their film or book;
- organising screenings or launch events;
- showing it to other people;
- evaluating the process and the films, presentations or books.

Reflecting on the work might include discussing their audiences' responses and the written reviews produced by other classes or parents. It might also involve asking the children why they chose to use close-ups, mid or long shots, or particular colours. They could also consider how they could improve their composition and what particularly satisfies them about their multimodal narratives. To support their own evaluative reflections, it is important for the teacher to comment on how they have used the technical devices they have learned about to make their own creative compositions.

CONCLUSION

The predominance of visual texts may make demands on teaching but, at the same time, liberates a wealth of children's text experience that can be shared, enjoyed and creatively built upon in the classroom. There is clear evidence (Warrington *et al.*, 2006; Walsh, 2007; Bearne and Bazalgette, 2010) that reading visual texts, composing them and using them as a basis for composition – either writing or multimodal texts – can help children find their own voices. In terms of reading, there is also evidence of children developing a critical eye (Maine, 2013; Parry, 2014) and becoming more discriminating and responsive readers of print texts as a result of viewing film. As it is likely that children will increasingly draw on screen texts for entertainment, information and enjoyment of narrative, the development of a critically analytical stance is essential. This will be made possible by the explicit discussion of how the different modes of communication and representation work together to make meaning. For this to happen, teachers themselves need to have confidence in their own knowledge of the structures and imaginative possibilities of digital texts and technologies. They also need to teach creatively, taking risks and being prepared to work with the full range of visual and digital texts that children encounter every day outside school.

FURTHER READING

Bearne, E. and Bazalgette, C. (2010) *Beyond Words: Developing children's response to multimodal texts*. Leicester, UK: United Kingdom Literacy Association.
Moline, S. (2012) *I See What You Mean: Visual Literacy, K-8* (2nd edn). Portland, ME: Stenhouse.

Parry, B. (2013) *Children, Film and Literacy*. Basingstoke, UK: Palgrave Macmillan.

Wohlwend, K. (2009) 'Early adopters: Playing new literacies and pretending new technologies in print-centric classrooms', *Journal of Early Childhood Literacy*, 9(7): 117–40.

CHILDREN'S TEXTS

Bird, B. (dir.) (1999) *The Iron Giant* [film]. Warner.

Hughes, T. (1968) *The Iron Man*. London: Faber & Faber.

Park, N. (dir.) (1993) *The Wrong Trousers* [film]. Aardman Animations.

Williams, M. (1998) *Mr William Shakespeare's Plays*. London: Walker.

PLANNING TO TEACH ENGLISH CREATIVELY

Teresa Cremin

INTRODUCTION

Teachers often plan assiduously to ensure curriculum coverage, cognisant of NC require-ments and assessment structures. Arguably, this view of the curriculum as planned, in response to the prescribed requirements, has dominated over the conception of the curriculum as lived/experienced. However, in the context of curriculum change, there is increased scope to make professional choices based on sound research evidence and teachers' own knowledge and understanding. More creative approaches to the curriculum are being developed.

In many schools, the creative process and its outcomes are being revalued and planned for more explicitly in English. Extended units of work that include experiential, enquiry-based and problem-solving pedagogic approaches are being planned, and these encourage teachers to develop more flexible and open-ended practices and to teach English across the curriculum. This chapter, in focusing on planning to teach English creatively, explores the significance of building a creative environment and the principles and practice of planning for creative learning. It also explores examples of teachers working alongside creative practitioners from outside the school community and highlights the importance of integrating the eight core elements of creative practice into the English curriculum experience.

BUILDING A CREATIVE ENVIRONMENT

It is difficult to draw a dividing line between a creative approach to English teaching and a creative ethos in the classroom: the teacher's approach towards English teaching significantly influences the climate created. Educators' attitudes to, and conceptions of, reading, writing, speaking and listening are very influential and are implicitly as well as explicitly shared and both frame and can constrain children's own identities as readers and writers (Hall, 2012). Teachers' perceptions of what is important are reflected, not only in the literal displays, role-play area, computers, writing table, message board, reading corners and so forth, but also in the climate created and the evocation of imaginative contexts for purposeful literacy learning.

In order for creativity to be fostered, children need to feel safe, valued and trusted and able to take risks as readers, writers, speakers and listeners and not be critiqued for suggesting alternative routes or trialling different ways forward. Research indicates strong links between creative learning and emotional security and suggests that creativity is best fostered in inclusive environments that foster, for both teachers and children, a high degree of ownership and control over the agenda, as well as emotional relevance and collaboration (Jeffrey and Woods, 2009; Craft, 2011). Positive relationships are crucial in fostering creativity. It flourishes in situations where there are trusting, mutually respectful teacher–learner relationships, when teachers not only respond to children's feelings and protect them from ridicule, but also value what children bring and the generation of child-initiated alternatives (Davies *et al.*, 2012). Individual creativity is affected by even very minor aspects of the immediate social environment (Amabile, 1988): the school ethos will affect the ethos created by teachers in their classrooms and, hence, the opportunities for creative teaching and learning in English and across the curriculum.

In reviewing research evidence on the characteristics of environments that are most effective in promoting creative-skills development in children for Learning and Teaching Scotland, Davies *et al.* (2012) note that the space within a classroom should be capable of being used flexibly (in terms of moving furniture, for example), that a wide range of appropriate materials (including texts) and other resources can stimulate creativity, and that using the outdoors or taking children to work in environments such as museums and galleries enhances their creative skills. In relation to the pedagogical environments, they conclude that, where children are given some control over their learning and are supported to take risks, this supports their creativity, as does the flexible use of time and opportunities for collaboration. In particular, they note there is very strong evidence that teacher–child relationships make a difference, including high expectations, mutual respect, modelling of creative attitudes, flexibility and dialogue (Davies *et al.*, 2012). All of these key features are examined within this book.

In classrooms with a secure ethos, children will be happy to ask and answer questions, confident enough to take sensible risks and get their risk taking rewarded. An ethos that encourages curiosity and profiles children's questions also encourages core elements of creativity, such as problem finding as well as problem solving, and the development of a speculative stance that expects and welcomes challenge. Teachers who show their own creativity tend to voice their exploratory thoughts and model tentative thinking in the classroom, revealing themselves as learners and as writers, for example. Such teachers are likely to deal positively with uncertainty, tolerate ambiguity and perceive failure as a learning opportunity.

There is a complex relationship between children's creativity and their development as independent enquirers, effective participants, team workers, self-managers and reflective thinkers, all of which are influenced by the ethos and environment established by the teacher (Davies *et al.*, 2012). Creative teachers not only seek to develop playful environments of possibility in which ideas are generated and privileged, but also help literacy learners share and review their ideas, subjecting them to serious scrutiny, so that action and reflection can lead to transformation and outcomes of value. They therefore profile judgement as well as playfulness and encourage reflection in multiple modes.

PRINCIPLES OF EXTENDED LEARNING JOURNEYS

If teachers are to move from being presenters of content to becoming leaders of creative learning journeys, which are, in essence, extended explorations set within purposeful units of work, then thoughtful use will need to be made of the key elements of creative English practice documented in this book. On such journeys, literacy is both taught and applied in meaningful contexts that enrich children's creativity, enhance their lateral thinking and develop their motivated and enthusiastic involvement in learning. The eight elements of creative English practice that need to be woven through such learning journeys are, as noted in Chapter 1:

1   profiling meaning and purpose;
2   foregrounding potent, affectively engaging texts;
3   fostering play and engagement;
4   harnessing curiosity and profiling agency;
5   encouraging collaboration and making connections;
6   integrating reflection, review, feedback and celebration;
7   taking time to travel and teach skills in context;
8   ensuring the creative involvement of the teacher.

In planning extended units of work, ranging from between a fortnight to half a term or more, all four language modes will be integrated, and opportunities for learners to direct some of their own learning will be planned from the outset. This can help create an increasingly negotiated and co-participative English curriculum. As creativity arises from interactions with ideas and others and is supported by open-ended discussions, improvisations, structured simulations and playful encounters, these experiences need to be threaded through each learning journey, and a wealth of opportunities for individual, pair and group work must be planned. In addition, formative assessment will be mapped into this flexible and creative approach, in order to enable teachers to be responsive to learners' needs and offer tailored instruction and focused feedback.

In seeking to adopt a creative approach, teachers work to temper the planned with the lived and let the learners lead more frequently, creating a responsive English curriculum that seeks to build coherently on unexpected contributions or enquiries and ensures the appropriate knowledge and skills are developed in the process. At its simplest, this might involve identifying children's key questions and puzzlements about a text and planning accordingly, or inviting the class to vote on whether *Lady Daisy* by Dick King Smith or Berlie Doherty's *Street Child* or *My Granny was a Buffer Girl* will be read during the Victorian focus. However, many teachers will wish to involve the learners more extensively in planning and developing the unit of work, in shaping their journeys and in negotiating their own goals and expectations. This enhances their agency and enables them to take more responsibility for their own learning, as Cochrane and Cockett (2007) demonstrate so effectively, ensuring they are clear about freedom and constraints and affording multiple opportunities for children to work together.

PLANNING EXTENDED LEARNING JOURNEYS

Extended explorations may focus entirely upon English or may seek to combine teaching and learning across the arts, integrating the teaching of English, music, art, dance and drama, for example. Alternatively, the core planning focus may be a cross-curricular theme in which literacy is both taught and applied in a humanities or science learning journey, for example, although, even in this context, the creative arts may well be involved. Whatever the particular combination of areas of learning sought, the following key steps will serve to help primary professionals identify a way forward when planning extended learning journeys.

Choose the focus, the duration and the text type(s) to be explored

Teachers will want to decide whether to tie literacy work into cross-curricular activities; if this is the case, a 5–6-week plan may not be excessive, or two mini-units may be chosen, both of which might relate to the Victorians, for example, with focus on narrative for three weeks, perhaps, and recounts/newspapers for the following two weeks. There is no hard and fast rule about length, but coherence is important, as is the need to allow time for the children to develop and complete an extended piece of work of which they can be proud. This relates to the second step in planning.

Identify an assessable outcome

Each extended unit of work needs to work towards a long-term outcome or product. This provides a clear aim for the children and enables the teacher to formatively assess their work as it develops over the weeks, knowing that the goal is, for example, to write a fairytale for inclusion in the class anthology, or to produce clear instructions on PowerPoint for another class to use in art and craft. There is no need for the outcome to be a written one in each case. The assessed piece may be focused on a performance of understanding, perhaps in the form of a documentary programme, poetry festival or storytelling event, or, alternatively, teachers may work towards the production of an audio tape or DVD of short stories written and read by the children. Making public the assessed outcomes is important, and a variety of these need to be included across a school year.

Collect and consider textual and other resources

Collecting a rich range of examples of the genre in focus and one or two that are likely to be examined in more detail is essential – for example, gathering together a range of traditional tales in picture books and anthologies, to be used in shared and guided time, as well as story tapes for children to read/listen to independently. A display of these may help to promote the genre and encourage the children to bring in their own examples to add to the loan collection. There is no need for these to be in the same medium; for example, films such as *Shrek* or *Aladdin*, YouTube videos or materials from the Literacy Shed website could be integrated into such a unit for comparison of screen-based and print-based versions, for exploration of the myriad of intertextual references to other tales or for examination of parody. Visual approaches to teaching literacy need to be integrated into the literacy curriculum and not left to chance. Much will depend upon the intended outcome and purpose of the unit and whether it is linked to cross-curricular work, as in the case of the storytelling focus being linked to a geographical examination of different cultures, for example.

Teachers will want to underpin the learning journey with potent, imaginatively engaging texts, but they may also want to supplement these with opportunities to work with storytellers, poets, authors, journalists, dancers, musicians and actors, for example, or with practitioners from a connected area of work, as well as members of the community whose expertise, stance and experience could enrich the children's travels.

Make appropriate NC connections

Teachers will want to select relevant elements from their NC documents to be explored and attended to, in order to achieve the final outcome. These may be identified in response to need and formative assessment, or may be from the programme of study for the age phase, but are likely to encompass reading, writing and spoken-word elements. On an extended learning journey, teachers will be involved in both supporting and challenging learning and seizing opportunities to integrate focused instruction when needed. Creative teachers do not ignore form and function, rules and language conventions, but actively seek to help children explore these in meaningful and imaginatively engaging contexts. Open-ended approaches, involving all the learners in a stimulating process of exploration and experimentation, can be planned and developed from statutory requirements and should have learning about conventions and codes embedded within them.

Although opportunities for explicit instruction in context will be planned into the unit from the outset, they are likely also to be seized by teachers in response to children's interests and the evolving nature of the work, as well as in response to ongoing formative assessment. Thus, whereas some objectives will be profiled throughout, others may be identified for closer examination as the unit develops. In addition, areas of PSHE may be woven through a unit, and cross-curricular threads and goals may also be linked into this work.

Alternatively, teachers may wish to look back retrospectively at the end of the unit, or periodically throughout a unit, to see which aspects of the statutory requirements and strands have been examined through the class's exploration. Such an approach has been found to enhance teachers' freedom, flexibility, creativity and professional autonomy (Bearne *et al.*, 2004) and is worth considering.

PLAN THE PROCESS OF TEACHING ENGLISH CREATIVELY

In planning a range of teaching and learning activities that explicitly build upon the eight elements of creative English practice, teachers will also want to map the journey towards the identified, assessable outcome and may wish to link this to the framework for teaching in Chapter 7.

Although the focus will initially be on familiarising the class with the genre and immersing them in the text type, time also needs to be set aside for the teacher to outline the challenge, purpose and relevance of the unit. Rather than presenting the work as 'a three-week unit on haiku', for example, teachers could seek to site this element of the children's journey within a wider exploration, perhaps of Japanese cultural habits and traditions. They might then frame an invitation to the class to create a Japanese tea ceremony/festival for members of the community, at which their poetry could be read, their Japanese dance and artwork shared, and their calligraphy displayed.

Another unit on poetry might be framed by inviting the class to organise a week-long poetry festival for the school community. After considerable discussion of possibilities, groups might be established to plan particular events at which their own and others' poetry could be shared, read, viewed, performed and published. This could involve working with parents and professional poets or musicians, and the class working as poetry ambassadors; much will depend on the combination of ideas finally agreed upon. Constructing learning journeys in consultation with the children in this way harnesses their curiosity and enhances their agency and sense of ownership of their learning, enriching both their commitment and their creativity.

Throughout the unit, teachers will plan to foster the children's playful engagement, perhaps through appealing to their interests and passions, involving them in imaginative experiences, finding powerful texts that inspire and/or connecting the learning to their lives. In a poetry unit, classroom drama might be used to investigate the issues in a narrative poem, poetry boxes might be established with a wide range of poetic texts, including jokes, playground rhymes, lyrics and riddles, and the Poetry Archive could be explored so that children can listen to poets reading their work and identify favourites. Music, dance and art could all be woven into the journey, triggering different interpretations and work on inference and deduction, as well as supporting the production of poetic compositions and performances. The identified objectives will be woven through the unit as appropriate to the activities and their purposes, so that children's knowledge and understanding of poetry will be developed through their engagement and accompanying tailored instruction.

Across each unit, teachers will want to ensure there are a range of opportunities for children to work individually and together, in pairs, groups and as a whole class, sometimes on set activities and sometimes in self-directed ways that nurture their capacity to collaborate and participate with one another. In such contexts, children will be generating ideas for the poetry festival, for example, and for their own compositions and performances, and will be evaluating and refining these together. Teachers may also want to widen the remit beyond the classroom, perhaps through establishing poetry partners in a neighbouring school and enabling the children to email their poems to them for comments and feedback. These partners might also be invited to visit during the poetry festival.

Teachers, as well as framing the exploration, will sensitively and spontaneously shape the unfolding journey in response to the children's interests and needs, while retaining a sense of the overall goal, learning intentions and curriculum requirements. They will also seek to inspire and engage the children through actively participating themselves as language artists and creative professionals, modelling the process of asking questions, making connections and taking risks, as well as trying alternatives, as they discuss, perform and compose their own poems, for example. In this way, they will be demonstrating many of the same creative attributes that they seek to foster in children, namely curiosity, perseverance, playfulness, resourcefulness and reflection.

Plan to review and celebrate

Throughout the extended learning journey, children will need time and space to play and explore, to speculate and question, and to critically review and evaluate their work. Time for this will need to be built in, both during the unit and towards the end of the journey, to involve the children in generating and appraising their work, reflecting on the insights gained, the ideas shared and the accomplishments achieved. This should encourage the capacity to reflect critically and support them as they seek to craft their work to a high standard over time.

Teachers will also want to celebrate the children's achievements by making public their work, in a variety of informal as well as more formal ways. This should trigger consideration of both the process and the product of their learning and should profile reflection, evaluation and feedback. It will also be important to help the children assess the degree to which their ongoing work, their responses to texts, work in groups and the multimodal texts that they produce are innovative or alternative and demonstrate their creativity.

Working in partnership to plan creative and critical events

The concept of critical events was coined by Woods (1994) to describe holistic projects that include external specialists and have unusually ambitious long-term goals, such as the production of a radio programme, an opera, a film or a play perhaps. Such projects often develop with external partners, seek to stimulate creative learning and encourage children to initiate activities and direct more of their own work. In many ways, the extended learning journeys described in this chapter are small-scale versions of creative and critical events, although not all will encompass working with specialists from beyond the school. Teachers learn to expect the unexpected when engaging in such events and need to be prepared to respond spontaneously, reframing the curriculum as the events unfold:

> Critical events are in large measure intended, planned and controlled. But the plans contain within them seeds for growth and scope for opportunities. There are elements, therefore, that are largely unforeseen, and unpredictable new pastures that all teachers and pupils alike are venturing into, with what consequences no one exactly knows.
>
> (Woods, 1994: 2)

Such opportunities to work on extended projects, with external visitors and learning partners from outside school, can significantly enrich children's learning experiences and make a real contribution to their literacy development (Brice-Heath and Wolf, 2004; Ellis and Safford, 2005; Pahl, 2007). This has been demonstrated in numerous studies, most recently in relation to a number of projects developed as part of the CP initiative in England (Creative Partnerships, 2008). This initiative sought to establish long-term, sustainable partnerships between schools, organisations and individuals, such as architects, theatre companies, museums, cinemas, film makers, installation artists, dancers, web designers, authors, poets, storytellers and many more. All schools can work on extended creative events with external partners and may choose to connect to English Heritage sites or a local gallery, library or museum, for example. This practice of working with artist partners and others from the business and cultural sectors has expanded significantly in recent years, and the 2008–11 pilot programme 'Find Your Talent', which sought to create a universal cultural offer of 5 hours of quality arts and culture a week, took this still further. Such programmes offer literacy learners the chance to work imaginatively with others, both inside and outside the classroom, and seek to foster their creativity.

Examples of creative and critical events

In one umbrella project entitled *Animating Literacy*, CP, working with the Centre for Literacy in Primary Education, spawned several school-based projects in drama, the performing arts, multimedia and film making (Ellis and Safford, 2005). These involved primary teachers in interpreting and adapting the curriculum more creatively and working with various artists over time. For example, in one project, short films were both devised and made by a class of 9–10-year-olds, working with their teacher, a film director and video makers/photographers. The teacher noted that the children all developed their speaking and listening skills through this work, as well as their self-esteem and capacity to collaborate with others.

In another project, a class of 10–11-year-olds worked closely both with the Young Vic Theatre and English National Opera. The former was staging a production of David Almond's book *Skellig*, and the youngsters became involved in this, watching it, interviewing the actors, producing their own scenes from it in the theatre and later performing on stage at the Young Vic as part of a Schools' Theatre festival. Their teacher successfully developed their curiosity and critical-thinking skills through this work, which was evident both in their talk and in their writing.

The success of such projects may be due, in part at least, to the real-world connections and relationships established and because the artists become role models, extending the children's horizons in various ways. In another CP project, an infant school worked with a resident artist and an architectural designer to create a reception area for the new school building. Oral language, visual literacies and strategic thinking were the focus of this research, which encompassed many themes and demonstrated, for example, the significance of constructing a creative vocabulary in the classroom and opportunities for learners to inhabit this discourse (Brice-Heath and Wolf, 2004). The artist's language seeped through into the children's everyday conversation, and his desire to talk about great works of art and remain open to different interpretations prompted the young children to look more closely, and take risks in responding and apply these skills to their conversations about picture books. This not only supported them as readers, but also, arguably, gave them insights into other possible worlds, as well as their own. Additionally, the evidence suggests it helped them develop a sense of the aesthetic and a language to comment upon and evaluate their own and others' creations.

Combining visual images and children's literature is also at the heart of the initiative 'Take One Picture', run by the National Gallery in London, which seeks to demonstrate the power of combining visual art forms and narrative/poetry. In one school, some 6–7-year-olds, in responding to Katsushiika Hokusai's 'Caught by the Ejiri Wind', arguably found their voices through the process of being physically, aesthetically and artistically engaged on their compositional journeys (Smith, 2007). The role of the body in enriching literacy learning is also evidenced in another collaborative project, in which three schools worked with a contemporary dance team and the Medway Arts and Literacy teams (Wells, 2008). The focus in this work was on folk tales from around the world, and Madonna's *The Adventures of Abdi* was selected as the core text because of the aesthetic qualities of the illustrations and the fact that the Arabic culture offered rich potential for dance and music connected to the theme of journeys. It led eventually to groups of children performing their final interpretations of parts of the narrative to their own school communities and creating multimedia presentations of the project for their school website, demonstrating again that weaving critical events around dance, literacy and art and working with experts beyond the school can be highly effective in fostering children's creative learning in English.

Such opportunities to work with creative partners and members of the community cost both time and money and demand flexibility on the part of all the professionals involved. They offer children the chance to work with talented colleagues from outside the school on holistic projects in which their literacy skills and understanding can be applied and developed in meaningful real-world contexts, over which they have some control.

THE TEACHER AS A CREATIVE PRACTITIONER

However, although such partnership projects are increasingly common and are to be welcomed, they may, inadvertently, focus the profession on external experts and under-estimate the creative capacity of classroom teachers. The conception of teachers as artists also deserves attention, support and development (Jeffrey, 2005). Teachers' ability to operate as co-participators and creative practitioners, apprenticing learners and modelling possibilities, is, Craft (2005) suggests, central to a creative approach to teaching and is one of the eight core elements of creative English practice articulated in this book. It represents a possible way to develop a balance between developing children's knowledge about language and creative language use and has the potential to offer increased job satisfaction to members of the profession, many of whom 'value the link between creative approaches and their own motivation and sense of pleasure in the job' (Barnes, 2003: 41).

Recent research exploring the signature pedagogies of artists who successfully fostered children's creativity revealed that they took a highly democratic approach to their work and adopted inclusive participatory practices, based on a fundamental belief that every child was capable of having ideas and contributing meaningfully to discussions and was integral to a collective 'performance' (Thomson *et al.*, 2012; Thomson and Hall, forth-coming). The artists sought to establish children's ways of knowing and 'funds of know-ledge' (Moll *et al.*, 1992) and saw themselves as contributors with expertise.

Teachers, although not professional artists and with the added challenges of wider responsibility for the curriculum and for assessment, can, however, learn from such work and seek, as this book has recommended, to more fully participate as playful, creative and curious adults in children's literacy learning. They can also seek to discover more about the children's home literacy practices, as practitioners involved in the *Researching Literacy Lives* project did (Cremin *et al.*, 2015). In this study, by positioning them-selves as researchers and learners and making Learner Visits to children's homes, the teachers expanded their knowledge of the children's literacy learning in different social, historical–cultural and linguistic contexts. Through examining their own literacy histories and practices, many of the teachers in this project began to: reconceptualise literacy in the twenty-first century and legitimise a wider view of literacy in school; acknowledge that they were in a position of power in defining, for parents and children, what 'counts' as valid and valuable literacy; develop a wider view of the inseparable relationship between literacy and learning; and appreciate the children's and families' diverse funds of know-ledge. Significantly, too, they began to build on these and design more creative and responsive learning opportunities, to connect home and school experience (Cremin, Mottram *et al.*, 2012). Several found that the more responsive curricula created increased children's engagement, independence and commitment as learners. The wider constructions of literacy that were legitimated also opened up opportunities for children to lead learning with their questions and interests. It would seem that developing deeper knowledge of the children, as individuals and as literacy learners, supports teachers in shaping a more responsive, tailored and potentially co-constructed literacy curriculum (Cremin *et al.*, 2015).

As literacy educators, teachers are personally and professionally involved, both as individuals and as managers of the learning. They can also be involved as fellow artists – 'meddlers in the middle' (McWilliam, 2008) – in the classroom, as creative practitioners themselves. In this role, they are arguably more personally and affectively involved, thinking and feeling their way through situations, asking questions, taking risks, and profiling pedagogies and language practices that help them develop their own and the children's creativity in action. Language arts activities, in particular, can help all members of the classroom community create environments of possibility, generating and evaluating alternative interpretations and insights and expressing themselves creatively.

The challenge of developing teachers' and children's imaginations is an exacting one; it depends in part upon adult involvement, with teachers and teaching assistants participating as writers, tale tellers, poetry performers, film makers and role-players, for example. This will not produce a profession of extroverts or performers in the flamboyant sense, but a creative profession, actively involved in the artistic processes in which the children are also engaged. The consequences of such educator engagement are manifold, particularly the pedagogical consequences. For example, with reference to reading, teachers can share their identities as readers and their emotional response to texts, demonstrating that this is a normal and legitimate part of being a reader. Through storytelling, teachers can share the challenges and satisfactions of spinning tales into existence and enticing the audience to wonder, feel and respond. Modelling their oral artistry in this way may also encompass teachers' reflecting upon the process of remembering and retelling tales, and their growing awareness of story structure, characterisation, vocabulary choices and so forth. Additionally, as teachers in role, professionals will experience the energising open-endedness of classroom drama and may seize the moment to write, as the tension mounts and multiple perspectives are explored. Furthermore, through engaging as writers in the classroom, teachers can experience the reflective, emergent nature of composing and identify insights from within the writing process, such as the emotional struggle, the role of incubation and experimentation, the importance of developing a listening ear and the value of authentic, meaning-focused feedback (Cremin, 2008).

Teachers' involvement as language artists in their classrooms may help them avoid routinising textual encounters, enabling them to raise possibilities rather than confirm probabilities; to open doors rather than close them. Their creative engagement in literacy teaching and learning may also help them to exploit the potential spaces, problems and possibilities that literature and other texts offer; gaps in texts increase the degree of uncertainty, provoking questions and potential for creative engagement. Teachers' widening experience of, and engagement in, the language arts and new technologies can also prompt them to use strategies that unsettle the status quo or open up new avenues for investigation, interpretation and problem solving. Teaching literacy creatively, therefore, demands high levels of professional assurance and artistry, the ability to tolerate uncertainty and the capacity to respond spontaneously, responsively and imaginatively.

CONCLUSION

Teachers are professionals who can exercise their own agency in the classroom and can choose to adopt a creative approach to teaching English that offers children a voice in the learning conversation and the chance to direct more of their own work. On purposeful and engaging learning journeys, children too can make more of their own choices and decisions, in collaboration with others. Such an approach can help teachers respond to the dual pressures of prescription and accountability and the demands to teach creatively and teach for creativity. Adopting a creative approach can help teachers construct a better balance between form and freedom, structure and innovation in their teaching. If teachers integrate the eight elements of teaching English creatively into their planning and work to extend their engagement as language artists, they will be fostering children's creativity: enriching their capacity to question, pose problems, make connections, generate, innovate and imagine alternatives and reflect critically as readers and writers, speakers and listeners. Creative English teaching fosters creative English learning.

FURTHER READING

Cremin, T. (2015) 'Creative teachers and creative teaching', in A. Wilson (ed.), *Creativity in Primary Education* (2nd edn). Exeter, UK: Learning Matters, pp. 33–44.

Davies, D., Jindal-Snape, D., Collier, C., Digby, R., Hay, P. and Howe, A. (2012) 'Creative environments for learning in schools', *Thinking Skills and Creativity*, 9: 80–91.

Marsh, J. (2010) *Childhood, Culture and Creativity: A literature review*. Newcastle upon Tyne, UK: Creativity, Culture and Education.

Thomson, P., Hall, C., Jones, K. and Sefton-Green, J. (2012) *The Signature Pedagogies Project: Final report* (1 June). London: Creativity, Culture and Education.

CHILDREN'S BOOKS

Almond, D. (1998) *Skellig*. London: Hodder.

Doherty, B. (1995) *Street Child*. London: Collins.

Doherty, B. (2007) *My Granny was a Buffer Girl* (new edn). London: Catnip.

King Smith, D. (1993) *Lady Daisy*. London: Puffin.

Madonna, with Dugina, O. and Digin, A. (illus.) (2004) *The Adventures of Abdi*. London: Puffin.

REFERENCES

Alexander, R. (2000) *Culture and Pedagogy*. Oxford, UK: Blackwell.

Alexander, R. (2008) *Towards Dialogic Teaching: Rethinking classroom talk*. Cambridge, UK: Dialogos.

Alexander, R. (ed.) (2010) *Children, Their World and Their Education: Final report and recommendations of the Cambridge Primary Review*. London and New York: Routledge.

Almond, D. (2001) 'Writing for children.' Lecture given at NLS Writing and Creativity Conference, 4 June, London.

Alper, M. (2013) 'Developmentally appropriate new media literacies: Supporting cultural competencies and social skills in early childhood education', *Journal of Early Childhood Literacy*, 1(2): 175–96.

Amabile, T.M. (1988) 'A model of creativity and innovation in organisations', in B.M. Staw and L.L. Cunnings (eds), *Research in Organisational Behaviour*. Greenwich, CT: JA, pp. 121–32.

Andrews, R. (1989) 'Beyond 'voice' in poetry', *English in Education*, 23(3): 21–7.

Andrews, R. (2008) 'Shifting writing practice: Focusing on the productive skills to improve quality and standards', in DCSF, *Getting Going: Generating, shaping and developing ideas in writing*. Nottingham, UK: DCSF, pp. 4–21.

Appleyard, J. (1990) *Becoming a Reader, The Experience of Fiction From Childhood to Adulthood*. Cambridge, UK: Cambridge University Press.

Arizpe, E. and Styles, M. (2003) *Children Reading Pictures: Interpreting visual texts*. London: RoutledgeFalmer.

Arizpe, E., Colomer, T. and Martínez-Roldán, C. (2014) *Visual Journeys Through Wordless Narratives*. London: Bloomsbury Academic.

Armstrong, M. (2006) *Children Writing Stories*. Berkshire, UK, and New York: Open University Press.

Arrow, A. and Finch, B.T. (2013) 'Multimedia literacy practices in beginning classrooms and at home: The differences in practices and beliefs', *Literacy*, 47(3): 131–41.

Arts Council England (2003) *From Looking Glass to Spy Glass: A consultation paper on children's literature*. London: Arts Council.

Auden, W.H. and Garrett, J. (1935) *The Poet's Tongue*. London: Bell.

Bakhtin, M. (1986) *Speech Genres and Other Late Essays* (trans. V.W. McGee). Austin, TX: University of Texas Press.

Bamford, A. (2008) *The Visual Literacy White Paper*. Adobe Systems, Australia. Available at www.adobe.com/uk/education/pdf/adobe_visual_literacy_paper.pdf (accessed 23 August 2014).

Barnes, J. (2003) 'Teacher's emotions, teacher's creativity: A discussion paper', *Improving Schools*, 6(1): 39–43.

Barrs, M. (1988) 'Maps of play', in M. Meek and C. Mills (eds), *Language and Literacy in the Primary School*. London: Falmer Press, pp. 101–12.

Barrs, M. and Cork, V. (2001) *The Reader in the Writer: The influence of literature upon writing at KS2*. London: Centre for Literacy in Primary Education.

Barrs, M. and Styles, M. (2013) 'Afterword', in S. Dymoke, A. Lambirth and A. Wilson, *Making Poetry Matter: International research on poetry pedagogy*. London: Bloomsbury, pp. 184–96.

Bearne, E. (2007) 'Writing at Key Stage 2', in T. Cremin and H. Dombey, *Handbook of Primary English in Initial Teacher Education*. Cambridge, UK: UKLA/NATE/Canterbury Christ Church University, pp. 83–95.

Bearne, E. and Grainger, T. (2004) 'Raising boys' achievements in writing', *Literacy*, 38(3): 153–9.

Bearne, E. and Wolstencroft, H. (2007) *Visual Approaches to Teaching Writing*. London: Sage and UKLA.

Bearne, E. and Bazalgette, C. (2010) *Beyond Words: Developing children's response to multi-modal texts*. Leicester, UK: United Kingdom Literacy Association.

Bearne, E., Grainger, T. and Wolstencroft, H. (2004) *Raising Boys' Achievements in Writing* (Joint research project). Baldock, UK: UKLA and the Primary National Strategy.

Bearne, E., Clark, C., Johnson, A., Manford, P., Mottram, M. and Wolstencroft, H., with Anderson, R., Gamble, N. and Overall, L. (2007) *Reading on Screen: Research report*. Leicester, UK: UKLA.

Benton, M. and Fox, R. (1985) *Teaching Literature 9–14*. Oxford, UK: Oxford University Press.

Bereiter, C. and Scardamalia, M. (1987) *The Psychology of Written Communication*. Hillsdale, NJ: Lawrence Erlbaum.

Berry, J. (2011) *A Story I Am: Selected poems*. Tarset, UK: Bloodaxe.

Bhojwani, P., Lord, B. and Wilkes, C. (2009) *I Know What to Write Now: Engaging boys (and girls) through a multimodal approach*. Leicester, UK: UKLA.

Black, P., Harrison, C., Lee, C., Marshall, B., and Williams, D. (2003) *Assessment for Learning: Putting it into practice*. Milton Keynes, UK: Open University Press.

Boden, M.A. (2001) 'Creativity and knowledge', in A. Craft, B. Jeffrey and M. Liebling (eds), *Creativity in Education*. London: Continuum, pp. 95–115.

Boden, M.A. (2004) *The Creative Mind* (2nd edn). London: Routledge.

Bourdieu, P. (1977) *Outline of a Theory of Practice* (trans. R. Nice). Cambridge, UK: Cambridge University Press.

Bradley, L. and Bryant, P. (1983) 'Categorising sounds and learning to read: A causal connection', *Nature*, 301: 419–21.

Brice-Heath, S. and Wolf, S. (2004) *Visual Learning in the Community School*. Kent: Creative Partnerships.

Britton, J. (1970) *Language and Learning*. London: Penguin.

Brown, J., Kim, K. and O'Brien Ramirez, K. (2012) 'What a teacher hears, what a reader sees: Eye movements from a phonics-taught second grader', *Journal of Early Childhood Literacy*, 12(2): 202–22.

Bruner, J. (1984) 'Language, mind and reading', in H. Goelman, A. Oberg and F. Smith (eds), *Awakening to Literacy*. London: Heinemann, pp. 136–54.

Bruner, J. (1986) *Actual Minds, Possible Worlds*. Cambridge, MA: Harvard University Press.

Buckley, J. (2012) *Pocket P4C: Getting started with philosophy for children*. Chelmsford, UK: One Slice Books.

Bunting, J. (2009) *Book Power: Literacy through Literature Year 1*. London: Centre for Literacy in Primary Education.

REFERENCES ▨ ▨ ▨ ■

Bunting, J., Ellis, S. and Vernon, J. (2010) *Book Power: Literacy through Literature Year 2*. London: Centre for Literacy in Primary Education.

Burnard, P., Craft, A. and Cremin, T. (2006) 'Documenting possibility thinking: A journey of collaborative inquiry', *International Journal of Early Years Education*, 14(3): 243–62.

Burns, C. and Myhill, D. (2004) 'Interactive or inactive? A consideration of the nature of interaction in whole class teaching', *Cambridge Journal of Education*, 34(1): 35–49.

Bus, A.G., Van Ijzendoorn, M.H. and Pellegrini, A.D. (1995) 'Joint book reading makes for success in learning to read: A meta-analysis on intergenerational transmission of literacy', *Review of Educational Research*, 65: 11–21.

Bussis, A.M., Chittenden, E.A., Amarel, M. and Klausner, E. (1985) *Inquiry Into Meaning: An investigation of learning to read*. Hillsdale, NJ: Lawrence Erlbaum.

Butler, K., Simpson E. and Court, J. (2011) 'Promoting excellence: Shadowing the CILIP Carnegie and Kate Greenaway Medals,' in J. Court (ed.), *Read to Succeed: Strategies to engage children and young people in reading for pleasure*. London: Facet, pp. 131–52.

Calkins, L.M. (1991) *Living Between the Lines*. Portsmouth, NH: Heinemann.

Carrington, V. and Robinson, M. (eds) (2009) *Digital Literacies: Social learning and classroom practices*. London: Sage.

Carter, R. (2004) *Language and Creativity: The art of common talk*. London: Routledge.

Chambers, A. (1993) *Tell Me: Children, reading and talk*. Stroud, UK: Thimble Press.

Chambers, A. (1995) *Book Talk: Occasional writing on literature and children*. London: The Thimble Press.

Chan, Y.P. (2009) 'In their own words: How do students relate drama pedagogy to their learning in curriculum subjects?', *Research in Drama Education: The Journal of Applied Theatre and Performance*, 14(2): 191–209.

Chappell, K., Craft, A., Burnard, P. and Cremin, T. (2008) 'Question posing and question responding: The heart of possibility thinking in the early years', *Early Years: An International Journal of Research and Development*, 28(3): 267–83.

Clark, C. (2013) *Children's and Young People's Reading in 2012: Findings from the 2012 National Literacy Trust's annual survey*. London: National Literacy Trust.

Clark, C. and Foster, A. (2005) *Children and Young People's Reading Habits and Preferences: The who, what, why, where and when*. London: National Literacy Trust.

Clarke, S. (2005) *Formative Assessment in Action: Weaving the elements together*. London: Hodder & Stoughton.

Claxton, G. (2000) 'The anatomy of intuition', in T. Atkinson and G. Claxton (eds), *The Intuitive Practitioner*. Buckingham, UK: Open University Press, pp. 32–52.

Claxton, G. (2002) *Building Learning Power: Helping young people become better learners*. Bristol, UK: TLO.

Cliff Hodges, G. (2010) 'Rivers of reading: Using critical incident collages to learn about adolescent readers and their readership', *English in Education*, 44(3): 180–99.

Cochrane, P. and Cockett, M. (2007) *Building a Creative School: A dynamic approach to school improvement*. Stoke-on-Trent, UK: Trentham.

Collins, F.M. and Kelly, A. (2013) 'Primary student teachers' attitudes towards poetry and poetry teaching', in S. Dymoke, A. Lambirth and A. Wilson, *Making Poetry Matter: International research on poetry pedagogy*. London: Bloomsbury, pp. 20–30.

Commeyras, M., Bisplinghoff, B.S. and Olson, J. (2003) *Teachers as Readers: Perspectives on the importance of reading in teachers' classrooms and lives*. Newark, DE: International Reading Association.

Cooper, H. (2013) *Teaching History Creatively*. London: Routledge.

Corden, R. (2000) *Literacy and Learning Through Talk Strategies for the Primary Classroom*. Birmingham, UK: Open University Press.

Corden, R. (2001) 'Teaching Reading–Writing Links (TRAWL) project', *Reading, Literacy and Language*, 35(1): 37–40.

Corden, R. (2003) 'Writing is more than "exciting": Equipping primary children to become reflective writers', *Reading Literacy and Language*, 37(1): 18–26.

Coulthas, V. (2012) 'Classroom talk: Are we listening to teachers voices?', *English in Education*, 46(2): 175–89.

Craft, A. (2000) *Creativity Across the Primary Curriculum: Framing and developing practice*. London: RoutledgeFalmer.

Craft, A. (2001) 'Little creativity', in A. Craft, B. Jeffrey and M. Leibling (eds), *Creativity in Education*. London: Continuum, pp. 45–61.

Craft, A. (2005) *Creativity in Schools: Tensions and dilemmas*. Oxford, UK: RoutledgeFalmer.

Craft, A. (2011) *Creativity and Educational Futures*. Stoke-on-Trent, UK: Trentham Books.

Craft, A., McConnon, L. and Matthews, A. (2012b) 'Creativity and child-initiated play', *Journal of Thinking Skills and Creativity*, 71: 48–61.

Craft, A., Cremin, T., Clack, J. and Hay, P. (2013) 'Creative primary schools', *Ethnography and Education*, 9(1): 16–34.

Craft, A., Cremin, T., Burnard, P., Dragovic, T. and Chappell, K. (2012a) 'Possibility thinking: Culminative studies of an evidence-based concept driving creativity?', *Education 3–13: International Journal of Primary, Elementary and Early Years Education*. Available at http://dx.doi.org/10.1080/03004279.2012.656671 (accessed 5 January 2015).

Creative Partnerships (2008) Available at www.creative-partnerships.com (accessed 12 August 2008).

Cremin, T. (2007) 'Revisiting reading for pleasure: Diversity, delight and desire', in K. Goouch and A. Lambirth (eds), *Teaching Phonics, Teaching Reading: Critical perspectives*. Milton Keynes, UK: Open University Press, pp. 166–90.

Cremin, T. (2008) 'Teachers as writers: Insights from inside the writing process.' Paper presented at the BERA Conference, 3–6 September, Edinburgh.

Cremin, T. (2015) 'Creative teachers and creative teaching', in A. Wilson (ed.), *Creativity in Primary Education*. Exeter, UK: Learning Matters, pp. 33–44.

Cremin, T. (2010) *Teachers as Writers: Writing alongside children* (Research and Development Project Report). London: Newham LA.

Cremin, T. and Baker, S. (2010) 'Exploring teacher–writer identities in the classroom: Conceptualising the struggle', *English Teaching: Practice and Critique*, 9(3): 8–25.

Cremin, T. and McDonald, R. (2012) 'Drama: A creative pedagogic tool', in D. Wyse and R. Jones, *Creative Teaching*. London: Routledge. pp. 83–97.

Cremin, T. and Myhill, D. (2012) *Writing Voices: Creating communities of writers*. London: Routledge.

Cremin, T. and Maybin, J. (2013) 'Language and creativity: Teachers and students', in K. Hall, T. Cremin, B. Comber and L. Moll, *The Wiley Blackwell International Research Handbook of Children's Literacy, Learning and Culture*. Oxford, UK: Wiley Blackwell, pp. 275–90.

Cremin, T. and Swann, J. (2015, forthcoming) 'Literature in common: Reading for pleasure in school reading groups', in L. McKechnie, K. Oterholm, P. Rothbauer and K.I. Skjerdingstad (eds), *Plotting the Reading Experience: Theory/practice/politics*. Stockholm: Wilfrid Laurier University Press.

Cremin, T., Burnard, P. and Craft, A. (2006a) 'Pedagogy and possibility thinking in the early years', *International Journal of Thinking Skills and Creativity*, 1(2): 108–19.

Cremin, T., Barnes, J. and Scoffham, S. (2009) *Creative Teaching for Tomorrow: Fostering a creative state of mind*. Deal, UK: Future Creative.

Cremin, T., Chappell, K. and Craft, A. (2012) 'Reciprocity between narrative, questioning and imagination in the early and primary years', *Thinking Skills and Creativity*, 9: 136–51.

Cremin, T. and Swann, J., with contributions from Mukherjee, S.J. (2012) *Report to Carnegie UK Trust and CILIP on a Two-Stage Study of the Carnegie and Kate Greenaway Shadowing Scheme.* Open University November, pp. 1–121.

Cremin, T., Mottram, M., Bearne, E. and Goodwin, P. (2008) 'Exploring teachers' knowledge of children's literature', *The Cambridge Journal of Education*, 38(4): 449–64.

Cremin, T., Bearne, E., Mottram, M. and Goodwin, P. (2008) 'Primary teachers as readers', *English in Education*, 42(1): 1–23.

Cremin, T., McDonald, R., Blakemore, L. and Goff, E. (2009) *Jumpstart! Drama.* London: David Fulton.

Cremin, T., Goouch, K., Blakemore, L., Goff, E. and McDonald, R. (2006) 'Connecting drama and writing: Seizing the moment to write', *Research in Drama in Education*, 11(3): 273–91.

Cremin, T., Mottram, M., Collins, F., Powell, S. and Safford, K. (2009) 'Teachers as readers: Building communities of readers', *Literacy*, 43(1): 11–19.

Cremin, T., Mottram, M., Collins, F., Powell, S. and Drury, R. (2012) 'Building communities: Teachers researching literacy lives', *Improving Schools*, 15(2): 101–15.

Cremin, T., Swann, J., Flewitt, R., Faulkner, D. and Kurcicova, N. (2013) *Report for MakeBelieve Arts and the Esmée Fairbairn Foundation on the Helicopter Technique of Storytelling and Story acting.* Available at www.makebelievearts.co.uk/helicopter (accessed 6 January 2015).

Cremin, T., Mottram, M., Collins, F., Powell, S. and Safford, K. (2014) *Building Communities of Engaged Readers: Reading for pleasure.* London and New York: Routledge.

Cremin, T., Mottram, M., Collins, F., Powell, S. and Drury, R. (2015) *Researching Literacy Lives: Building home school communities.* London and New York: Routledge.

Crumpler, T. and Schneider, J. (2002) 'Writing with their whole being: A cross study analysis of children's writing from five classrooms using process drama, *Research in Drama Education*, 7(2): 61–79.

Davies, D., Jindal-Snape, D., Collier, C., Digby, R., Hay, P. and Howe, A. (2012) 'Creative environments for learning in schools', *Thinking Skills and Creativity*, 8: 80–91.

D'Arcy, P. (1999) *Two Contrasting Paradigms for the Teaching and Assessment of Writing.* Leicester, UK: NATE.

Dawes, L., Mercer, N., and Wegerif, R. (2004) *Thinking Together: Developing speaking, listening and thinking skills for children aged 8-11.* Birmingham, UK: Imaginative Minds.

DENI (2011) The National Curriculum. Available at www.nicurriculum.org.uk/docs/key_stages_1_and_2/statutory_requirements/ks2_language_literacy.pdf (accessed 30 September 2014).

Department for Children, Education, Lifelong Learning and Skills (DCELLS) (2008a) *Framework for Children's Learning for 3 to 7-Year-Olds in Wales.* Cardiff: DCELLS.

Department for Children, Education, Lifelong Learning and Skills (DCELLS) (2008b) *Skills Framework for 3–19 Year Olds.* Cardiff: DCELLS.

Department for Children, Schools and Families (DCSF) (2008) *The Impact of Parental Involvement on Children's Education* (DCSF-00924-2008). London: DCSF.

Dezuanni, M. and Jetnikoff, A. (2011) 'Creative pedagogies and the contemporary school classroom', in J. Sefton Green, P. Thomson, K. Jones and L. Bresler, *The Routledge International Handbook of Creative Learning.* London: Routledge, pp. 264–72.

DfE (2010) *The Importance of Teaching: The Schools White Paper.* London: The Stationery Office.

DfE (2013) *The National Curriculum Framework Document.* London: DfE.

DfE (2014) *Statutory Framework for the Early Years Foundation Stage: Setting the standards for learning, development and care for children from birth to five.* London: DfE.

DfEE (1989) *English for Ages 5 to 16: The National Curriculum.* London: DfEE and the Welsh Office.

DfEE (1998) *The National Literacy Strategy Framework for Teaching.* London: DfEE.

DfES (2003) *Excellence and Enjoyment.* London: HMSO.

DfES (2006) *Primary National Strategy: Primary framework for literacy and mathematics.* Nottingham, UK: DfES.

DfES (2007) *Letters and Sounds.* London: DfES.

DfES (2013) *National Literacy and Numeracy Framework (LNF).* Cardiff: Welsh Assembly.

Dickie, J. and Shuker, M.J. (2014) 'Ben 10, superheroes and princesses: Primary teachers' views of popular culture and school literacy', *Literacy*, 48(1): 32–8.

Dix, S. and Cawkwell, G. (2011) 'The influence of peer group response: Building a teacher and students' expertise in the writing classroom', *English Teaching: Practice and Critique*, 10(4): 41–57.

Dweck, C. (2012) *Mindset: How you can fulfil your potential.* London: Robinson.

Education Scotland (2012) *A Curriculum for Excellence – Literacy and English experiences and outcomes.* Available at www.educationscotland.gov.uk/learningteachingandassessment/curriculumareas/languages/litandenglish/eandos/index.asp (accessed 30 September 2104).

Ee Loh, C. (2009) 'Reading the world: Reconceptualising reading multicultural literature in the English language arts classroom in a global world', *Changing English: Studies in Culture and Education*, 16(3): 287–99.

Ellis, S. and Safford, K. (2005) *Animating Literacy.* London: CLPE.

Engel, S. (2005) 'The narrative worlds of *what is* and *what if*', *Cognitive Development*, 20: 514–25.

English, E., Hargreaves, L. and Hislam, J. (2002) 'Pedagogical dilemmas in the National Literacy Strategy: Primary teachers' perceptions, reflections and classroom behaviour', *Cambridge Journal of Education*, 32(1): 9–26.

Essex County Council (2003) *Visually Speaking Using Multimedia Texts to Improve Boys Writing.* Chelmsford, UK: The English Team, Essex Advisory and Inspection Service.

Fang, Z., Fu, D. and Lemme, L. (2004) 'From scripted instruction to teacher empowerment: Supporting literacy teachers to make pedagogical transitions', *Literacy*, 38(1): 58–64.

Faulkner, D. (2011) 'Angels, tooth fairies and ghosts: Thinking creatively in an early years classroom', in D. Faulkner and E. Coates (eds), *Exploring Children's Creative Narratives.* Abingdon, UK: Routledge, pp. 39–61.

Fecho, B. (2011) *Writing in the Dialogical Classroom: Students and teachers responding to the texts of their lives.* Urbana, IL: National Council of Teachers of English.

Fisher, R. (2013) *Teaching Thinking* (4th edn). London: Bloomsbury.

Fisher, R. and Williams, M. (2004) *Unlocking Creativity: Teaching across the curriculum.* London: David Fulton.

Fisher, R., Jones, S., Larkin, S. and Myhill, D. (2010) *Using Talk to Support Writing.* London: Sage.

Fleming, M., Merrell, C. and Tymms, P. (2004) 'The impact of drama on pupils' language, mathematics and attitude in two primary schools', *Research in Drama Education*, 9(2): 177–97.

Flower, L. and Hayes, J.R. (1980) 'The dynamics of composing: Making plans and juggling constraints', in L.W. Gregg and E.R. Steinberg (eds), *Cognitive Processes in Writing.* Hillsdale, NJ: Lawrence Erlbaum, pp. 31–50.

Fox, C. (1993a) *At the Very Edge of the Forest: The influence of literature on storytelling by children.* London: Cassell.

Fox, C. (1993b) 'Tellings and retellings: Educational implications of children's oral stories', *Reading*, 27(1): 14–20.

Frater, G. (2001) *Effective Practice in Writing at Key Stage 2: Essential extras*. London: Basic Skills Agency.

Frater, G. (2004) 'Improving Dean's writing: What shall we tell the children?', *Literacy*, 38(2): 45–56.

Freebody, K. (2010) 'Exploring teacher–student interactions and moral reasoning practices in drama classrooms', *Research in Drama Education: The Journal of Applied Theatre and Performance*. 15(2): 209–25.

Freire, P. (1985) 'Reading the world and reading the word: An interview with Paulo Friere', *Language Arts*, 62(1): 15–21.

Galton, M. (2010) 'Going with the flow or back to normal? The impact of creative practitioners in schools and classrooms', *Research Papers in Education*, 25(4): 355–75.

Gamble, N. and Yates, S. (2008) *Exploring Children's Literature* (2nd edn). London: Sage.

Gardner, H. (1993) *Frames of Mind: The theory of multiple intelligences*. London: Fontana Press.

Geekie, P., Cambourne, B. and Fitzsimmons, P. (1999) *Understanding Literacy Development*. Stoke-on-Trent, UK: Trentham.

Goouch, K., Cremin, T. and Lambirth, A. (2009) *Writing is Primary: Final report*. London: Esmée Fairbairn Foundation.

Goswami, U. (1999) 'Causal connections in beginning reading: The importance of rhyme', *Journal of Research in Reading*, 22: 217–40.

Graham, L. (2012) 'Unfolding lives in digital worlds: Digikid teachers revisited', *Literacy*, 46(3): 133–9.

Graham, L. and Johnson, A. (2003) *Children's Writing Journals*. Royston, UK: UKLA.

Grainger, T. (1997) *Traditional Tales: Storytelling in the primary classroom*. Leamington Spa, UK: Scholastic.

Grainger, T. (1998) 'Drama and reading: Illuminating their interaction', *English in Education*, 32(1): 29–37.

Grainger, T. (2003) 'Exploring the unknown: Ambiguity, interaction and meaning making in classroom drama', in E. Bearne, D. Dombey and T. Grainger (eds), *Classroom Interactions in Literacy*, Maidenhead, UK: Open University Press, pp. 105–14.

Grainger, T. (2005) 'Teachers as writers: Travelling together', *English in Education*, 39(1): 77–89.

Grainger, T., Goouch, K. and Lambirth, A. (2002) 'The voice of the writer', *Reading Literacy and Language*, 36(3): 39–142.

Grainger, T., Goouch, K. and Lambirth, A. (2005) *Creativity and Writing: Developing voice and verve in the classroom*. London: Routledge.

Graves, D. (1994) *A Fresh Look at Writing*. Portsmouth, NH: Heinemann.

Greenwood, J. (2009) 'Drama education in New Zealand: A coming of age?', *Research in Drama Education: The Journal of Applied Theatre and Performance*, 14(2): 245–60.

Guildford, J.P. (1973) *Characteristics of Creativity*. Springield, IL: Illinois State Office of the Superintendent of Public Instruction, Gifted Children Section.

Hague, C. and Williamson, B. (2009) *Digital Participation, Digital Literacy, and School Subjects: A review of the policies, literature and evidence*. Slough, UK: Futurelab.

Hall, C. and Coles, M. (1999) *Children's Reading Choices*. London: RoutledgeFalmer.

Hall, K. (2013) 'Effective literacy teaching in the early years of school: A review of the evidence', in J. Larson and J. Marsh, *The Sage Handbook of Early Childhood Literacy* (2nd edn). London: Sage, pp. 533–40.

Hall, L.A. (2012) 'Rewriting identities: Creating spaces for students and teachers to challenge the norms of what it means to be a reader in school', *Journal of Adolescent and Adult Literacy*, 55: 368–73.

Hardy, B. (1977) 'Towards a poetics of fiction: An approach through narrative', in M. Meek, A. Warlow and G. Barton (eds), *The Cool Web*. London: Bodley Head, pp. 290–312.

Harrison, C. (2002) 'What does research tell us about how to develop comprehension?', in R. Fisher, G. Brooks and M. Lewis (eds), *Raising Standards in Literacy*. London: Routledge, pp. 9–22.

Honan, E. (2008) 'Barriers to teachers using digital texts in literacy classrooms', *Literacy*, 42(1): 36–43.

Hope, J. (2008) 'One day we had to run': The development of the refugee identity in children's literature and its function in education', *Children's Literature in Education*, 39: 295–304.

Hughes, J. (2013) 'Digital poetry, power and social justice', in S. Dymoke, A. Lambirth and A. Wilson, *Making Poetry Matter: International research on poetry pedagogy*. London: Bloomsbury, pp. 167–79.

Hughes, T. (1967) *Poetry in the Making*. London: Faber.

Hyland, K. (2003) *Second Language Writing*. Cambridge, UK: Cambridge University Press.

Jeffrey, B. (2005) *Final Report of the Creative Learning and Student Perspectives Research Project (CLASP), A European Commission funded project through the Socrates Programme, Action 6.1* (no 2002–4682/002–001. SO2–61OBGE). Milton Keynes, UK: Open University Press.

Jeffrey, B. (ed.) (2006) *Creative Learning Practices: European experiences*. London: Tufnell Press.

Jeffrey, B. and Woods, P. (2003) *The Creative School: A framework for success, quality and effectiveness*. London: RoutledgeFalmer.

Jeffrey, B. and Craft, A. (2004) 'Teaching creatively and teaching for creativity: Distinctions and relationships', *Educational Studies*, 30(1): 77–87.

Jeffrey, B. and Woods, P. (2009) *Creative Learning in the Primary School*. Oxford, UK: Routledge.

Jeffrey, G. (ed.) (2005) *The Creative College: Building a successful learning culture in the arts*. Stoke-on-Trent, UK: Trentham.

Jesson, R., Parr, J. and McNaughton, S. (2013) 'The unfulfilled pedagogical promise of the diloagic in writing: Intertextual writing instruction for diverse settings', in K. Hall, K., T, Cremin, B. Comber and L. Moll (2013) *The Wiley Blackwell International Research Handbook of Children's Literacy, Learning and Culture*. Oxford: Wiley Blackwell, pp. 215–27.

Johns, J.L. and Berglund, R.L. (2006) *Fluency: Strategies and assessment*. Dubeque, IA: Kendall Hunt.

Kelley, M.J. and Clausen-Grace, N. (2007) *Comprehension Shouldn't Be Silent: From strategy instruction to student independence*. Newark, DE: International Reading Association.

Kennedy, R. (2014) 'Being authors: Grammar exploration', *English 4–11*, 50: 2–4.

King, C. and Briggs, J. (2005) *Literature Circles: Better talking, more ideas*. Royston, UK: UKLA.

Krashen, S.D. (2011) *Free Voluntary Reading*. Santa Barbara, CA: Libraries Unlimited.

Kress, G. (1997) *Before Writing: Rethinking the paths to literacy*. London: Routledge.

Kress, G. and Knapp, P. (1992) 'Genre in a social theory of language', *English in Education*, 26(2): 2–11.

Kress, G. and van Leeuwen, T. (2006) *The Grammar of Visual Design*. Routledge: London.

Kucirkova, N. (2013) 'Role of iPads in Early Years', *Early Years Educator*, 14(1): 24–6.

Kucirkova, N., Willans, D. and Cremin, T. (2014) 'Spot the dog! Spot the difference', *English 4–11*, Summer: 11–14.

Kuntz, A.M., Presnall, M.M., Priola, M., Tilford, A. and Ward, R. (2013) 'Creative pedagogies and collaboration: An action research project', *Educational Action Research*, 21(1): 42–58.

Kyle, F., Kujala, J., Richardson, U., Lyytinen, H. and Goswami, U. (2013) 'Assessing the effectiveness of two theoretically motivated computer-assisted reading interventions in the United Kingdom', *Reading Research Quarterly*, 48(1): 61–76.

Lambirth, A., Smith, S. and Steele, S. (2012) 'Poetry is happening but I don't exactly know how. Literacy subject leaders' perceptions of poetry in their primary schools', *Literacy*, 16(2): 73–80.

Lambirth, A., Smith, S. and Steele, S. (2013) 'Responding to children's poetry', in S. Dymoke, A. Lambirth and A. Wilson, *Making Poetry Matter: International research on poetry pedagogy*. London: Bloomsbury, pp. 71–83.

Landay, E. and Wootton, K. (2012) *A Reason to Read: Linking literacy and the arts*. Cambridge, MA: Harvard.

Lefebre, P., Trudeau, N. and Sutton, A. (2011) 'Enhancing vocabulary, print awareness and phonological awareness through shared storybook reading with low income pre-schoolers', *Journal of Early Childhood Literacy*, 11(4): 453–79.

Levy, R. (2008) 'Third spaces are interesting places: Applying "third space theory" to nursery-aged children's construction of themselves as readers', *Journal of Early Childhood Literacy*, 8(1): 43–66.

Lin, Y.-S. (2011) 'Fostering creativity through education – A conceptual framework of creative pedagogy', *Creative Education*, 2(3): 149–55.

Lintner, T. (2010) 'Using children's literature to promote critical geographic awareness in elementary classrooms', *The Social Studies*, 101: 17–21.

Littleton, K. and Mercer, N. (2013) *Interthinking: Putting talk to work*. London: Routledge.

Lockwood, M. (2008) *Promoting Reading for Pleasure in the Primary School*. London: Sage.

Luce-Kapler, R., Chin, J., O'Donnell, E. and Stoch, S. (2001) 'The design of meaning: Unfolding systems of writing', *Changing English*, 8(1): 43–52.

McAdam, J. and Arizpe, E. (2011) 'Journeys into culturally responsive teaching', *Journal of Teacher Education and Teachers Work*, 2(1): 135–58.

McPake, J., Plowman, L. and Stephen, C. (2013) 'Preschool children creating and com-municating with digital technologies at home', *British Journal of Educational Technology*, 44(3): 421–31.

McWilliam, E. (2008) 'Unlearning how to teach', *Innovations in Education and Teaching International*, 45(3): 263–9.

Maine, F. (2013) 'How children talk together to make meaning from texts: A dialogic perspective on reading comprehension strategies', *Literacy*, 47(3): 150–6.

Malaguzzi, L. (1998) 'History, ideas and basic philosophy: An interview with Lella Gandini', in C. Edwards, L. Gandini and G. Forman (eds), *The Hundred Languages of Children* (2nd edn), Greenwich, CT: Ablex, p. 45.

Mallet. M (2005) 'First encounters with non-fiction', *Books for Keeps*, 153. Available at http://booksforkeeps.co.uk/issue/153/childrens-books/articles/other-articles/early-years-reading-first-encounters-with-non-fiction (accessed 6 January 2015).

Marsh, J. (2004) 'The techno-literacy practices of young children', *Journal of Early Childhood Research*, 2(1): 51–66.

Marsh, J. (ed.) (2005) *Popular Culture, New Media and Digital Literacy in Early Childhood*. London: RoutledgeFalmer.

Marsh, J. (2008) 'Productive pedagogies: Play creativity and digital cultures in the classroom', in R. Willet, M. Robinson and J. Marsh (eds), *Play, Creativity and Digital Cultures*. New York and Abingdon, UK: RoutledgeFalmer, pp. 200–21.

Marsh, J. (2011) 'Young children's literacy practices in a virtual world: Establishing an online interaction order', *Reading Research Quarterly*, 46(2): 101–18.

Marsh, J. and Millard, E. (2005) *Popular Literacies, Childhood and Schooling*. London: RoutledgeFalmer.

Marsh, J. and Bearne, E. (2008) *Moving Literacy On: Evaluation of the BFI Lead Practitioner Scheme for moving image media literacy*. Leicester, UK: University of Sheffield and United Kingdom Literacy Association.

Marsh, J. and Bishop, J. (2014) *Changing Play: Play, media and commercial culture from the 1950s to the present day*. Maidenehead, UK: The Open University.

Marsh, J., Brooks, G., Hughes, J., Ritchie, L., Roberts, S. and Wright, K. (2005) *Digital Beginnings: Young children's use of popular culture, media and new technologies*. Sheffield, UK: University of Sheffield.

Maybin, J. (2013) 'What counts as reading? PIRLS, EastEnders and the man on the flying trapeze', *Literacy*, 47(2): 59–66.

Medwell, J., Strand, S. and Wray, D. (2007) 'The role of handwriting in composing for Y2 children', *Journal of Reading, Writing and Literacy*, 2(1): 18–36.

Medwell, J., Wray, D., Poulson, L. and Fox, R. (1998) *Effective Teachers of Literacy: A report of a research project commissioned by the Teacher Training Agency*. Exeter, UK: University of Exeter.

Meek, M. (1988) *How Texts Teach What Readers Learn*. Stroud, UK: Thimble Press.

Meek, M. (1991) *On Being Literate*. London: Bodley Head.

Mercer, N. (2000) *Words and Minds: How we use language to think together*. London: Routledge.

Mercer, N. and Littleton, K. (2007) *Dialogue and the Development of Children's Thinking*. London: Routledge.

Moline, S. (2012) *I See What You Mean: Visual literacy, K-8* (2nd edn). Portland, ME: Stenhouse.

Moll, L., Amanti, C., Neff, D. and Gonzalez, N. (1992) 'Funds of knowledge for teaching: Using a qualitative approach to connect homes and classrooms', *Theory into Practice*, 31: 132–41.

Morgan, D. (2010) 'Pre-service teachers as writers', *Literacy Research and Instruction*, 49(4): 352–65.

Motion, A. (2014) *What is Poetry by heart?* Available at www.poetrybyheart.org.uk/what-is-poetry-by-heart (accessed 12 September 2014).

Mullis, I.V.S., Martin, M., Foy, P. and Drucker, K. (2012a) *PIRLS 2011 International Results in Reading*. Boston: TIMSS & PIRLS International Study Center, and Amsterdam: International Association for the Evaluation of Educational Achievement.

Mullis, I.V.S., Martin, M.O., Foy, P. and Drucker, K.T. (2012b) *Progress in International Reading Literacy Study in Primary Schools*. Chestnut Hill, MA: TIMSS & PIRLS International Study Center, Boston College.

Myhill, D.A. (2001) 'Crafting and creating', *English in Education*, 35(3): 13–20.

Myhill, D.A. (2009) 'Becoming a designer: Trajectories of linguistic development', in R. Beard, D. Myhill, J. Riley and M. Nystrand (eds), *The Sage Handbook of Writing Development*. London: Sage, pp. 402–14.

Myhill, D.A. (2011) 'Grammar for designers: How grammar supports the development of writing', in S. Ellis, E.McCartney and J. Bourne (eds), *Insight and Impact: Applied linguistics and the primary school*. Cambridge, UK: Cambridge University Press, pp. 72–94.

Myhill, D.A., Jones, S.M., Lines, H. and Watson, A. (2011) 'Re-thinking grammar: The impact of embedded grammar teaching on students' writing and students' metalinguistic understanding', *Research Papers in Education*, 2(27): 1–28.

National Advisory Committee on Creative and Cultural Education (NACCCE) (1999) *All Our Futures: Creativity, Culture and Education*. London: DfEE.

National Literacy Trust (NLT) (2012) *Boys' Reading Commission: The report of the All-Party Parliamentary Literacy Group Commission*. London: The National Literacy Trust.

Neelands, J. (2011) 'Drama as creative learning', in J. Sefton-Green, P. Thomson, K. Jones and L. Bresler (eds), *The Routledge International Handbook of Creative Learning*. New York: Routledge, pp. 168–76.

Nestlé Family Monitor (2003) *Young People's Attitudes Towards Reading*. Croydon, UK: Nestlé Family Monitor.

Neumann, N., Acosta, C. and Neumann, D. (2014) 'Young children's visual attention to environmental print as measured by eye-tracker analysis', *Reading Research Quarterly*, 49(2): 157–68.

Nicholson, H. (2000) 'Dramatic literacies and difference', in E. Bearne and V. Watson (eds), *Where Texts and Children Meet*. London: Routledge, pp. 113–24.

Nystrand, M. (2006) 'Research on the role of classroom discourse as it affects reading comprehension', *Research into the Teaching of Reading*, 40(4): 392–412.

OECD (2010) *PISA 2009 Results: Learning to learn – Student engagement, strategies and practices* (vol. III). Available from http://dx.doi.org/10.1787/9789264083943-en (accessed 5 January 2014).

Office for Standards in Education (Ofsted) (2003) *Expecting the Unexpected: Developing creativity in primary and secondary schools* (HMI 1612). Available at www.ofsted.gov.uk (accessed 12 June 2006).

Office for Standards in Education (Ofsted) (2006) *Creative Partnerships: Initiative and impact* (HMI 2517). Manchester, UK: Ofsted.

O'Sullivan, O. and McGonigle, S. (2010) 'Transforming readers: Teachers and children in the Centre for Literacy in Primary Education Power of Reading project', *Literacy*, 44(2): 51–9.

Pahl, K. (2007) 'Creativity in events and practices: A lens for understanding children's multimodal texts', *Literacy*, 41(2): 81–7.

Paley, V.G. (1990) *The Boy Who Would Be a Helicopter*. Cambridge, MA: Harvard University Press.

Paley, V.G. (2004) *Child's Play: The importance of fantasy play*. Chicago, IL: Chicago University Press.

Park, N. (dir.) (1993) *The Wrong Trousers*. Bristol, UK: Aardman Animations.

Pennac, D. (2006) *The Rights of the Reader*. London: Walker.

Parry, B. (2014) 'Popular culture, participation and progression in the literacy classroom', *Literacy*, 48(1): 14–22.

Poetry Archive, The (2005) Available at www.poetryarchive.org/childrensarchive/home.do (accessed 13 June 2008).

Poddiakov, N. (2011) 'Searching, experimenting and the heuristic structure of a preschool child's experience', *International Journal of Early Years Education*, 19(1): 55–63.

Pound, L. and Lee, T. (2015) *Teaching Mathematics Creatively*. London: Routledge.

Powling, C. (2003) 'Introduction', in C. Powling, B. Ashley, P. Pullman, A. Fine and J. Gavin (eds), *Meetings with the Minister*. Reading, UK: National Centre for Language and Literacy, pp. 1–5.

Powling, C., Ashley, B., Pullman, P., Fine, A. and Gavin, J. (eds) (2005) *Beyond Bog Standard Literacy*. Reading, UK: National Centre for Language and Literacy.

Prentice, R. (2000) 'Creativity: A reaffirmation of its place in early childhood education', *The Curriculum Journal*, 11(2): 145–58.

Pressley, M., Wharton-McDonald, R., Allington, R., Block, C.C., Morrow, L. (2001) 'A study of effective first grade literacy instruction', *Scientific Studies of Reading*, 5(1): 35–58.

Priestley, M. and Humes, W. (2010) 'The development of Scotland's Curriculum for Excellence: Amnesia and déjà vu', *Oxford Review of Education*, 36(3): 345–61.

Progress in International Reading Literacy Study (PIRLS) (2011) Available at http://timss.bc.edu/pirls2011/index.html (accessed 5 January 2015).

Purcell-Gates, V. (1988) 'Lexical and syntactic knowledge of written narrative held by wellread-to kindergartners and second graders', *Research in the Teaching of English*, 22(2): 128–60.

Qualifications and Assessment Authority (QAA)/United Kingdom Literacy Association (UKLA) (2004) *More Than Words: Multimodal texts in the classroom*. London: QCA.

Qualifications and Assessment Authority (QAA)/United Kingdom Literacy Association (UKLA) (2005) *More Than Words 2: Creating stories on page and screen*. London: QCA.

Reedy, D. and Lister, B. (2007) ' "Busting with blood and gore and full of passion": The impact of an oral retelling of the *Iliad* in the primary classroom', *Literacy*, 41(1): 3–9.

Reedy, D. and Bearne, E. (2013) *Teaching Grammar Effectively in Primary Schools*. Leicester, UK: United Kingdom Literacy Association.

Riley, J. and Reedy, D. (2005) 'Developing young children's thinking through learning to write argument', *Journal of Early Childhood Education*, 5(1): 29–52.

Roberts, P. (2006) *Nurturing Creativity in Young People: A report to government to inform future policy*. London: DCMS.

Robinson, C. (2014) *Children, Their Voices and Their Experiences of School: What does the evidence tell us?* Available at http://cprtrust.org.uk/research/childrens-voice/ (accessed 6 January 2015).

Robinson, M. and Mackey, M. (2006) 'Assets in the classroom: Comforts and competence with media among teachers present and future', in J. Marsh and E. Millard (eds), *Popular Literacies, Childhood and Schooling*. London: RoutledgeFalmer, pp. 200–20.

Rogers, R. and Elias, M. (2012) 'Storied selves: A critical discourse analysis of young children's literate identification', *Journal of Early Childhood Literacy*, 12(3): 259–92.

Rosen, H. (1988) 'The irrepressible genre', in M. Maclure, T. Phillips and A. Wilkinson (eds), *Oracy Matters*. Milton Keynes, UK: Open University Press, pp. 13–23.

Rosen, M. (1989) *Did I Hear You Write?* London: André Deutsch.

Rosenblatt, L. (1978) *The Reader, the Text, the Poem: The transactional theory of literary work*. Carbondale, IL: South Illinois University Press.

Rosenblatt, L. (1985) 'The transactional theory of the literary work: Implications for research', in C. Cooper (ed.), *Researching Response to Literature and the Teaching of English*, Norwood, NJ: Ablex, pp. 58–69.

Rothery, J. (1985) *Teaching Writing in the Primary School: A genre based approach*. Sydney, Australia: Department of Linguistics, University of Sydney.

Rumelhart, D. (1985) 'Towards an interactive model of reading', in H. Singer and R. Rundell (eds), *Theoretical Models and Processes of Reading*. Newark, DE: International Reading Association, pp. 76–98.

Sæbø, A.B. (2009) 'Challenges and possibilities in Norwegian classroom drama practice', *Research in Drama Education*, 14(2): 279–94.

Sawyer, K. (2011) 'Improvisation and narrative', in D. Faulkner and E. Coates, *Exploring Children's Creative Narratives*. London: Routledge, pp. 11–38.

Sharples, M. (1999) *How We Write: Writing as creative design*. London: Routledge.

Smith, A. (2007) 'In what ways can a creative pedagogy feed narrative writing?', unpublished MA dissertation, Canterbury Christ Church University, UK.

Smith, F. (1982) *Writing and the Writer*. London: Heinemann.

Smith, P., Rudd, P. and Coghlan, M. (2008) *Harnessing Technology: Schools survey 2008*. National Foundation for Education Research and Becta. Available at www.nfer.ac.uk/publications/TSV01/TSV01.pdf (accessed 23 August 2014).

Soalt, J. (2005) 'Bringing together fictional and informational texts to improve comprehension', *The Reading Teacher*, 58(7): 680–3.

Spiro, J. (2007) 'Teaching poetry: Writing poetry – Teaching as a writer', *English in Education*, 41(3): 78–93.

Sternberg, R.J. (1997) *Successful Intelligence*. New York: Plume.

Sternberg, R.J. (ed.) (1999) *The Handbook of Creativity*. New York: Cambridge University Press.

Taylor, B.M. and Pearson, P.D. (eds) (2002) *Teaching Reading: Effective schools, accomplished teachers*. Mahwah, NJ: Lawrence Erlbaum.

Taylor, P. and Warner, C.D. (2006) *Structure and Spontaneity: The process drama of Cecily O'Neil*. Stoke-on-Trent, UK: Trentham.

Thomson, P. and Hall, C. (forthcoming) '"Everyone can imagine their own Gellert": The democratic artist and "inclusion" in primary and nursery classrooms', *Education 3–13*, Special issue on Creativity.

Thomson, P., Hall, C., Jones, K. and Sefton-Green, J. (2012) *The Signature Pedagogies Project: Final report*. London: Creativity, Culture and Education.

Twist, L., Sizmur, J., Bartlett, S. and Lynn, L. (2012) *PIRLS 2011 Reading Achievement in England* (Research Brief DFE-RB262). Available at www.education.gov.uk/publications/standard/publicationDetail/Page1/DFE-RB262 (accessed 6 January 2014).

Vandewater, E.A., Rideout, V.J., Wartella, E.A., Huang, X., Lee, J.H. and Shim, M.S. (2007) 'Digital childhood: Electronic media and technology use among infants, toddlers, and preschoolers', *Pediatrics*, 119(5): e1006–15.

Vass, E. (2004) 'Friendship and collaboration: Creative writing in the primary classroom', *Journal of Computer Assisted Learning*, 18: 102–11.

Vass, E. (2007) 'Exploring processes of collaborative creativity: The role of emotions in children's joint creative writing', *Thinking Skills and Creativity*, 2: 107–17.

Vera, D. (2011) 'Using popular culture to increase emergent literacy skills in one high-poverty urban school district', *Journal of Early Childhood Literacy*, 11(3): 307–30.

Vygotsky, L.S. (1978) *Mind in Society*. Cambridge, MA: Harvard University Press.

Walsh, C.S. (2007) 'Creativity as capital in the literacy classroom: Youth as multimodal designers', *Literacy*, 41(2): 79–85.

Warrington, M., Younger, M. and Bearne, E. (2006) *Raising Boys' Achievement in Primary Schools: Towards a holistic approach*. Maidenhead, UK: Open University Press.

Watts, R. (2007) 'Harnessing the power of film in the primary classroom', *Literacy*, 41(2): 102–9.

Wells, G. (1999) *Dialogic Inquiry*. Cambridge, UK: Cambridge University Press.

Wells, R. (2008) 'Dancing into writing: Adventures into the world of Abdhi', *English 4–1*, 33: 9–13.

Whitehead, F. (1977) *Children and Their Books*. London: Macmillan.

Williams, M. (2006) *Greek Myths*. London: Walker.

Wigfield, A., Guthrie, J.T., Tonks, S. and Perencevich, K.C. (2004) 'Children's motivation for reading: Domain specificity and instructional influences', *Journal of Educational Research*, 97(6): 299–309.

Wilson, S. and Ball, D.L. (1997) 'Helping teachers meet the standards: New challenges for teacher educators', *The Elementary School Journal*, 97(2): 121–38.

Wohlwend, K. (2009) 'Early adopters: Playing new literacies and pretending new technologies in print-centric classrooms', *Journal of Early Childhood Literacy*, 9(7): 117–40.

Wohlwend, K. (2011) *Playing Their Way Into Literacies: Reading, writing and belonging in early childhood classrooms*. New York: Teachers College Press.

Woods, P. (1994) *Critical Events in Teaching and Learning*. London: Falmer Press.

Woods, P. (2001) 'Creative literacy', in A. Craft, B. Jeffrey and M. Liebling (eds), *Creativity in Education*. London: Continuum, pp. 62–79.

Wray, D. and Lewis, M. (1997) *Extending Literacy: Children reading and writing non-fiction*. London: Routledge.

Wray, D., Medwell, J., Poulson, L. and Fox, R. (2002) *Teaching Literacy Effectively in the Primary School*. London: RoutledgeFalmer.

Yeo, M. (2007) 'New literacies, alternative texts: Teachers' conceptualisations of composition and literacy', *English Teaching: Practice and Critique*, 6(1): 113–31.

Zephaniah, B. (2001) 'Poetry writing', in J. Carter (ed.), *Creating Writers: A creative writing manual for schools*. London: Routledge, pp. 42–8.

INDEX